SKIALETHEIA

T.

SKIALETHEIA

OR

A Shadowe of Truth, in Certaine Epigrams and Satyres

By
EVERARD GUILPIN

Edited by
D. ALLEN CARROLL

THE UNIVERSITY OF NORTH CAROLINA PRESS
CHAPEL HILL

Manufactured in the United States of America
Library of Congress Catalog Card Number 73-14841
ISBN 0-8078-1220-X

Library of Congress Cataloging in Publication Data

Guilpin, Edward, fl. 1598.
  Skialetheia; or, A shadowe of truth, in certaine
epigrams and satyres.

Bibliography: p. 27
  I. Carroll, Daniel Allen, 1938-   ed.   II. Title.
PR2283.G7S5 1974   821'.3   73-14841
ISBN 0-8078-1220-X

Contents

Acknowledgments

For kindnesses that include but go far beyond a number of helpful suggestions I want to thank O. B. Hardison, Jr., of the Folger Shakespeare Library, Jerry Leath Mills of The University of North Carolina at Chapel Hill, and Norman Sanders and Paul Merchant of The University of Tennessee at Knoxville. For a Summer Research Grant I am indebted to The University of Tennessee Graduate School. And for generous assistance in defraying a portion of the considerable cost of publication I am grateful to The University of Tennessee Better English Fund, established by John C. Hodges.

D.A.C.

INTRODUCTION

Content and Date

Skialetheia, entered in the Stationers' Register on 15 September 1598 (STC 12504), and published anonymously, contains seventy epigrams and seven formal verse satires—a "*Satyre Preludium*" and six numbered satires, without descriptive titles. Modeled after Martial and Juvenal, the major classical influences on Elizabethan satire, its tone is that of vigorous and outraged pessimism, its method that of direct rebuke, and its objects of attack now "gulls and fooles" in general, now very real persons, former friends, poets, people in high places, and so on, and now something of both, from that misty mid-region between "type" and real. In accounts of the rise of formal satire in England it belongs just after Donne, Hall, and Marston, and in studies of the influence of Martial, after Davies and Harington. To these contemporaries it is heavily indebted. It was among the first to sound that peculiarly negative, melancholic, and malicious note that we associate with the late nineties, with the verse satirists, Jonson's *Humour* plays, and *Hamlet*. *Every Man In* was probably performed first in this same September. *Skialetheia* was partly responsible for the order that "noe *Satyres* or *Epigrams* be printed hereafter" and was among those called in and burnt on 1 and 4 June 1599.[1] Of its reception otherwise we have Marston's word, perhaps not completely objective: "those bookes that are cald in, are most in sale and request."[2] Francis Meres included "the Author of *Skialetheia*" among those best for satire.[3]

The epigrams, approximately a third of which are based ultimately on Martial, treat subjects traditional with epigrammatists, such as loose women, absurd fashions, dishonest lawyers and merchants, fops and fantastics, and poetasters, under the conventional type-names of Lais, Clodius, Matho, Licus, Nævia, and so on. A number are especially topical, such as Epigram 68 with its list of London sights and sounds, Epigram 8 "*To Deloney*," and Epigram 24 "*Of Fuscus*," who is probably Nashe. All give the impression not of Martial's Rome but rather of Elizabeth's London.

Satyre Preludium, on poets and poetry, attacks contemporary tastes and particular works by way of defending epigram and satire as literary forms.

Satyra Prima, on hypocrisy, lashes out at the times in general, listing various guises of hypocrisy.

Satyra Secunda, against cosmetics, describes them and details the horror of their effects.

Satyra Tertia, on inconstancy, attacks one overly fashionable former friend in particular, and others in passing.

Satyra Quarta, on jealousy, portrays the jealous husband's antics and exposes his guilt.

Satyra Quinta, on vanity, presents in the form of a city walk the variety of vanities to be met in the streets of London.

Satyra Sexta, on opinion, attacks the sway this inferior function has over Reason in the times.

Most if not all of *Skialetheia* was written within a year or perhaps eighteen months of its entry.[4] The allusion to a ballad of "the *Burgonians* tragedy" (V. 56) could have been made only after July 1598, when John Barrose, the Burgonian fencer, was executed. Guilpin's reference to "*Reactio*" (VI. 96) would probably follow the publication of *Certaine Satyres* in May 1598, to which Marston's satire by that name was added. The incident with "*Fabian*" and the "*Prince d'Amour*" (III. 93-100) almost certainly took place during the Christmas revels at the Middle Temple in 1597/98. And the "vnfrequented Theater" (V. 84) was closed on 28 July 1597. More generally, the "*Cads*-beard" mentioned three times (Ep. 53, III. 65, V. 75) we may presume to have been fashionable for a number of months after that military success in the summer of 1596. Such evidence suggests that little would have been written much before the end of 1596, and the whole gives the impression of late 1597 and 1598. *Skialetheia* would not of course have been composed *seriatim,* parts having been written at various times. Epigrams and satires are by nature pieces and compounds of pieces, certainly a number of these are. Clearly, however, the author could not have finished the book as it is now until a few weeks before publication.

EVERARD GUILPIN: LIFE AND LITERARY RELATIONS

John Payne Collier first noticed that seven extracts from the anonymous *Skialetheia* included in *England's Parnassus* (1600) are assigned to Guilpin, and scholars have since confirmed his identification and provided sufficient detail for a limited biographical sketch.[5] Everard (sometimes Edward) Guilpin (sometimes Gilpin) was the eldest of six children of John Guilpin and Thomasin Everard of Highgate, who were married, according to the register of Gillingham St. Mary, Norfolk, on 27 February 1570/71. John seems to have been prominent and reasonably well-to-do, having been elected governor of the Highgate Grammar School in 1580 and serving as clerk of the pleas in the Court of Exchequer. In his will dated 1 March 1586/87 he left all his property, which he perhaps too modestly refers to as "soe smale a portion," and which apparently included some in Swain's Lane, Highgate, to his wife, trusting her to use it and her discretion in bringing up their children. He was buried in St. Andrews, Holborn, on 11 March 1590/91, and his will was proved on 10 May following.[6]

On 29 June 1592 Thomasin married William Guarsi (Guercy, etc.), grandson of Andrew Guarsi of London, and the brother of John Marston's mother Mary. The two apparently lived in Highgate for a period and removed thereafter to William's house in Aldermanbury parish. Such seems to be the case from a lawsuit of 1596 involving them in the Court of Requests—prepared by "Marston," presumably the satirist's father and William's brother-in-law—an attempt to retain certain property in Hornsey Great Park, which Thomasin had leased for terms of eight or nine years in September 1591 and March 1592 to one Walter Pewes, a butcher of St. Sepulchre's, Holborn, who was delinquent in rent and upkeep.[7] As a witness for his mother and stepfather, Everard Guilpin submitted two signed quarto pages of testimony in answer to eight set questions in which he described himself as of Gray's Inn and of the age of twenty-four or thereabouts. By the late nineties the Guarsies had moved to Ilketshall (near Bungay) in Suffolk. Thomasin, the daughter of John Everard of Gillingham (near Bungay), was apparently related to a number of Norfolk and Suffolk Guilpins. Her elder brother Edward, who owned property in Bungay and elsewhere, provided the farm for the Guarsies, and in his will of 24 February 1598/99 (he died 21 November 1599), he arranged for legacies to the six Guilpin children, Everard's portion being £100 (£50 for two years).

In all probability Everard Guilpin (b. 1572?) attended Highgate Grammar School, founded by Sir Roger Chomley in 1565, of which his father was governor. He matriculated at Cambridge in 1588, and was entered as a pensioner of Emmanuel College on 1 June of that year. He did not apparently proceed to a degree. On 29 April 1591, shortly after his father's death, he entered Gray's Inn, probably with a view to completing his legal studies without delay. He alludes to his education in Epigram 22 :

> I haue sized in Cambridge, and my friends a season
> Some exhibition for me there disburst :
> Since that, I haue beene in Goad his weekly role,
> And beene acquaint with *Mounsieur Littleton,* etc.

There is no evidence that he was ever thereafter called to the bar. According to the register of St. Mary's, Bungay, on 3 February 1606/7 Everard married Sarah Guarsi of "Boxcot" (in or near Bungay), almost certainly the daughter of William, his stepfather, by a first marriage, and thus Marston's first cousin. Along with his stepfather, Guilpin disposed of property and land in Highgate on 19 March 1607/8, by which time it may be assumed that Thomasin had died. He is described as of Boyscott, Suffolk, where it seems likely, near relatives, he took up residence. He may have, like Donne and Marston, entered the Church.

Beyond this outline we are left with assumptions based on his work and on literary allusions to him. He can easily be identified with that extraordinary set of young men who came from the universities in the 1590s to the Inns of Court to study law and by some means to find preferment at court. All were well educated, of fairly good family, ambitious, quick-witted, frustrated, active almost to the point of desperation, it seems, and quickly and thoroughly skilled in the ways of city and court. All sought admission into circles of possibility, and saw display of literary wit as one means of advancement. "The history of each poet is in outline the same," says John Wilcox, referring to the satiric wits Donne, Davies, Hall, Marston, Weever, and (so far as his biography admits) Guilpin, all of whom follow a pattern established earlier by Harington.[8] For these satirists literature was a form of self-advertisement, argues Wilcox, albeit inversely so, as they usually delayed publication, circulating their manuscripts privately, or else they published them anonymously. *Skialetheia* is a product of the limited world of the Inns of Court, with its special values and private sensibilities. The realistic and satiric tendency it shares with other literature of this world is, according to Philip J. Finkelpearl, a compound of many elements: "youthful, self-conscious cynicism nurtured in the catalytic atmosphere of the law schools; a sense of belonging to an elite of wits in a world of gulls; a tradition of free and candid speech; upper-class condescension to the taste of professional writers; a tradition of plain style in language which tended to be associated with the Inns and the courtly writers; and perhaps the dominance of one powerful and admirable figure in Donne."[9] *Skialetheia* is above all a display of "wit." But beneath its pose of the almost manic satirist, outraged that former friends now arrived should forget him, there runs a tendency toward despondency, as though from disillusionment with a chance for place. Guilpin, so far as we know, never received preferment.

From his place in this special set and from his little book, it is clear that Guilpin was thoroughly aware of the literary currents of the mid-nineties—one reason that *Skialetheia* should appeal to the literary historian. He enjoyed the familiarity of at least two significant rising literary lights of his day. Donne's verse letter "To Mr. E. G." is certainly addressed to him.[10] Probably written in the summer of 1593, while Guilpin vacationed away from the city at Highgate and Suffolk, it presumes an established intimacy both personal and literary. My "rimes," Donne writes from London,

> bred in our vale below,
> Bearing with them much of my love and hart,
> Fly unto that Parnassus, wher thou art.

Already, the poem implies, Guilpin was something of a poet. By this time Donne had begun writing satires, and Guilpin doubtless drew inspiration from his success, and may already have made his first attempts. The opening of Guilpin's fifth satire is a close imitation of the opening of Donne's first (probably written in 1593).[11] Scholars therefore have sought allusions to Donne in *Skialetheia*.

Guilpin's relation with Marston is more evident and relevant. The most striking impression one receives from Guilpin's satires is the close affinity they have with Marston's. "To all appearances," says John Peter, "the book is simply Marston's work all over again."[12] The similarity of image, idea, tone, and overall structure, which the commentary points out time and again, gives witness to a sympathy over and above "literary influence." Their family tie, we know, dates from the early nineties. They shared a number of interests, including law (Marston became a member of the Middle Temple in 1592), the theater, and apparently an antagonism toward Hall, who had been a member of Guilpin's college, Emmanuel, at Cambridge. Some offense by Hall against Guilpin may have prompted Marston's attack, which otherwise seems largely gratuitous or at least extremely difficult to explain.[13] Whatever the case, Guilpin probably supplied Marston with accounts of Hall. When in his roll call of poets in Satire VI Guilpin refers to Hall's satires, he notes with

apparent satisfaction that Marston has put Hall down (alluding
to Marston's "*Reactio*"):

> The double volum'd *Satyre* praised is,
> And lik'd of diuers for his Rods in pisse,
> Yet other-some, who would his credite crack
> Haue clap'd *Reactioes* Action on his back.
>   [ll. 93-96]

And one of Marston's more vigorous attacks against Hall,
"Satyra Noua," added to the 1599 edition of *The Scourge of
Villanie*, is dedicated "*To his very friend, maister E.G.*," that is,
to Guilpin.

Guilpin further participated alongside Marston in what
Arnold Davenport has labeled the "Hall-Marston-Guilpin-
Jonson-Weever-Breton quarrels," exchanges in a series of pam-
phlets that moved from the literary enmity between Hall and
Marston into spirited attempts to deprecate or justify satire.[14] In
The Whipping of the Satyre (1601), which seems to be an attempt to capitalize on the Archbishop's ban of satire, one
"W. I.," who may be John Weever, attacks the work in particular of three authors—a "Satyrist, Epigrammatist, and Hu-
mourist." Davenport has successfully identified the three as
Marston, Guilpin, and Jonson. All "W. I." 's descriptive charges
in his epistle readily apply to Guilpin. *Skialetheia* is certainly
"bawdery"; one could say, with regard to the bulk of them, that
"the whole Epigram doth make way for the last two lines";
Fabius, Felix, and Clodius, included, as "W.I." says, in "such a
companie of Imaginarie persons," do appear in *Skialetheia* (but
not Rufus, who is in Davies's epigrams); and Guilpin does turn
from "knaue" to "scholler" in the end, the last satire, of Reason
and Opinion, being uncharacteristically academic. Moreover,
the section of the poem devoted to the Epigrammatist (ll. 619-
834), accusing him of breaching the peace, of relying on personal
abuse, and of hypocrisy, contains numerous additional, con-
firming allusions. Nicholas Breton's *No Whippinge, nor trip-
pinge: but a kinde friendly Snippinge* (1601), which gives gentle

guidelines for inoffensive, constructive satire, refers to the Epigrammatist, again clearly Guilpin, in its opening stanza:
    The Epigrammatist in his quips displaies
    A wicked course in shadowes of corrections.
But Breton does not pursue the particular person or work. It is
Guilpin without question, as Davenport contends, who joins the
quarrel in defense of Marston and himself against "W. I." (ig-
noring Breton) in the little anonymous pamphlet *The Whipper of
the Satyre his Pennance*, etc. (1601), arguing, in his abusive and
difficult style, almost exclusively the value of the father's "rod":
"Better be whipt on Earth, then scourg'd in Hell" (l. 114).
Guilpin's rejoinder apparently terminates the quarrel, for we
hear no more of it. And there is not firm evidence that Guilpin
wrote again after *The Whipper*.[15]

Just as we have trouble, moving from one to the other,
realizing any distinction between the styles of Marston and Guilpin, we cannot establish with any certainty, for purposes of
literary history, the direction of indebtedness. Publication dates,
not altogether trustworthy in this respect, give a slight priority
to Marston. *Certaine Satyres* was registered on 27 May 1598,
and there may have been, as Davenport thinks, an earlier edition. *The Scourge of Villanie*, to which *Skialetheia* bears the
greatest resemblance, was registered on 8 September 1598, one
week before *Skialetheia*. We might assume because of its reference to *"Reactio"* that Satire VI, the last, was written after
Certaine Satyres. But otherwise there is little evidence. Guilpin
was presumably several years older than Marston (who was
baptized in October 1576), and thus could be expected to exert
influence. We also can infer from Donne's verse letter that Guilpin was writing poetry of some sort by the summer of 1593.
Such evidence falling short, however, we must rely on impressions of their respective work, and these, I think, encourage the
assumption that Marston was the inspirer. In addition to the
slightly earlier publication dates, Marston's style seems more
independent and consistent. Guilpin is more given to imitation,

following Donne, Davies, Shakespeare, and so on. Marston is more productive, more compulsive in his dedication to literature, as his longer career testifies. Besides, Marston, who concentrated his efforts at this time on satire, was the "Satyrist" to contemporaries, Guilpin, the "Epigrammatist." Finally, impressions indicate that Marston's was the more aggressive and commanding personality. But we cannot easily separate them or be certain of the debt. The important feature is that the two were "in close contact, sharing ideas and books,"[16] as the similarity of their works suggests. One is inclined to detect a hint of their literary friendship, perhaps friendly rivalry, when the "satirist," in the opening lines of Satire I (following Juvenal's First), refuses any longer to remain "in silence and giue ayme [encouragement], / To other wits which make court to bright fame."

Moving in such circles Guilpin was extremely sensitive to the literary climate of his day. We know from his book that he had read much of the best written by his contemporaries, that he knew first- or second-hand many significant literary figures, and held estimates of them, literary and personal, which he sought to express or imply, and that he undertook seriously to make a real contribution to his tradition. He makes explicit references to Chaucer, Gower, Spenser, Sidney, Drayton, Daniel, Markham, and Deloney. Openly or covertly he alludes to Marlowe, Nashe, Davies, Lodge, Harvey, and more. Frequently he tantalizes the reader into a near recognition of some important contemporary only to stop him short, a little embarrassed, as is the satirist's wont. And he constantly echoes passages from other works. *Satyre Preludium,* large parts of Satires I and VI, and several epigrams he devotes to discussions of literary genre, especially satire, and of literary tastes. His preoccupation with his craft and contemporary craftsmen renders *Skialetheia* a delightful, if frustrating on occasions, sourcebook for the literary scholar.

But behind these few facts and impressions Guilpin himself remains shadowy. We know he loved the theater (he refers to Theatre, Rose, and Curtain), and took a special interest in dancing and music, in the major events at home and abroad, in intrigue and gossip among the high and low. It is clear, moreover, that in his special way he loved the London of his day, its streets, people, sins, and its words. He participated in it all, and has recorded with sensitivity for us one fleeting moment in England's palmiest hour.

Skialetheia AND ELIZABETHAN FORMAL VERSE SATIRE

The feature most characteristic of verse satire in the 1590s and immediately after, and that which readily distinguishes it from earlier satire, is the presence of a voice of a special quality, and one that participates dramatically in the satiric process. Whereas medieval satire had stressed the "scene," that is, the estates, the "fair field full of folk," and relegated to a minor role a plain and humble "satirist," Elizabethan satire exaggerated the interaction with the "scene" of a different, more exciting "satirist," stressing both, and as a consequence produced significantly different satire. According to Professor Alvin Kernan, whose *Cankered Muse* is the best account of this new satire, Elizabethan verse satire is "a poem in which the author playing the part of the satyr attacks vice in the crude, elliptic, harsh language which befits his assumed character and his low subject matter."[17] No longer the morally earnest, blunt Piers or Colin (and not yet the urbanely ironic wits to be found in Dryden and Pope), the satirist is "satyr," outraged, rough, abusive, lascivious, and frank, according to the popular conception of the satyr as half-man half-goat, from which it was thought the word *satire* derived, and in keeping with the spirit of the persona of Juvenal, whom Elizabethans were trying to imitate. Guilpin shares with his immediate contemporaries Hall, Marston, Rankins, and others this general understanding of satire, which accounts for certain qualities of his practice.

He does not, however, present the woodland satyr in a consistent, fully realized form, as does Rankins, for example.

Instead he sends his satirist through a series of "characters," shifting from one to another, as if trying under various shapes to acclimate him to English experience in general and to each specific satiric situation, as if determined to outmask the many masks he meets wherever he turns in a fast-moving, changing scene. The "satyr" is Beadle with "whip and cord" (I. 157), the puritan lecturer warning against the wiles of women (II), a fencer with rapier in fist, "a careless Prince," a "foule-mouth Iester" (Ep. 70), a physician, who "heale[s] with lashing" (*Sat. Pre.* 71), a wayward, testy child (VI. 129 ff.), and so on. Frequently the satirist attributes to his female Muse comparable impulses; she "play[s] the scold" (I. 12), and must be encouraged, lest she "fall from brawling to a blubbering passion" (I. 44). She is the promiscuous whore, who repays sins after the whore's fashion, with venereal disease. In places Guilpin appears not completely practiced in the recently received technique. He disregards the satirist's persona (that is, the satirist does not call attention to himself) in Satire IV, for example, where the distinct voice is not heard. Elsewhere the satirist sounds very like Guilpin himself, the Inns of Court man, as in the first part of Satire III, or else his tone slips from stuttering abuse to passive reflection, as in parts of Satire VI. On the whole, however, despite the lapses and audible whatever the mask, the satirist is the furious, vicious, and impatient satyr, righteously indignant, "the Strappado, rack," "the scourge, the *Tamburlaine* of vice" (*Sat. Pre.* 82, 89), who takes pleasure in applying the whip.

For the satirists of the nineties, it followed that the style of satire should be rough, crude, and licentious, as would be appropriate to a "satyr" and as followed from their understanding of crabbed Persius and jerking Juvenal. Guilpin makes an effort to render his lines rough, referring more than once to his "harsh stile" (VI. 177):

> I know they are passing filthy, scuruey lines,
> I know they are rude, harsh, vnsauory rimes:
> Fit to wrap playsters, and odd vnguents in, etc.
>
> [Ep. 70]

His Muse "must haue words compact of fire & rage" (I. 50). His
diction, always extreme, unlaureate, mixes gutter with academy.
Spitting and stuttering, he has "lousie," "whimpring," "puling,"
"chitterlings," "ulcerous," "toad housing sculs," alongside such
pretensions as "Polypragmon," "manumission," "Genius," "Fanonian," "opinionate," and other extreme latinates. He affects the
irritating, shrill pipe and the pounding drum of Pan rather than
the melodic lute of Apollo, urging his antagonists on a verbis
ad verbera. Moreover, his lines are intentionally difficult and
obscure in varying degrees. Elizabethans believed that satires
should be "ridle-like obscuring their intent," according to Hall,
or "palpable darke, and so rough writ, that the hearing of them
read, would set a mans teeth on edge," according to Marston
(with some exaggeration).[18] They may have questioned the
degree of obscurity that would be effective, apologized for or
tried to justify what they took to be their own frequent "plain-
ness," as Hall and Marston do, falling back in part on the traditional notion from earlier practice of the blunt, straightforward
satirist; but their satires betray what is, by Elizabethan stan-
dards, a cultivated obscurity, an allegiance to the idea implicit to
them in Juvenal and Persius that there is a "peculiar kinde of
speech for a Satyres lips."[19]

　　Guilpin's satires are hard to read. They exploit a number of
techniques calculated to perplex, including rapidly shifting dialogues, abrupt shifts in syntax, wild, ambiguous expressions,
allusions and puns in line after line, suppressed transitions,
questions, and irregular metrical qualities. They make sense
finally, but only at the demand of an alert reader and full commentary. The line, for example, despite its displaced accent and
variously placed caesura, is almost always iambic pentameter,
with five clear stresses and ten syllables. For us, after the meta-
physicals the sound is not so grating, but beside the lyric poetry
of the nineties and the elegant lyrics of the tribe of Ben, it is
rugged.

　　A final characteristic of the satyr which helped establish the

new decorum of satire, and one likewise encouraged by attempts
to imitate the classical satirists, was his lasciviousness. The Muse
of *Skialetheia* is a prostitute, "To womens loose gownes suting
her loose rimes" (Ep. 69). "Wanton words," Guilpin says, "are
the language of an Epigrame" (Ep. 47). The satirist attacks vice
and folly of all forms, but none rouses his wrath more or holds
his attention longer than sexual perversion in all its forms. With
detailed description or glancing implication the satirist exposes
the activities of whore, bawd, homosexual, and randy, and the
ribaldry of popular love poetry. It is not without justice that
"bawdery" constitutes "W. I." 's primary complaint against the
"Epigrammatist": "How your tongue rioted in bawdery, I am
ashamed to rehearse. . . . For, touching examples of Venerie, I
thinke, you had gotten a whole Sampler-full from Venus her
selfe, so that you might well haue a place and applause aboue all
others for that faculty."[20] The traditionally promiscuous character of the satyr, along with a decorum which required that style
fit the subject, gave writers of satire at least partial excuse for
their liberty and one argument against constant criticism of
which "W. I." 's is typical. But there remains about their satire,
and *Skialetheia*, a little more than convention if less than out-
right perversion itself. Of the satirists we may say with
Harington: "Lechers learn to stir vp Lust with lashes."[21] At the
basis of all satire rests this paradox, that the satirist is himself
guilty. "The satirist attacks *in others* the weaknesses and temp-
tations that are really *within himself*," as Kenneth Burke
observes, and he "thereby *gratifies* and punishes the vice within
himself. Is he whipped with his own lash? He is."[22] Guilpin's
satirist castigates contemporary love poems as "Panders vnto
lusts, and food to sinnes" (*Sat. Pre.* 10) in the face of his own
obsession with sex and the innuendos he gives, an attitude
permissible, presumably, through the agency of the wanton
"satyr." Aware that what he describes is filthy and his own work
so, his satirist appeals to Decorum (Ep. 70):

Viewing this sin-drownd world, I purposely,
Phisick'd my *Muse*, that thus vnmannerly,
She might beray our folly-soyled age,
And keepe *Decorum* on a comick stage, etc.

"Genius," according to Northrop Frye, "seems to have led prac-
tically every great satirist to become what the world calls
obscene."[23] If no satiric genius, Guilpin found the symptoms
congenial, for *Skialetheia* is extremely obscene, and satire of
love as much as of disgust. This salacity more than anything
else, John Peter thinks, caused the Archbishop to burn it.[24]

The satirist involves himself not only in a basically para-
doxical position of moral hypocrisy, but also in a number of
other related inconsistencies, all more or less attributable to
what Kernan calls the "contradictory and twisted nature of the
satyr."[25] He presumes to give an accurate picture of the way
things are, "to speake the truth" (*Sat. Pre.* 76), but what he
renders could hardly be called "realistic," so distorted as it is by
his special vision. At times he poses as the plain, unlettered
satirist of the early tradition, referring to his "lean play"
(Ep. 70), his "lewd" style, and calling his epigram "a plaine
dealing lad" who "calls a iade, a iade" (*Sat. Pre.* 75-76). But his
satire displays the widest range of rhetorical tricks, of conscious
literary devices, and is anything but plain. He extols the virtues
of reason and stoic calm, but is himself given to wildly irrational
rage. He denies concern for critical estimation of his satire, but
clearly, considering the vehemence and frequency of his denials,
protests too much. He despises critics, and is himself one. And
so on. Such inconsistencies are primarily implicit in his general
character, the result of specific uses made of him at specific
moments throughout. In at least two significant places, however, Guilpin turns on the satirist, exploiting his inadequacies to
give additional (mild) point to the conclusions of satires. At the
end of Satire I the speaker admits to having sought praise by
exposing hypocrites and chides himself. At the end of Satire II he
concludes himself a "foole" since no one heeds his admonitions.

His complexity, which seems to have been conventional, con-
tributes to the total complexity of the satires, wherein it is his
presence that first strikes the reader.

In addition to encouragement for those more obvious
features of persona and tone, Elizabethan satirists drew other,
less notable features from their classical models. The formal
structure of the satires, a series of short satires in one book, of
about a thousand lines in length, followed from the classics.[26]
Like Persius, Guilpin has a prologue and six satires. The use of
personal type-names likewise derives from the classics, as do
certain stylistic characteristics: the forceful, dramatic insertion
into the scene in the openings, the rapid movement from object
to object within the scene, and the extravagant profusion of
rhetorical and linguistic devices throughout. Moreover, there
are specific debts to the Romans that would tend to indicate an
overall similarity. At least a third of Guilpin's epigrams are
imitations of Martial. The attack on contemporary literature in
Satyre Preludium was undoubtedly inspired by the opening
attacks of Juvenal and Persius. Satire II, with its criticism of
women, fits neatly alongside Juvenal's celebrated Sixth, from
which, as Dryden has it, "all the Moderns have notoriously
stollen their sharpest Raileries."[27] Satire V takes its form from
Horace's city walk (I. ix), following Donne's imitation, and its
substance from Juvenal's vicious, protracted account of city evils
in his Third. And the reflective elements of VI has precedents in
Horace and Persius. Thus Guilpin gives the impression that his
satires are classically correct, as they certainly are in spirit and
general conception.

But when one looks closely for direct borrowings, with the
exception of the epigrams, not properly satires though associated with them in the Elizabethan mind, one finds very few, as
the notes indicate. Most of the detail is English, the humor in a
vernacular especially homespun, and whatever is traceable to
classical sources could easily have been taken from current
English intermediaries.[28] It need not disturb one's sense that the

satirists affected the classical vein to note that they nonetheless drew most of their statement and power from native sources. The fact, for example, that there are seven satires manifests the latent hold which the old Seven Deadly Sins maintained on Guilpin's mind. A slight shift in perspective reveals that Satire I is the old personification of Dissimulation, Satire II, the anti-feminist tract (cf. Tertullian, *De cultu feminarum*), III, a description of Pride, V, of Vanity Fair, and VI, of the Goddess Fortuna. In Satire IV Jealousy is a beast in medieval manner. In the various vignettes under Elizabethan cover remain the traditional sins or branches thereof. Gnatho of Epigram 25, for example, is Idleness; Fœlix (Essex in the passage drawn from Shakespeare, I. 63-76), Ambition; the Traveller and Antiquary (I. 123-42), old Lying with his tricks. In many instances even the epigrams take their points from traditional English proverbs, after Heywood's earlier manner, being partly, as Davies of Hereford refers to his, *"Descants vpon English Proverbs"*; or else they rely on the bawdy jest, after the popular jestbooks.

But it is to an immediately Elizabethan expression of this native tradition that Guilpin goes, more than to any other, for the stuff of his satire. As has long been noted, no essential difference exists between the tone and matter of Elizabethan verse satire and that of the puritan pamphlets of Gosson and Stubbes. There rarely occurs an image, pun, or other point in *Skialetheia* not already present or hinted at in the works of Greene, Harvey, Lodge, and especially in Nashe, the brilliant "young Iuvenall" of his day. In Nashe's *Pierce Penilesse* (1592), the most important influence after Marston for Guilpin, the satirist bursts with moral indignation and proceeds on the street to point out various objects for rebuke just as does Guilpin's satirist. Nashe's work, as James B. Leishman has pointed out, is in the manner of the medieval allegory complete with traditional sins.[29] And *Christ's Tears*, wherein the "second Daughter of Pryde [who] is Gorgeous attyre" closely resembles parts of Satire II,[30] simply marshals the Seven Deadly Sins and their offspring in Elizabethan dress. Nashe and other prose satirists parade all the types familiar in the verse satirists: flatterers, gulls, malcontents, spendthrifts, whores, etc., all based ultimately on traditional conceptions. Leishman, whose argument for the primacy of native influence over the classical is convincing, has aptly commented on the continuity of the English tradition.

> If anyone will make the experiment of reading, one after the other, a few pages of, let us say, Nashe's *Pierce Penilesse*, Lodge's *Wits Miserie*, Rowlands's *Letting of Humours Blood*, Hall's Satires, Jonson's *Every Man out of His Humour*, and almost any of the prose characters from Overbury to Earle, he will, I think, perceive a fundamental resemblance, and will feel that the form chosen—prose satire, verse satire, "humour" comedy, prose Character—is, in a sense, almost accidental. Behind them all he will feel, far more powerfully than that of Horace or Juvenal or Persius, or Plautus or Terence or Theophrastus, the presence of that allegorical and realistic representation of the Seven Deadly Sins and their followers which is as old as the medieval pulpit and the medieval homily.[31]

To put it another way, from an Elizabethan point of view Guilpin's satires are classical; from ours they are native.

Guilpin's gull of Epigram 20, for example, is Davies's and Greene's before him, Dekker's and others' after him. He not only follows the types, he takes over the manner of treatment. His "circle" of Idleness in Epigram 25 is in manner like that of Stubbes's idle "gentlewomen": "For some of them lye in bed (I will not saie with whom) till nine or tenne of the clocke euery mornyng; . . . thei are twoo or three howers in puttyng on their Robes, . . . thei go to dinner . . . thei walke abrode for a time. . . . Thus some spende the daie till suppertime, and then the night as before."[32] Guilpin simply alters the sex, compresses the detail into verse, and applies an ironic point, maintaining the theme and approach, the circularity. How the satirists worked within a limited and consistent tradition, taking what was already familiar and varying it more or less for different effect, should be clear to one who observes the various treatment the same "circle" gets in Nashe, Harington, Davies, the *Parnassus Plays,* and Rowlands.[33] Lodge's description of Lying, to take one of the examples Leishman adduces to show the satirists' overall interdependence (Rowlands appropriates it almost verbatim from Lodge), has parallel in Guilpin.

> he wil tell you of monsters that haue faces in their breasts, and men that couer their bodies with their feet in stead of a Penthouse. . . . hee will offer you . . . a piece of CAESARS chaire wherein hee was slaine in the Senate house. Etc.

> He shewes a peece of blacke-iack for the shooe,
> Which old *Ægeus* bequeathd his valiant sonne:
> A peece of pollisht mother of pearle's the spoone
> *Cupid* eate pappe with; and he hath a dagger
> Made of the sword wherwith great *Charles*
> did swagger.
>
> [I. 138-42][34]

By shuffling character, sin, and stock situation, satirists usually avoided (except in Rowlands's case) repeating their predecessors exactly. Guilpin's Traveller, for example, a braggart exposed as a coward, could just as easily be given to lust and bear the marks of venereal disease, or vain and wear in ostentation the evidence of his travels. The point is that *Skialetheia* fits solidly into a very precise English contemporary satiric environment for all its apparent indebtedness to the classics. A strong sense of the nature of this "literary" environment, which the commentary attempts to give, revitalizes *Skialetheia,* easing the difficulties caused by unfamiliar images, allusions, and puns native to that environment. When Guilpin says of the Malcontent that "To his sights life, his hat becomes a toombe" (Ep. 52), he points indirectly to one of the Malcontent's conspicuous, established features, his failure to wear a hatband. And when he speaks of "the sharp tart veriuice of his [the critic's] snap-haunce hate" (VI. 134), he varies, rather extremely, the popular epithet for critics, "crabbed and snappish."

In Guilpin's satire as in all Elizabethan satire, the "scene" is active and packed with all sorts of grotesques. "London is as rich in apes / As *Affricke Tabraca*" (V. 70-71), which is his way of giving the satirist's "Stultorum plena sunt omnia." And he delights in pointing at each fool: "But see yonder," "Here's one," "whom haue we here?" in a gallery of freaks, "Brokers, Coblers, slaues, / Black-men, trap-makers, and such kind of knaues" (VI. 161-62). His major stylistic device is *accumulatio*, filling his scene with scrap after scrap, until, like Rome (in the allusion of Epigram 1) it "orewhelms" itself by its own weight. *Satire*, after all, was related to the Latin adjective *satur* meaning full or charged with a mixture, and because a *mixture*, impure. *Skialetheia* is heavy with things as well as characters, all of which to the satirist are filthy: clothes, money, food, drink, coaches, paints, masks, horses, asses, muck, cosmetics, hair, books, rheum—all "durt, and sensualitie" (VI. 20). Like all outraged moralists, Marston, Jonson, Swift, Martin Luther, his vision of the world is excremental; it is a "folly-soyled age" (Ep. 70). Satire for him is catharsis—he "phisicks" his Muse (Ep. 70)—a catharsis for the world, and itself excrement, or else flatulence (cf. Ep. 7), taking its place naturally in the privy (VI. 174-78). He is determined to untruss the "humorous" (in its scatological sense) times, "to rende the foggie cloude," as he says, "whose al black wombe far blacker vice doth shrowd" (I. 15-16). There is in Guilpin, says Whipple, "filth for filth's sake," says Peter, "dirt for dirt's sake."[35] His obsession with sex, which to him is always dirty, with disease, and with ordure leads one to conclude of him, as Kernan and others have of Marston, that his attitude "passes the bounds of reason and borders on the psychotic."[36] But we need not dwell on the point as it is familiar to anyone who knows Elizabethan satire and the images in the satirists' descriptions of their own work ("purge," etc.).

A number of characteristics of the "scene" or texture of the satires, beyond these, follow from Guilpin's attitude. As the commentary indicates, *Skialetheia* is charged with allusions, bits and pieces picked up from a wide variety of sources, in line after line, giving it a sense of weight ("gravity"), and requiring the reader to strain at understanding. It is heavy with words: "words, words, words," as Professor Ellis-Fermor, echoing Hamlet, says of Marston.[37] Its diction resembles what Jonson forces Marston to throw up in *Poetaster*, "heapes of huge words uphoorded hideously," as Spenser would say.[38] Moreover, it betrays a prepossession with the distinction between appearance and reality, shadow and substance. Compulsively the satirist points to "masks," to that which is painted over, women, pictures, posts, repeating such words as "daub," "varnish," "oil." He grows irascible over clothes, skin, gestures, and counterfeits—these being what Eliot calls, referring to Jonson, the "superficies" of life, that, we might say, which is smeared on. Otherwise he concentrates on extreme image polarities appropriate to his obsession, of lightness and weight, emptiness ("puffed") and fullness ("stuff"), movement-noise-rage ("business," "activity," "wind") and quietude ("calm," "content"), and so on, all related to what one would call an anal personality. The consequence of such a dual vision is that the meaning of individual words in context becomes problematical. Words are slippery, duplicitous, masking in one signification only to function underneath toward a different, more significant end. Next to *accumulatio*, wordplay is Guilpin's central literary device, and, incidentally, not the least symptomatic of his pathology. Hardly a line passes without evidence of manipulation which the reader must attend to for the pun or quibble. A few should alert the reader: *conceit=con-seat, close=clothes, vain=vein, back and all=bacchanal, rare=rear, pens=penis, growst stale=*(one suspects) *gross tail, court=cart.* Any word our experience with Elizabethan wordplay has led us to suspect of a backside must be be considered: *light, discourse, wind, proud, occupation, cunning,* etc. It is impossible to relax one's attention or choose to ignore the wordplay and at the same time participate in the satiric event. Epigrammatists usually called the reader's attention to this conventional complexity of the words in the opening epistles. Heywood's admonition, for example, describes this conception of the word:

> Ere ye full reiecte these trifles folowyng here
> Perceiue (I praie you) of the woordes thententes clere.
> In whiche (maie ye like to looke) ye shall espie
> Some woordes, shewe one sence, a nother to disclose,
> Some woords, them selues sondrie senses signifie:
> Some woordes, somewhat from common sence, I
>   dispose,
> To seeme one sence in text, a nother in glose.
> These words in this work, thus wrought your
>   working toole
> Maie woorke me to seeme (at least) the les a foole.[39]

Finally as concerns the satirist's scene, there is little in the way of the good and blessed in these satires to be held up as a standard against the press of filth and depravity. We have only hints, the impressive account of the satirist's study, his *"Eden of content"* (V. 1-36), the brief passage in praise of Epictetus (VI. 140-54), and the praise of the corrective function of satire and epigram (*Sat. Pre.*). The last two of these resort to the peculiarly negative imagery characteristic of the texture generally. One has the impression that were Guilpin to call on the Prince of Light he would be distracted by the sexual quibble on *light*, that there is no *grace* for him, only *grease*.

Neither Elizabethan nor classical verse satires have "plots" in the usual sense of the word—no sequences of interrelated events that bring about a change in satirist or object of attack. The Inconstant Friend of Satire III for all the castigation remains proud and distant at the end; the Jealous Husband of IV jealous forever. The reader's emotions are excited and controlled not so much by response to the large shape of the satire, which provides little in the way of real variation of quality or quantity of effect from beginning to end, but rather out of response to particular fragments within the whole, which call attention to themselves with slight regard for the large context. Guilpin and his contemporaries are, however, aware of the normal requirements of unity and climax. Guilpin treats in each satire a single topic, to which the fragments pertain, and he provides most with a distinct "frame," ending where he begins. Moreover, he manages with some success to bring each to a climax. Satires II and IV, of rather limited topics, end with exposés. Satires I, III, and VI, on more general themes, all conclude by engaging the satirist in a final, highly intense dramatic scene with his respective antagonists. And V, using the opposite technique, closes with an exasperated understatement.

But the impression of an overall, careful design does not strike the reader. It is not as though each conclusion is probably or inevitably anticipated beforehand, that each is, as one might imagine, the last fatal blow in a series of blows of ever-increasing intensity. What the reader remembers are the separate parts, and the fragmentary nature of the whole, as though fragments were the only forms the satirist could trust. The satires are episodic, encyclopedic, a form amenable to the exposure of a succession of different aspects of a single subject. Each satire is a grab bag, *sated* with *ire* (to borrow an Elizabethan play), in which are collected the satirist's effects, loosely thrown together after the name of each bag. As it is with characters, things, allusions, and puns, *Skialetheia* is "stuffed" with an innumerable variety of purely rhetorical devices: proverbs, dialogues, anecdotes, allegoric descriptions, portraits, miniature dramas, brief sermons, apostrophes, invocations to abstractions, each with its sharpened irony for summary exposure, understatement, overstatement, innuendo, contradiction, and so on. The tone varies with periodic intervals, at times the calm, slow accumulation of mild climaxes, at other times the wild, sometimes strained, outburst of invective. Whatever special device he may be using, the satirist, like the angry man, loves the series, of climaxes, of deprecations, the string of abuses. Opinion is, for example,

> *Fooles bawble, innouations Mistris,*
> *The Proteus Robin-good-fellow of change,*

> Smithfield of iaded fancies, and th'Exchange
> Of fleeting censures, nurse of heresie,
> Begot by Malice on Inconstancie:
> It's but the hisse of Geese, the peoples noyse,
> The tongue of humours, etc.
>
> [VI. 58-64]

In this phase of satire, according to Northrop Frye, the satirist harks back to the old giant-killer who "would have to bear down his opponent by sheer weight of words, and hence be a master of that technique of torrential abuse which we call invective"; and the satirist's poem, says Frye, describing Nashe and Marston, displays "a creative exuberance of which the most typical and obvious sign is the verbal tempest, the tremendous outpouring of words in catalogues, abusive epithets and erudite technicalities."[40] It is the general rush of such details and their combined weight that belabors the victim and impresses the reader, not the calculated destruction.

A final significant feature of Elizabethan satire is its topicality. We have stressed the literary environment of the satires, their conventional and derivative elements. Equally conventional was the desire to give the impression of "realism," however distorted this "real" might be. Guilpin, more than most satirists of his day, loads his lines with matter contemporary and recognizable. He gives scores of London place-names—St. Pancras, Ludgate, St. Martin, Westminster, "Bloome is Ordinary," Smithfield, Bridewell, Mercer's Chapel, Paris-Garden, etc. He gives countless street sights and sounds which must have been familiar to his audience, the Irish fruitmonger crying "pippe, fine pippe" (Ep. 68), the two car-men fighting for passageway (V. 49), the troop of "wanton schoole-boys" returning from a play (V. 164). And he reports with precision social and literary events special to his own day, what mode of dress was popular, the closing of the Theatre, contemporary attitudes toward poets past and present. He takes pains to suggest his London at his time, an important time from the viewpoint of literary history, and his "realism" has led scholars repeatedly to rely on his

support for generalizations about Shakespeare's London. *Skialetheia* is "one of the most important" of Elizabethan satires, says
G. B. Harrison, "because of its vivid and detailed picture of the
manners, fashions, and follies of London society at the time
when Shakespeare was writing the two parts of *Henry the
Fourth*, and Ben Jonson the two *Every Man* plays."[41] The
satirist's distortion arises from the formation of grotesque hy-
brids out of concrete details and a peculiarly obsessional viewpoint, and of course from the density of the scene.

Behind such characters there lurk, one suspects, real and
identifiable persons. Satire for Elizabethans was invective, and
thus could be personal, separated from "libel" by a very fine
line. Anonymous publications, such as *Skialetheia*, were certain
to be considered so. "It is good," says Harington, "to set a name
to the booke: For a booke without name may be called a
libell."[42] In his attack on the "Epigrammatist," "W. I." hints at
the libelous nature of *Skialetheia*, referring twice to "lyes." With
obvious reference to Satire III (cf. ll. 80-82), he says,

> But what a Gods name meane you to negotiate in euery
> mans matter? Doubtlesse you were super-fantastically
> infatuated, when you skipt vp and downe from one
> estate to another, like a Squirrell on a tree, and snapt at
> euery man, as though he had been a venison Pasty. O,
> ye were as busie as a Bee, . . . and the liberality of
> your tongue mayntained most absolute lyes for the
> atchieuing of the whetstone.[43]

The description of Fœlix (I. 63-76), imitated from Shakespeare's
account of Bolingbroke's progress in *Richard II*, would certainly
have been taken by contemporaries as an attack on Essex, indicating that Guilpin had no inclination to spare the person, and
struck high. The Fuscus of Epigrams 8 and 19 may be Marlowe,
that of Epigram 24 Nashe. *Satyre Preludium* alludes to Nashe's
Choice of Valentines (ll. 43-50). Occasionally we hit on or close
to an identification we feel fairly certain of, especially those that
relate to literature and writers, about whom we are naturally

more sensitive and better informed. Always the suspicion remains that others, Titus, Matho, Cælius, Paule, and so on, are modeled after real persons available to contemporaries, if only to a select few, and lost to us. That we suspect is sufficient and conventional, part of the satirist's complexity and appeal. To us Guilpin would say what Harington says:

> . . . though I by yow am often prest
> To know the secret drift of mine entent
> In these my pleasent lynes, and who are meant
> By *Cinna, Lynus, Lesbia* and the rest,
> Yet pardon though I graunte not your request;
> Tis such as I thereto may not assent.[44]

Invariably the true object slips safely from our glance behind a screen of wit. Satire, as Kenneth Burke reminds us, thrives and is most inventive when satirists are most repressed and censorship imminent.[45] By burning *Skialetheia* society, wisely it seems, betrayed certain suspicions we should share when reading it.

Text: Compositors and Bibliography

It is possible on the basis of recent studies of the compositors in James Roberts's shop to recognize in *Skialetheia* clear traces of the same orthographic habits that were a little later to produce *Merchant of Venice* (1600), *Titus* Q2 (1600), and *Hamlet* Q2 (1604/5).[46] Of the two compositors, customarily referred to as X and Y, Y is responsible for the larger part of the work, and is more readily identifiable. In keeping with later habits,.Y spells *deere, deerely*, etc., X *deare*, etc.; Y *theyr/their*, X *their*; Y prefers *I'le*, X *Ile/ile*; only Y has *bee, beeing*; Y prefers *oo* to *o* in *doost*; and only Y has the tilde. Otherwise, Y uses the *-all, -ell* endings, X *-ale, -aile*; Y uses *-ie* endings where spelling conflicts with *-y* occur; and Y has a tendency to use fewer elision marks with *o're, e're*, etc., with preterites and past participles.

These and other distinctions permit a tentative assignment to Y of the following formes: *A-inner, A-outer, C-inner* (exception 6ʳ?), *C-outer* (7ʳ?), and *D-inner;* and to X the following: *B-inner, B-outer, D-outer,* and *E-half sheet* (probably, or else another hand). Y thus seems primarily responsible for five formes, X for four. Such assignments must remain tentative, however, as there are too few gatherings to permit certainty, and there are not yet corroborative studies of the shop at this early date.

There are seven stop-press corrections, six of which occur in the *B-outer* forme, with the uncorrected instances appearing only in the Bodleian copy, and one in the *C-outer* forme, with the uncorrected instance only in the British Museum copy.

Ep. 45, l. 5 (B3ʳ): "turue" to "turne"

Ep. 57, l. 11 (B5ʳ): "sir, she'spainted" to "sir, she's painted"

Ep. 60, title (B5ʳ): *"De Ignoto. 50"* to *"De Ignoto. 60."*

Ep. 68. l. 17 (B6ᵛ): *"obsequie,"* to *"obsequie)"*

Sat. Pre. 21 (B8ᵛ): indentation added

Sat. Pre. 32 (B8ᵛ): "word" to "word:"

II. 42 (C6ᵛ): "scaus" to "scauls"

Skialetheia

Edition, 1598 (first and only)

Registered: 15 September 1598. Entered to Nicholas Ling.

Title Page: Reproduced on p. 37.

Collation: 8ᵒ: A-D8, E3. (4-8 not signed. Not paginated.)

Contents: A1, blank; A2ʳ, title page; A2ᵛ, blank; A3ʳ-B7ᵛ, "EPIGRAMS." [with small device top of A3ʳ]; B7ᵛ, [ornamental band] "SA-"; B8ʳ-C2ʳ, "SATYRE PRE-ludium." [with small device top of B8ʳ]; C2ᵛ-C5ᵛ, "Satyra prima."; C5ᵛ-C7ᵛ, "Satyra secunda."; C7ᵛ-D2ʳ, "Satyra tertia."; D2ᵛ-D4ʳ, "Satyra Quarta."; D4ʳ-D7ᵛ, "Satyra Quinta."; D7ᵛ-E3ᵛ, "Satyra sexta."

Running Titles: A3ᵛ-B7ᵛ, "EPIGRAMS."; B8ᵛ-C2ʳ, "Sat. prœludium."; C3ʳ-C5ᵛ, "SATYRE. I."; C6ʳ-C7ᵛ, "SATYRE. II."; C8ᵛ, "SATYRE. III."; D1ʳ-D2ʳ, "SATIRE.

III.": D3^r-D4^r, "SATIRE. IIII."; D4^v-D7^r, "'SATIRE. V.";
D7^v-D3^v, "SATIRE. VI."

Copies Collated (all those known to exist, from photo-
stats):

Folger Shakespeare Library

British Museum, C. 40. b. 54.

Bodleian Library (which lacks C4 and C5)

Henry E. Huntington Library

There have been four reprintings of *Skialetheia* by 1) E. V.
Utterson at the Beldornie Press (London, 1843), sixteen copies;
2) John Payne Collier, in *Miscellaneous Tracts temp. Eliz. and
Jac. I* [no. 4] (London, 1870); 3) A. B. Grosart, with introduction and notes, in *Occasional Issues* (Manchester, 1878), fifty
copies; and 4) Humphrey Milford, for The Shakespeare Association, Facsimile no. 2, with an introduction by G. B. Harrison
(Oxford, 1931).

The text has been normalized only slightly, the intention
being at once to ease the reader over minor, perhaps irritating
Elizabethan printing and pointing unfamiliarities, and at the
same time to preserve much of the Elizabethan impression.
Ligatures, tildes, *VV, vv,* long *s,* wrong font type, obviously
misplaced or misturned letters have all been silently normalized.
The *u* for *v, i* for *j* practice, however, is continued. It has seemed
advisable on occasions, for clarity's sake, to strengthen the
comma that served compositors to stop an independent clause, a
convention unfamiliar to us. Such changes are duly acknowledged. For the most part, however, these clauses offer no
difficulty, and the compositor's comma is retained, which
should not distract the reader alert to the practice. Quotation
marks are not added to signal utterances; such are indicated in
the commentary.

NOTES TO THE INTRODUCTION

1. Edward Arber, *A Transcript of the Registers* (London, 1876), 3:677-78.

2. *The Dutch Courtesan* 3. 1, in *The Plays of John Marston*, ed. H. Harvey Wood, 3 vols. (Edinburgh, 1938), 2:99.

3. Francis Meres, *Wits Treasury* (1598), in *Elizabethan Critical Essays*, ed. G. Gregory Smith, 2 vols. (Oxford, 1904), 2:320.

4. G. B. Harrison thinks most of *Skialetheia* was written about eighteen months before publication; see his introduction to The Shakespeare Association, Facsimile no. 2 (Oxford, 1931), p. viii.

5. See John Payne Collier's edition of *Skialetheia*, in *Miscellaneous Tracts temp. Eliz. and Jac. I* [no. 4] (London, 1870), p. i; and Charles Crawford, ed., *England's Parnassus* (Oxford, 1913), items 372, 652, 784, 1243, 1255, 1414, 1565. The signatures include four "E"s, two "Ed."s, one "Edw.," four "Guilpin"s, and three "Gilpin"s.

I rely primarily on the discoveries of R. E. Bennett, "John Donne and Everard Gilpin," *Review of English Studies* 15 (1939): 66-72; Philip J. Finkelpearl, "Donne and Everard Gilpin," ibid., n.s. 14 (1963): 164-67; and especially R. E. Brettle, "Everard Guilpin and John Marston (1576-1634)," ibid., n.s. 16 (1965): 396-99. These articles should be consulted for additional details and references.

6. Prerogative Court of Canterbury, Prob. 11/77 f36.

7. Court of Requests, P.R.O. Req. 2. 26/27 and 144/77.

8. John Wilcox, "Informal Publication of Late Sixteenth-Century Verse Satire," *Huntington Library Quarterly* 13 (1949-50): 194. For an accurate sense of the social and literary climate of the Inns see Philip J. Finkelpearl, *John Marston of the Middle Temple* (Cambridge, Mass., 1969), pp. 1-80.

9. Finkelpearl, *John Marston*, p. 73.

10. The letter is in John Donne's *The Satires, Epigrams and Verse Letters*, ed. W[esley] Milgate (Oxford, 1967), p. 64.

11. So Milgate dates the first, during Donne's second year of residence at Lincoln's Inn (ibid., p. 117).

12. John Peter, *Complaint and Satire in Early English Literature* (Oxford, 1956), p. 143.

13. Arnold Davenport speculates as to the origin of the quarrel, implicating Guilpin to some extent, and refers to other attempts at explanation, in his introduction to *The Collected Poems of Joseph Hall* (Liverpool, 1949), pp. xxviii-xxxiv; and in "The Quarrel of the Satirists," *Modern Language Review* 37 (1942): 123-30. See also his introduction to his edition of *The Poems of John Marston* (Liverpool, 1961), pp. 1-3.

14. Davenport, "The Quarrel of the Satirists," p. 123. Davenport has edited the so-called *Whipper Pamphlets* (Liverpool, 1951), in two parts, one containing *The Whipping*, which he attributes to John Weever (others think William Ingram), and two containing *No Whippinge* and *The Whipper of the Satyre his Pennance*, which he attributes, respectively, to Breton and Guilpin. His introduction (to Part One) should be consulted.

15. Guilpin contributed two prefatory sonnets to Markham's *Devoreux* (1597), on which see the note in the commentary to Satire VI. 79-84. And he seems very likely to have been the "E. G." who contributed prefatory sonnets to Sylvester's *Du Bartas* (1604) and Dekker's *Lanthorne* (1609).

16. *Poems of John Marston*, ed. Davenport, p. 2.

17. Alvin Kernan, *The Cankered Muse* (New Haven, 1959), p. 62. I rely on Kernan's concepts of "satirist," "scene," and "plot."

18. *Virgidemiae* 3. Prol. 3, in *Poems of Joseph Hall*, ed. Davenport; *Scourge of Villanie*, "To those that seeme iudiciall perusers," in *Poems of John Marston*, ed. Davenport. For discussions of this widely acknowledged literary convention see Arnold Stein, "Donne's Obscurity and the Elizabethan Tradition," *English Literary History* 13 (1946): 98-118; Kernan, *Cankered Muse*, pp. 58-63, and, on Marston's practice, pp. 94-108; and R. M. Alden, *The Rise of Formal Satire in England*

(Philadelphia, 1899), pp. 102-8, who argues that the degree of obscurity is overemphasized.

19. Marston, *Scourge of Villanie*, "To those that seeme iudiciall perusers."

20. *The Whipping*, ed. Davenport, p. 6. The passage echoes the conclusions of *Satyre Preludium* and Satire IV.

21. Ep. 84, in *The Letters and Epigrams of Sir John Harington*, ed. Norman E. McClure (Philadelphia, 1930), p. 180.

22. Kenneth Burke, *Attitudes toward History* (Boston, 1959), p. 49.

23. Northrop Frye, *Anatomy of Criticism* (Princeton, 1957), p. 235.

24. Peter, *Complaint and Satire*, pp. 148-52. Peter discusses in some depth the various suggestions, such as that of G. B. Harrison in *The Elizabethan Journals*, 2 vols. (New York, 1965), 2:97n., and Arnold Davenport in *Poems of Joseph Hall*, p. xxvi, that their seditious and libelous character was the real issue. Both Harrison and Davenport acknowledge their obscenity as a partial cause.

25. Kernan, *Cankered Muse*, p. 115.

26. Mary C. Randolph discusses formal parallels in "The Structural Design of the Formal Verse Satire," *Philological Quarterly* 21 (1942): 378.

27. John Dryden, *Poems*, ed. James Kinsley, 4 vols. (Oxford, 1958), 2:694.

28. Alden has the same impression, in *Rise of Formal Satire*, p. 154. For John Peter, "the classical influence is obvious throughout" (*Complaint and Satire*, p. 146).

29. James B. Leishman, ed., *The Three Parnassus Plays (1598-1601)* (London, 1949), pp. 46-47.

30. See *The Works of Thomas Nashe*, ed. Ronald B. McKerrow, rev. F. P. Wilson, 5 vols. (Oxford, 1958), 2:136-44.

31. Leishman, ed., *Three Parnassus Plays*, p. 45.

32. Philip Stubbes, *Anatomy of Abuses*, ed. Frederick J. Furnivall, New Shakespeare Society, ser. 6, no. 4 (London, 1877), pt. 1, p. 87.

33. For references see the commentary on Ep. 25.

34. *Wits Miserie* (1596), in *The Complete Works of Thomas Lodge*, 4 vols., Hunterian Club (Glasgow, 1883), 4:41. See Leishman's discussion in *Three Parnassus Plays*, pp. 48-49, and Kernan's in *Cankered Muse*, pp. 85-86.

35. T. K. Whipple, *Martial and the English Epigram from Sir Thomas Wyatt to Ben Jonson* (Berkeley, 1925), p. 350; Peter, *Complaint and Satire*, p. 163.

36. Kernan, *Cankered Muse*, p. 121. See Kernan's summary of similar estimates of Marston on pp. 26-27.

37. Una M. Ellis-Fermor, *The Jacobean Drama* (London, 1936), p. 79.

38. *Teares of the Muses*, l. 553.

39. "To the Reader," in John Heywood, *Works*, ed. Burton A. Milligan (Urbana, 1956), p. 104. See also Harington's "Epistle to All," *Letters and Epigrams*, ed. McClure, p. 147; and Jonson's "To the Reader," in *Ben Jonson*, ed. Charles H. Herford and Percy and Evelyn Simpson, 11 vols. (Oxford, 1925-52), 8:27. The commentary does not record all wordplays: many are obvious, many are lost to us, and many are so extreme as to require evidence extending the comment beyond reasonable length.

40. Frye, *Anatomy of Criticism*, p. 236.

41. Introduction to Harrison's facsimile of *Skialetheia*, pp. v-vi. For opposing views on the degree to which Elizabethan satire is an accurate account of the times see Leishman, ed., *Three Parnassus Plays*, p. 49, and C. R. Baskervill, *English Elements in Jonson's Early Comedy* (Chicago, 1911), who argue for the traditional nature of the content and treatment, and Hallett Smith, *Elizabethan Poetry* (Cambridge, Mass., 1952), chap. 4, and L. C. Knights, *Drama and Society in the Age of Jonson* (London, 1937), who see contemporary men and activities.

42. John Harington, *A New Discourse of a Stale Subject, Called The Metamorphosis of Ajax*, ed. Elizabeth Story Donno (New York, 1962), p. 204, and see note.

43. *The Whipping*, ed. Davenport, p. 6.

44. Ep. 423, "Of the obiects of his satire," in Harington, *Letters and Epigrams,* ed. McClure, p. 319.

45. See Robert C. Elliott, "The Satirist and Society," *English Literary History* 21 (1954): 245. The strong similarity between satire (especially Guilpin's) and libel becomes evident from a quick look at "A libell against some Grayes Inn gentlemen and Reuellers," probably written in 1594-95, reproduced from the manuscript by James L. Sanderson, *Notes and Queries,* n.s. 10 (1963): 298-300.

46. See the important studies by John Russell Brown, "The Compositors of *Hamlet* Q2 and *The Merchant of Venice,"* *Studies in Bibliography* 7 (1955): 17-40, and Paul L. Cantrell and George W. Williams, "Roberts' Compositors in *Titus Andronicus* Q2," ibid. 8 (1956): 27-38.

TEXT

SKIALETHEIA.

OR,

A shadowe of Truth, in certaine Epigrams and Satyres.

At London,
Printed by I. R. for Nicholas Ling, and are
to bee solde at the little West doore of
Poules. 1598.

Insteede of Ingling *termes for thy good will,*
Reader fall to, reade, iest, and carpe thy fill.

Epigrams

Prooemium. I.

As in the greatest of societies,
    The first beginners, like good natur'd soules,
    Beare with their neighbors poore infirmities:
    But after, when ambition controules
Theyr calme proceedings, they imperiously   5
"(As great things still orewhelme themselues with
        weight)
    Enuy their countrimens prosperity,
    And in contempt of poorer fates delight.
So *Englands* wits (now mounted the full height,)
Hauing confounded monstrous barbarismes,   10   [A3v]
Puft vp by conquest, with selfe-wounding spight,
Engraue themselues in ciuill warres *Abismes*,
    Seeking by all meanes to destroy each other,
    The vnhappy children of so deere a mother.

To the Reader. 2.

Whose hap shall be to reade these pedler rimes,
Let them expect no elaborat foolery,
Such as Hermaphroditize these poore times,
With wicked scald iests, extreame gullerie:
    Bunglers stande long in tinck'ring their trim Say,   5
    Ile onely spit my venome, and away.

To the Reader. 1 will,] will.

[39]

Of Titus. 3.

Titus oft vaunts his gentry euery where,
Blazoning his coate, deriuing's pedegree;
What needest thou daily Titus iade mine eare?
I will beleeue thy houses auncestry;
    If that be auncient which we doe forget,   5
    Thy gentry is so; none can remember it.

To Liuia. 4.

Liuia, I kon thee thanke, when thou doost kisse
Thou turn'st thy cheeke: see what good nature is!
For well thou knowst thy breaths infection,
Able to turne my stomack vpside downe.
    Which when I thinke on, but for manners sake,   5   [A4]
    I'ld pray thee thy cheeke too away to take.

Of Matho. 5.

Matho in credite bound to pay a debt,
His word engagde him for, doth still replie,
That he will aunswere it with sophistrie,
And so deferres daily to aunswere it:
    Experience now hath taught me sophistrie,   5
    He gaue me his word; that is, he coussend me.

Of Faber. 6.

Since marriage, Faber's prouder then before,
Yfayth his wife must take him a hole lower.

Of a railing humour. 7.

(Good Lord) that men should haue such kennel wits
To thinke so well of a scald railing vaine,
Which soone is vented in beslauered writs,
As when the cholicke in the gutts doth straine,

Of a railing humour. 3 writs,] writs.

With ciuill conflicts in the same embrac't.   5
But let a fart, and then the worst is past.

To Deloney. 8.

Like to the fatall ominous Rauen which tolls,
The sicke mans dirge within his hollow beake,
So euery paper-clothed post in Poules,
To thee (*Deloney*) mourningly doth speake,   [A4ᵛ]
And tells thee of thy hempen tragedie.   5
The wracks of hungry Tyburne naught to thine,
Such massacre's made of thy balladry,
And thou in griefe, for woe thereof maist pine:
        At euery streets end *Fuscus* rimes are read,
        And thine in silence must be buried.   10

Of Paule. 9.

Paule daily wrongs me, yet he daily sweares
He wisheth me as well as to his soule:
I know his drift, to damne that he naught cares
To please his body: therefore (good friend *Paule*)
        If thy kind nature will affoord me grace,   5
        Heereafter loue me in thy bodies place.

Of Syluio. 10.

Syluio the Lawyer, hunting for the fame
Of a wise man, studies Phylosophie,
And odly in his singularitie,
From being odde, thinks wisedome hath her name.
So long hath he turnde ouer *Scaliger*,   5
Old *Cardan* and the other chimick wits,
Which haue to after-times demisde their writs,
That a fift Element he doth auerre:

Of a railing humour. 5 embrac't.] embrac't, To Deloney.
5 tragedie.] tragedie, 6 thine,] thine.

Deserues not he to make the wise men euen,
Who odly thus makes odd the *Nerues* of heauen?   10

To Gue. 11.   [A5]
Gue, hang thy selfe for woe, since gentlemen
Are now growne cunning in thy apishnes:
Nay, for they labour with their foolishnes
Thee to vndoe, procure to hang them then:
    It is a strange seeld seene vncharitie,   5
    To make fooles of themselues to hinder thee.

Of Cotta. 12.
Behold a wonder, neuer seene before,
Yonder's *Cotta's* picture, dauncing trenchmore.

Of the same. 13.
I saw not *Cotta* thys halfe yeere before,
When he was angry that I spoke not to him,
He hath no reason to take it so sore,
Being so painted that I did not know him.

To Licus. 14.
Licus, thou often tell'st me iestingly,
I am a fine man, and so tyrannously
Hast thou now tired that phrase, that euery one
Is a fine man in thine opinion:
In thine opinion? no it's but thy word,   5
Which doth that fine addition affoord:
And yet I see no cause but many may,
Be euen as fine as *Licus* euery way;   [A5v]
In dauncing, vaulting, and in riming too,
In theyr conceits there are as good as you.   10
Then wherein is't that you so farre surpasse

Other plaine iades, like *Lucius* golden Asse?
I heare thee say the foulest day that is,
Thou art shodde in Veluet, and in Naples bisse:
Nay then I yeeld, for who will striue in it,   15
May haue fine clothes, but a most filthy wit.

Of Zeno. 15.

Zeno desirous of the idle fame
Of Stoicke resolution, recklesly
Seemes to esteeme of good report or blame;
So prouing himselfe dull, most foolishly,
    To euery thing he heares, he saith he cares not: 5
    He cares not for his booke, nor yet for wit,
    For pleasant catch-fooles in like sort he spares not
    To sweare hee's carelesse, carelesse to forget
Or thinke vpon his dutie, soules comfort;
Carelesse to thriue, or liue in decencie;   10
Carelesse of vertuous, and a good consort,
Carelesse of wisedome, and of honestie;
    To all this carelesnes, should one declare
    His fathers death, I am sure he would not care.

Of Riuus. 16.   [A6]

Once *Riuus* saw a pretty lasse,
And liquorous tooth'd desir'd to tast,
But knowing not how to bring't to passe,
He vow'd to hange himselfe in hast:
    I feard him not, the wench was gone,   5
    And he was loth to hang alone.

Of Clodius. 17.

Clodius oft sayth he hath chaleng'd beene by many,
But neuer tells me he hath answered any.

Of Curio. 18.

Curio threats my death in an Epigrame,
Yfayth hee'le eate his word, he is too blame,
And yet I think hee'le write; then ware of bleeding,
Nay feare not, he writes nothing worth the reading.

Of Faustus. 19.

Faustus in steede of grace, saith Fuscus rimes,
Oh gracelesse manners! oh vnhallowed times!

To Candidus. 20.

Friend Candidus, thou often doost demaund,
What humours men by gulling vnderstand:
Our English Martiall hath full pleasantly,
In his close nips describde a gull to thee: [A6ᵛ]
I'le follow him, and set down my conceit   5
What a Gull is: oh word of much receit!
He is a gull, whose indiscretion,
Cracks his purse strings to be in fashion;
He is a gull, who is long in taking roote
In barraine soyle, where can be but small fruite: 10
He is a gull, who runnes himselfe in debt,
For twelue dayes wonder, hoping so to get;
He is a gull, whose conscience is a block,
Not to take interest, but wastes his stock:
He is a gull, who cannot haue a whore,   15
But brags how much he spends vpon her score:
He is a gull, that for commoditie
Payes tenne times ten, and sells the same for three:
He is a gull, who passing finicall,
Peiseth each word to be rhetoricall: 20
And to conclude, who selfe conceitedly,
Thinkes al men guls, ther's none more gull then he.

To Candidus. 20 rhetoricall] thetoricall

Of Procus. 21.

Procus insteede of more fitting discourse
To entertaine his Mistris eares withall,
Tells her a long tale of a rosted horse,
Of a great brabble did to him befall;
     When she demaunds the occasion of the braule,   5
     He in a gallant brauery, gull-like swore,
     The reason that he foorth with him did fall,   [A7]
     Was, for the other grutcht him of his whore:
(Ye who doe loue your loues better conceit,)
Iudge if this gull deserued his mistris fauour,   10
Who thus his goatish humours did relate:
Or what paine wish you for this rude behauiour?
     Whomsoe're he marries may she a whore proue,
     For this speech shewes that he a whore doth loue.

To Clodius. 22.

I prethee *Clodius*, tell me what's the reason,
Thou doost expect I should salute thee first,
I haue sized in Cambridge, and my friends a season
Some exhibition for me there disburst:
Since that, I haue beene in Goad his weekly role,   5
And beene acquaint with *Mounsieur Littleton*,
I haue walkt in Poules, and duly din'd at noone,
And sometimes visited the dauncing schoole:
     Then how art thou my better, that I should
     Speake alwaies first, as I incroch faine would?   10
     But in a whore-house thou canst swagger too,
     Clodius good day; tis more then I can doo.

Of Sextilius. 23.

Sextilius sigh'd, for *Leuca* let a fart,
Hath not the youth a meruailous kind hart?

Of Fuscus. 24. [A7ᵛ]

When *Fuscus* first had taught his Muse to scold,
He gloried in her rugged vaine so much,
That euery one came to him, heare her should,
First *Victor*, then *Cinna*, nor did he grutch
To let both players, and artificers,   5
Deale with his darling, as if confident,
None of all these he did repute for Lechers,
Or thought her face would all such lusts preuent :
    But how can he a bawdes surname refuse,
    Who to all sorts thus prostitutes his Muse?   10

Of Gnatho. 25.

My Lord most court-like lyes in bed till noone,
Then, all high-stomackt riseth to his dinner,
Falls straight to Dice, before his meate be downe,
Or to disgest, walks to some femall sinner.
Perhaps fore-tyrde he gets him to a play,   5
Comes home to supper, and then falls to dice,
There his deuotion wakes till it be day,
And so to bed, where vntill noone he lies.
    This is a Lords life, simple folke will sing.
    A Lords life? what, to trot so foule a ring?   10
    Yet thus he liues, and what's the greatest griefe,
    Gnatho still sweares he leads true vertues life.

To Pollio. 26. [A8]

Th'art a fine fellow trust me *Pollio*,
And euery one reputes thee so to be,
Both for thy ingles face, and goodly show,
Of thyne apparraile and thy naperie :
Then, for thou pertly knowes to wagge thy head,   5
Like some old palsey-strucken vsurer,

Of Gnatho. 10 what, to] what to

Chiefely, for that this Christmas thou hast led
An vnthrifts life, (gramercy Creditor,)
But for this last thou must be faine to goe,
Into the country for a yeere or two.   10

Of the same. 27.

Pollio at length's fallne in my good conceit,
Not for his wanton face and curled haire,
Nor his fatte buttocke, nor that I delight
In his french Galliard, which is nothing rare,
    Nor for that others thinke him to be so,   5
    (For others credits cannot better me,)
    But for he thinks himselfe a fine fellow,
    For his owne state who better knowes then hee?

Of Zeno. 28

Zeno would faine th'old widdow Æagle haue,
Trust me hee's wise, for shee is rich and braue:
But *Zeno, Zeno,* shee will none of you,
In my mind shee's the wiser of the two.

Of Arion. 29.   A8v

Arions thoughts are growne so musicall,
That all his talke's of crotchets, and of quauers,
His very words to sembriefe time doe fall,
And blowing of his nose of musicke sauours:
Hee'le tell you of well fretting of a Lute,   5
Euen til you fret, and of the harmonie,
Is either in a still Cornet or Flute,
Of rests, and stops, and such like trumperie,
    Yet loues he more, for all sweet musick sence,
    His mistris belly, then these instruments.   10

Of Chrysogonus. 30.

Chrysogonus each morning by his glasse,
Teacheth a wrinckled action to his face,

And with the same he runnes into the street,
Each one to put in feare that he doth meet:
I prythee tell me (gentle *Chrysogone*)   5
What needs a borrowed bad face to thine owne?

Of Torques. 31.

Torques a Knight, and of indifferent liuing,
Is neyther free of house-keeping, nor giuing:
Yet stands he in the *Debet* booke vncrost:
Wonder not man, he keepes a whore to his cost.

Of Lais. 32.   B

Wanton young *Lais* hath a pretty note,
Whose burthen is, pinch not my petticoate:
Not that she feares close nips, for by the rood,
A priuy pleasing nip will cheare her blood:
But she which longs to tast of pleasures cup,   5
In nipping wòuld her petticoate weare vp.

Of Fidens. 33.

Fidens instructs young Gentlemen to play,
Who teach his wife, they get true fingring:
But she learnes to play false; no meruaile, they
Of a Maister, she of Schollers got her learning.

Of Orpheus. 34.

Orpheus hath wed a young lusty wife,
And all day long vpon his Lute doth play:
Doth not this fellow lead a merry life,
Who playes continually both night and day?

Of Cotta. 35.

I wonder (*Cotta*) Paynters Art can like thee,
Who drew thy picture being nothing like thee.

Of Metius. 36.

Metius of late hath greatly cosend me,
I tooke him for an earnest Catholike,
He talk'd so much of almes and charity;   [B₁ᵛ]
But I was mightily deceau'd belike.
    He praiseth charity and almes, because   5
    He was made Barrister for almes, not lawes.

Of the same. 37.

With what conscience can *Metius* sell law deare,
When of meere almes he was made Barrister?

To Licus. 38.

Licus, thou art deceau'd in saying, that
I'me a fine man: thou saist thou knowst not what.
He's a fine fellow who is neate and fine,
Whose locks are kem'd, & neuer a tangled twine,
Who smels of Musk, Ciuet, and Pomander,   5
Who spends, and out-spends many a pound a yeare,
Who piertly iets, can caper, daunce, and sing,
Play with his Mistris fingers, her hand wring,
Who companying with wenches nere is still:
But either skips or mowes, or prates his fill,   10
Who is at euery play, and euery night
Sups with his *Ingles,* who can well recite,
Whatsoeuer rimes are gracious. (*Licus*) leaue,
Iniure not my content then, to bereaue
My fortune of her quiet: I am I,   15
But a fine fellow in my fantasie
Is a great trouble, trouble me not then,   B₂
For a fine fellow, is a fine foole mongst men.

To Licus. 13 gracious. (*Licus*)] gracious (*Licus*)

Of Chrestina. 39.

I told *Chrestina* I would lie with her,
When she with an old phrase doth me aduise,
To keepe my selfe from water and from fier,
And she would keepe me from betwixt her thighs,
    That there is water I doe make no doubt,   5
    But Il'e be loth (wench) to be fired out.

Of Nœuia. 40.

Nœuia is one while of the Innes of Court,
Toyling in *Brooke, Fitzherbert,* and in *Dyer:*
Another while th'Exchange he doth resort,
Moyling as fast, a seller, and a buyer:
    Will not he thriue (think yee) who can deuise,   5
    Thus to vnite the law and merchandise?
    Doubtlesse he will, or cosen out of doubt;
    What matter's that? his law will beare him out.

Of the same. 41.

Nœuia's a Merchant, and a Gentleman:
That is, scarce honest, liue he how he can.

Of the same. 42.

Pardon me (Reader) I will not bewray
Who *Nœuia* is, not that I feare to say,
But that he should be punishd I am loth,   [B2ᵛ]
For engrossing occupations as he doth.
He is a Lawyer, and a Merchant to,   5
And shortly will I doubt haue more to do:
He is a busie fellow, and may be
A knaue Promoter for his honesty.

Of Clodius. 43.

Clodius me thinks looks passing big of late,
With *Dunstons* browes, and *Allens Cutlacks* gate:

What humours haue possest him so, I wonder,
His eyes are lightning, and his words are thunder:
What meanes the Bragart by his alteration?   5
He knows he's known too wel, for this fond fashion
To cause him to be feard: what meanes he than?
Belike, because he cannot play the man,
Yet would be awde, he keepes this filthy reuell,
Stalking and roaring like to *Iobs* great deuill.   10

Of Phrix. 44.
Phrix hath a nose; who doubts what ech man knows;
But what hath *Phrix* know-worth besides his nose?

In Zelotypum. 45.
Thy wife so nimph-like sitting at the board,
Why frown'st thou that I look on her? good Lord.
What sinne is't to looke on a pretty lasse!
We look on heauen, the Sun & Moons bright face.   B3
Would'st haue me turne away, as I did see   5
Some filthy slut, or lewd deformity?
Why, Iealousie her selfe may suffer sight;
Sight cannot cuckold thee, nor do thee spight:
If thow'lt not haue her look'd on by thy guests,
Bid none but Harpers hence-forth to thy feasts.   10

Of Gellia. 46.
The world finds fault with *Gellia,* for she loues
A skip-iack fidler, I hold her excus'd,
For louing him, sith she her selfe so proues:
What, she a fidler? tut she is abus'd?
No in good faith; what fidle hath she vs'd?   5
    The *Viole Digambo* is her best content,
    For twixt her legs she holds her instrument.

Of Clodius. 6 fashion] fashion: 8 man,] man. *Of Phrix.*
1 knows;] knows

To the Reader. 47.

Excuse me (Reader) though I now and than,
In some light lines doe shew my selfe a man,
Nor be so sowre, some wanton words to blame,
They are the language of an Epigrame.

To Lydia. 48.

(*Lydia*) so mote I thee thou art not faire,
A plaine brownetta when thou art at best:
Yet darst not thou come forth into the ayre,
When no wind stirres, and Sunne's hid in the west,   [B3ᵛ]
    But mask'd forsooth, I prethy what's thy reason,   5
    That hauing (God he knowes) no faire to loose,
    Thou hid'st that pitteous *None* so out of season?
    Oh th'art a mummer, and perhaps dost choose,
A faire calme euen as fittest for thy gaine:
Sayest thou me so? nay, then we'le haue about,   10
Come, trip the dice, haue at your box (*Madame*)
Ile cast at all, for sure I goe not out.
    Nothing but mum? nay then we are agreed,
    Be I well chanc'd, my chance may be to speed.

To Cotta. 49.

Be not wrath, *Cotta,* that I not salute thee,
I vs'd it whilst I worthy did repute thee:
Now thou art made a painted Saint, and I
Cotta will not commit idolatry.

To Women. 50.

Yee that haue beauty and withall no pitty,
Are like a prick-song-lesson without ditty.

To Lydia. 4 west,] west.

Of Chrestina. 51.

Talke bawdery and *Chrestina* spets and spals,
So much her chast thoughts hate it, tut that's false,
She loues it well, wherfore then should she spet?
Her teeth doe water but to heare of it.

Of Pansa. 52.   [B4]

Fine spruce yong *Pansa's* growne a malcontent,
A mighty malcontent though young and spruce,
As heresie he shuns all merriment,
And turn'd good husband, puts forth sighs to vse,
Like hate-man *Timon* in his Cell, he sits   5
Misted with darknes like a smoaky roome,
And if he be so mad to walke the streetes,
To his sights life, his hat becomes a toombe.
What is the cause of this melancholly,
His father's dead: no, such newes reuiues him,   10
Wants he a whore? nor that, loues he? that's folly,
Mount his high thoughts? oh no, then what grieues him?
Last night which did our *Ins* of court men call
In silken sutes like gawdy Butterflies,
To paint the Torch-light sommer of the hall,   15
And shew good legs, spite of slops-smothering thies,
         He passing from his chamber through the Court,
         Did spoile a paire of new white pumps with durt.

Of Cornelius. 53.

See you him yonder, who sits o're the stage,
With the Tobacco-pipe now at his mouth?
It is *Cornelius* that braue gallant youth,
Who is new printed to this fangled age:
         He weares a Ierkin cudgeld with gold lace,   5
         A profound slop, a hat scarce pipkin high,   [B4^v]

Of Pansa. 16 thies,] thies 18 durt.] durt

For boots, a paire of dagge cases; his face,
Furr'd with *Cads*-beard: his poynard on his thigh.
He wallows in his walk his slop to grace,
Sweares *by the Lord*, daines no salutation   10
But to some iade that's sick of his owne fashion,
As *farewell sweet Captaine*, or (*boy*) *come apace*:
    Yet this Sir *Beuis*, or the fayery Knight,
    Put vp the lie because he durst not fight.

Of Issa. 54.

Issa from me to a player tooke her way,
No meruaile, for she alwaies lou'd to play.

To Mira. 55.

Many aske *Mira*, why I nam'd thee so:
Let them aske Nature why she fram'd thee so.

De Ignoto. 56.

There's an odd fellow, (ile not tell his name,
Because from my lines he shal get no fame:)
Reading mine Epigrams bathes euery limb,
In angry sweat swearing that I meane him:
Content thy selfe, I write of better men,   5
Thou art no worthy subiect for my pen.

Of Nigrina. 57.   [B5]

Why should *Nigrina* weare her mask so much?
Her skins lawn's not so fine, so soone to staine,
Her tendrest poultry may endure the touch,
Her face, face and out-face the wind againe:
    The cherry of her lip's a winter Cherry,   5
    Then weather-proof, & needs no masks defence:
    Her cheeks best fruit's a black, no Mulberry,

De Ignoto. 5 selfe, I] selfe I

But fearelesse of sharp gustes impouerishments:
And to be briefe, she being all plaine *Ione*,
Why is she mask'd to keepe that where is none?　　　10
　　O sir, she's painted, and you know the guise,
　　Pictures are curtaind from the vulgar eyes.

Of Drus. 58.
Drus for a Cuckold, and miserable's fam'd,
May not he well a hard-head then be nam'd?

To Mira. 59.
Thou fearst I loue thee, for I prayse thee so:
Should I dispraise thee, what wouldst feare I trow?

De Ignoto. 60.
Yon fellow thinks mine Epigrams him meane,
Then let me write of euery bawd and queane.

Of Nigrina. 61.　　　　　　　　　　　　　　　[B5ᵛ]
Painted *Nigrina* vnmask'd comes ne're in sight,
Because light wenches care not for the light.

Of the same. 62.
Painted *Nigrina* with the picture face,
Hauing no maske thinks she's without grace,
So with one case she doth another case,
Doth not her maske become her then apace?

Of Bassus. 63.
Eloquent *Bassus* speakes all with a grace,
Not so much but good morrow, and good night:
I wonder when the Somner did him cite,
For his sweet sinne, how he spake in that case:
　　I am sure he could with no grace well refuse it　　5
　　And worse I doubt with any grace excuse it.

To Mira. 64.

Thou fear'st I am in loue with thee (my Deare);
I prethy feare not, *It comes with a feare.*

Of Nigrina. 65.

Because *Nigrina* hath a painted face,
Many suspect her to be light and base:
I see no reason to repute her such,
For out of doubt she will abide the tuch.

Of Gellia. 66.   [B6]

Gellia intic'd her good-man to the Citty,
And often threatneth to giue him the lurch,
See how this sweet sinne makes the simplest witty:
She (*too prophane*) whilst he is at the church,
    Ringing the first peale at the greatest bels   5
    At home will ring all in with some one els.

Ad Crocum. 67.

Crocus, thou sai'st that thou do'st know more queans
Then many a poore man ears in Autum gleans?
But *Crocus*, *Crocus*, if they all know you,
I feare I-faith you haue too much to do.

Of Caius. 68.

As *Caius* walks the streets, if he but heare
A blackman grunt his note, he cries *oh rare!*
He cries *oh rare*, to heare the *Irishmen*
Cry pippe, fine pippe, with a shrill accent, when
He comes at Mercers chappell; and, *oh rare,*   5
At *Ludgate* at the prisoners plaine-song there:
Oh rare sings he to heare a Cobler sing,
Or a wassaile on twelfe night, or the ring

To Mira. 1 Deare);] Deare)

At cold S. *Pancras* church; or any thing:
He'le cry, *oh rare*, and scratch the elbow too   10
To see two Butchers curres fight; the Cuckoo,
Will cry *oh rare*, to see the champion bull,   [B6v]
Or the victorious mastife with crown'd scull:
And garlanded with flowers, passing along
From *Paris*-garden he renewes his song,   15
To see my L. Maiors Henchmen; or to see,
(*At an old Aldermans blest obsequie*)
The Hospitall boyes in their blew æquipage,
Or at a carted bawde, or whore in cage:
He'le cry, *oh rare*, at a Gongfarmers cart,   20
Oh rare to heare a ballad or a fart:
Briefely so long he hath vsde to cry, *oh rare*,
That now that phrase is growne thin & thred-bare,
But sure his wit will be more rare and thin,
If he continue as he doth begin.   25

To the Reader. 69.
Some dainte eare, like a wax-rubd Citty roome,
Wil haply blame my *Muse* for this salt rhume,
Thinking her lewd and too vnmaidenly,
For dauncing this Iigge so lasciuiously:
But better thoughts, more discreet, will excuse   5
This quick *Couranto* of my merry *Muse*;
And say she keeps *Decorum* to the times,
To womens loose gownes suting her loose rimes:
But I, who best her humorous pleasance know,
Say, that this mad wench when she iesteth so   10
Is honester then many a sullen one,   [B7]
Which being more silent thinks worse being alone
Then my quick-sprighted lasse can speake: for who
Knowes not the old said saw of the *Still Sow*.

   To the Reader. 12 alone] alone:

Conclusion to the Reader. 70.
(*Reader*) when thou hast read this mad-cap stuffe,
Wherein my *Muse* swaggers as in her ruffe:
I know these Orphants shal be soone renounced,
Of euery one, and vnto death denounced:
I know thow'lt doome them to th'*Apotheta,*   5
To wrap Sope in, and *Assifœtida:*
And iustly to: for thou canst not misuse,
More then I will, these bastards of my *Muse:*
I know they are passing filthy, scuruey lines,
I know they are rude, harsh, and vnsauory rimes: 10
Fit to wrap playsters, and odd vnguents in,
Reedifiers of the wracks of *Synne.*
Viewing this sin-drownd world, I purposely,
Phisick'd my *Muse,* that thus vnmannerly,
She might beray our folly-soyled age,   15
And keepe *Decorum* on a comick stage,
Bringing a foule-mouth Iester who might sing
To rogues, the story of the lousie King.
I care not what the world doth think, or say,
There lies a morral vnder my leane play: 20
And like a resolute Epigrammatist,   [B7ᵛ]
Holding my pen, my Rapier in my fist:
I know I shall wide-gaping *Momes* conuince.
My *Muse* so armed is a carelesse Prince.

Satyre Preludium

Fie on these *Lydian* tunes which blunt our sprights
And turne our gallants to *Hermaphrodites*:
Giue me a *Doricke* touch, whose *Semphony*,
And dauncing aire may with affinity
Moue our light vaulting spirits and capering.   5
Woo *Alexander* from lewd banquetting
To armes. Bid *Haniball* remember *Cannas*,
And leaue *Salapian Tamyras* embrace.
      Hence with these fidlers, whose oyle-buttred lines,
Are Panders vnto lusts, and food to sinnes,   10
Their whimpring Sonnets, puling Elegies
Slaunder the Muses; make the world despise,
Admired poesie, marre *Resolutions* ruffe,
And melt true valour with lewd ballad stuffe.
      Heere one's Elegiack pen patheticall,   15
His parting from his Mistris doth bewaile:
Which when young gallant *Mutio* hath perus'd,
His valour's crestfalne, his resolues abusd,
For whatsoe're his courage erst did moue,
He'le goe no voyage now to leaue his Loue.   20
      Another with his supple passion
Meaning to moue his Pigsney to compassion,
Makes puisne *Lucius* in a simpathy
In loue with's pibald Laundres by and by.
      A third that falls more roundly to his worke,   25
Meaning to moue her were she Iew or Turke:
Writes perfect *Cat and fidle*, wantonly,
Tickling her thoughts with masking bawdry:
Which read to Captaine *Tucca*, he doth sweare,

And scratch, and sweare, and scratch to heare   30
His owne discourse discours'd: and *by the Lord*
It's passing good: oh good! at euery word:
When his Cock-sparrow thoughts to itch begin,
He with a shrug sweares't *a most sweet sinne.*
    Some others Lady Muse is comicall,   35
Thalia to the back, nay back and all,
And she with many a salt *La volto* iest
Edgeth some blunted teeth, and fires the brest
Of many an old cold gray-beard Cittizen,
Medea like making him young againe;   40
Who comming from the Curtaine sneaketh in,
To some odde garden noted house of sinne.
    But oh worse yet! for some Capritcious humor
Making an issue of his vlcerous tumor,
Some prophane Clodian pen daring display   45
(Like connicatching) bawdries Orgia,
With the prouost Martiall, ransacks euery roome
Of a vaulting house, and ribbald doth presume,
With Midwife *Albert*, or the womans booke
To anatomize each corner, and fond nooke.   50
    Let *Rablais* with his durtie mouth discourse
No longer blush, for they'le write ten times worse:
And *Aretines* great wit be blam'd no more,
They'le storie forth the errant arrant whore:
And speaking painters excuse *Titian*,   55
For his *Ioues* loues; and *Elephanticke* vaine.
    Thus all our Poets as they had carousde
A health to *Circes*, are in hogsties housde,
Or els transformd to Goates lasciuiously,
Filthing chast eares with theyr pens *Gonorrhey*,   60
For euen the stateliest and most generous,
The heroicke Poem is lasciuious,

      61 stateliest] staliest

Which midst of *Mars* his field, & hote alarmes,
Will sing of *Cupids* chiualrie and armes.
     The Satyre onely and Epigramatist,   65
(Concisde Epigrame, and sharpe Satyrist)
Keepe diet from this surfet of excesse,
Tempring themselues from such licenciousnes.
The bitter censures of their Critticke spleenes,
Are Antidotes to pestilentiall sinnes,   70   [C₁ᵛ]
They heale with lashing, seare luxuriousnes,
They are Philosophicke true *Cantharides*
To vanities dead flesh. An Epigrame
Is popish displing, rebell flesh to tame:
A plaine dealing lad, that is not afraid   75
To speake the truth, but calls a iade, a iade.
And *Mounsieur Guulard* was not much too blame,
When he for meat mistooke an Epigrame,
For thought it be no cates, sharp sauce it is,
To lickerous vanitie, youths sweet amisse.   80
But oh the Satyre hath a nobler vaine,
He's the Strappado, rack, and some such paine
To base lewd vice; the Epigram's Bridewell,
Some whipping cheere: but this is follies hell.
The Epigram's like dwarfe Kings scurrill grace,   85
A Satyre's Chester to a painted face;
It is the bone-ach vnto lechery,
To Acolastus it is beggery:
It is the scourge, the *Tamberlaine* of vice,
The three square Tyborne of impieties.   90
     But to come neere the verses of our time,
It is (oh scuruey) to a Lenten rime;
It is the grand hisse to a filthy play,
Tis peoples howts and showts at a pot fray.
Itch farther yet, yet nerer to them, fie   95
Their wits haue got my Muse with Tympanie: C₂
And with their loose tayld penns to let it loose,

It's like a Syring to a Hampshire Goose.
These critique wits which nettle vanitie,
Are better farre then foode to foppery: 100
And I dare warrant that the hangingst brow,
The sowrest Stoicke that will scarce allow
A riming stone vpon his fathers graue,
(Though he no reason haue no rime to haue:)
The stricktest (*Plato*) that for vertues health: 105
Will banish Poets forth his common-wealth,
Will of the two affoord the Satyre grace,
Before the whyning loue-song shall haue place:
And by so much his night-cap's ouer awde,
As a Beadle's better states-man then a Bawde.   110

Explicit the Satyres flourish before
his fencing.

Alterius qui fert vitia ferendo
facit sua.

106 common-wealth,] common-wealth.

Satire I

Shall I still mych in silence and giue ayme,
To other wits which make court to bright fame?
A schoole boy still, shall I lend eare to other,
And myne owne priuate Muses musick smother?
Especially in this sinne leapered age,   5
Where euery Player vice comes on the stage:
Maskt in a vertuous robe? and fooles doe sit
More honored then the *Prester Iohn* of wit?
Where vertue, like a common gossop shieldes
Vice with her name, and her defects ore-guilds: 10
No no, my Muse, be valiant to controule,
Play the scold brauely, feare no cucking-stoole,
Begall thy spirit, like shrill trumpets clangor,
Vent forth th'impatience, and allarme thine anger:
Gainst sinnes inuasions, rende the foggie clowde,   15
Whose al black wombe far blacker vice doth shrowd.
    Tell Gyant greatnes a more great did frame,
Th'imaginary Colosse of the same;
    And then expostulate why *Titus* should
Make shewe of Ætnas heat, yet be as cold   20
As snow-drownd *Athos* in his frozen zeale,
Both to Religion and his Common-weale?
    Or why should *Cælius* iniure thrift so much,
As to entitle his extortion such?
    Or desperat *Drus* cloke the confusion,   25
Of heady rage with resolution?   C3
    Pale trembling *Matho* dies his milke-staind liuer

16 shrowd.] shrowd 26 resolution?] resolution,

In colour of a discreet counsell-giuer:
And coole aduisement: yet the world doth know,
Hee's a rancke coward: but who dares tell him so?   30
    The world's so bad that vertue's ouer-awde,
And forst poore soule to become vices bawde:
Like the old morrall of the comedie,
Where Conscience fauours Lucars harlotry.
In spight of valour martiall *Anthony,*   35
Doth sacrifice himselfe to lecherie:
Wasting to skin & bones (true map of ruth,)
Yet termes it solace, and a trick of youth.
    Oh world, oh time, that euer men should be
So blinde besotted with hipocrisie: 40
Poyson to call an wholsome *Antidote,*
And make carouse the same, although they know't.
    How now my *Muse,* this is right womans fashion,
To fall from brawling to a blubbering passion?
Haue done haue done, and to a nimbler key,   45
Set thy winde instrument, and sprightly play.
Thys leaden-heeled passion is to dull,
To keepe pace with this Satyre-footed gull:
This mad-cap world, this whirlygigging age:
Thou must haue words compact of fire & rage: 50
Tearms of quick Camphire & Salt-peeter phrases,
As in a myne to blow vp the worlds graces,   [C3ᵛ]
And blast her anticke apish complements.
Her iugling tricks and mists which mock the sence,
Make *Catiline* or *Alcibiades,*   55
To seeme a *Cato,* or a *Socrates.*
    This vizar-fac't pole-head dissimulation,
This parrasite, this guide to reprobation,
Thys squynt-eyde slaue, which lookes two wayes at once,
This forkt Dilemma, oyle of passions,   60

    42 make] made

Hath so bereyde the world with his foule myre,
That naked truth may be suspect a lyer.
    For when great *Fœlix* passing through the street,
Vayleth his cap to each one he doth meet,
And when no broome-man that will pray for him,   65
Shall haue lesse truage then his bonnets brim,
Who would not thinke him perfect curtesie?
Or the honny-suckle of humilitie?
The deuill he is as soone: he is the deuill,
Brightly accoustred to bemist his euill: 70
Like a Swartrutters hose his puffe thoughts swell,
With yeastie ambition: *Signior Machiauell*
Taught him this mumming trick, with curtesie
T'entrench himselfe in popularitie,
And for a writhen face, and bodies moue,   75
Be Barricadode in the peoples loue.
    Yonder comes *Clodius*, giue him the salute,
An oylie slaue: he angling for repute,   [C4]
Will gently entertaine thee, and preuent
Thy worse conceit with many a complement: 80
But turne thy backe, and then he turnes the word,
The foul-mouthd knaue wil call thee goodman *Tord*.
    Nothing but cossenage doth the world possesse,
And stuffes the large armes of his emptines.
    Make sute to *Fabius* for his fauour, he   85
Will straight protest of his loues treasurie:
Beleeu'st thou him, then weare a motly coate,
He'le be the first man which shall cut thy throat.
    Come to the Court, and *Balthazer* affords
Fountaines of holy and rose-water words: 90
Hast thou need of him? & wouldst find him kind?
Nay then goe by, the gentleman is blind.
    Thus all our actions in a simpathy,
Doe daunce an anticke with hypocrisie,
And motley fac'd Dissimulation,   95

Is crept into our euery fashion,
Whose very titles to are dissembled:
The now all-buttockt, and no-bellied
Doublet and hose which I doe reuell in,
Was my great grandsires when he did begin   100
To wooe my grandame, when hee first bespake her,
And witnesse to the ioynture he did make her:
(Witnes some auntient painted history
Of *Assuerus, Haman, Mardoche.*   [C4ᵛ]
For though some gulls me to beleeue are loth,   105
I know thei'le credite print, and painted cloth)
Yet, like th'olde Ballad of the Lord of *Lorne*,
Whose last line in King *Harries* dayes was borne,
It still retaines the title of as new,
And proper a fashion, as you euer knew.   110
        All things are different from their outward show,
The very poet, whose standish doth flow
With Nectar of *Parnassus*, and his braine
Melts to *Castalian* dew, and showres wits raine,
Yet by his outward countnaunce doth appeare   115
To haue beene borne in wits dearths deerest yeere.
So that *Zopirus* iudging by his face,
Will pronounce *Socrates* for dull and base.
        This habite hath false larumd-seeming wonne
In our affections, that whatsoere is done   120
Must be newe coynd with slie dissemblance stamp,
And giue a sunne-shine title to a lampe.
        This makes the foisting trauailer to sweare,
And face out many a lie within the yeere.
And if he haue beene an howre or two aboarde,   125
To spew a little gall: then, by the Lord,
He hath beene in both the *Indias*, East and West,
Talkes of *Guiana, China,* and the rest:

115 countnaunce] coutnaunce

The straights of *Gibraltare, and Ænian,*
Are but hard by, no nor the *Magellane;*   130   [C5]
Mandeuile, Candish, sea-experienst *Drake*
Came neuer neere him, if he truly crake;
Nor euer durst come where he layd his head,
For out of doubt he hath discouered
Some halfe a dozen of th'infinity   135
Of *Anaxarchus* worlds. Like foppery
The Antiquary would perswade vs to:
He shewes a peece of blacke-iack for the shooe,
Which old *Ægeus* bequeathd his valiant sonne:
A peece of pollisht mother of pearle's the spoone   140
Cupid eate pappe with; and he hath a dagger
Made of the sword wherwith great *Charles* did swagger.
Oh that the whip of fooles, great *Aretine,*
Whose words were squibs, and crackers euery line,
Liu'd in our dayes, to scourge these hypocrites,   145
Whose taunts may be like gobblins and sprights:
To haunt these wretches forth that little left them
Of ayery wit; (for all the rest's bereft them.)
Oh how the varges from his blacke pen wrung,
Would sauce the *Idiome* of the English tongue,   150
Giue it a new touch, liuelier Dialect
To heare this two-neckt goose, this falshood checkt.
      Me thinks I see the pie-bald whoresone tremble
To heare of *Aretine:* he doth dissemble,
There is no trust to be had to his quaking,   155
To him once more, and rouse him from his shaking   [C5ᵛ]
Feauer of fained feare, hold whip and cord,
Muse, play the Beadle, a lash at euery word:
No, no, let be, he's a true cosoner still,
And like the Cramp-fish darts, euen throgh my quil   160
His slie insinuating poysonous iuice,

130 *Magellane;*] *Magellane,*

And doth the same into my Spirit infuse:
Me thinks already I applaud my selfe,
For nettle-stinging thus this fayery elfe:
And though my conscience sayes I merit not   165
Such deere reward, dissembling yet (God wot)
I hunt for praise, and doe the same expect:
Hence (crafty enchaunter) welcome base neglect,
Scoffes make me know my selfe, I must not erre,
Better a wretch then a dissembler.   170

Satire II

Heere coms a Coach (my Lads) let's make a stand,
And take a view of blazing starres at hand:
Who's here? who's here? now trust me passing faire,
Thai're most sweet Ladies: mary and so they are.
Why thou young puisne art thou yet to learne,   5
A harper from a shilling to discerne?
I had thought the last mask which thou caperedst in
Had catechiz'd thee from this errors sinne,
Taught thee S. *Martins* stuffe from true gold lace,   [C6]
And know a perfect from a painted face: 10
Why they are Idols, Puppets, Exchange babies,
And yet (thou foole) tak'st them for goodly Ladies:
Where are thine eyes? But now I call to mind,
These can bewitch, and so haue made thee blind;
A compound mist of May deaw and Beane flowre,   15
Doe these *Acrasias* on thy eye lids powre:
Thou art enchaunted (*Publius*) and hast neede
Of *Hercules*, thy reason, to be freede.
    Consider what a rough worme-eaten table,
By well-mix'd colours is made saleable: 20
Or how toad-housing sculs, and old swart bones,
Are grac'd with painted toombs, and plated stones:
And think withall how scoffe-inspiring faces
From dawbing pencils doe deriue their graces:
Their beauties are most antient Gentlemen,   25
Fetch'd from the deaw-figs, hens dung, & the beane.
Nay, this doth rather prooue them bastard faires,
For to so many fathers they are heires,
Yet their effronted thoughts adulterate,

Think the blind world holds them legitimate.   30
(Madame) you gull your selfe, thinking to gull
Young puisnes eyes with your ore-varnish'd scull:
For now our Gallants are so cunning growne,
That painted faces are like pippins knowne:
They know your spirits, & your distillations,   35   [C6v]
Which make your eies turn diamonds, to charm passions,
Your cerusse now growne stale, your skaine of silke,
Your philterd waters, and your asses milke,
They were plaine asses if they did not know,
Quicksiluer, iuyce of Lemmons, Boras too,   40
Allom, oyle Tartar, whites of egges, & gaules
Are made the bawdes to morphew, scurffs, & scauls.
Then whats a wench but a quirke, quidlit case,
Which makes a Painters pallat of her face?
Or would not *Chester* sweare her downe that shee   45
Lookt like an Elench, logicke sophistrie?
Or like a new sherifes gate-posts, whose old faces
Are furbisht ouer to smoothe times disgraces?
        Then how is man turnd all *Pygmalion*,
That knowing these pictures, yet we doate vpon   50
The painted statues, or what fooles are we
So grosly to commit idolatry?
What, are we Ethnicks that we honour beasts?
(They are beasts which paint themselues) or els papists
Whose ouer-fleeting brittle memories   55
Right worshipfull intitle Images?
But be we any thing; these wenches know
We are but fooles to be deluded so:
Who for deluding vs, to plague their sinne,
Are turnd to counterfaits, which their vncasde skin,   60
Quickly discouers, and to shadowes too,   [C7]
For making louers shadowes as they doo.

        42 scauls.] scauls

Is not he fond then which a slip receaues
For currant money? she which thee deceaues
With copper guilt is but a slip, and she   65
Will one day shew thee a touch as slippery:
She's counterfait now, and it will goe hard,
If e're thou find her currant afterward:
A painted wench is like a whore-house signe,
The old new slurred ouer: or mix'd wine,   70
Sophisticate, to giue it hew and tast;
A dudgin dagger that's new scowr'd and glast:
Or I could sute her were she not prophane,
To a new painted, and churchwarden'd fane:
Or generall pardons, which speake gloriously,   75
Yet keepe not touch: or a Popish *Iubily*.
Thus altering natures stamp, they're altered,
From their first purity, innate maydenhead:
Of simple naked honesty, and truth,
And giuen o're to seducing lust and youth: 80
Whose stings when they are blunted, & these freede,
Then shall they see the horror of this deede:
And leauing it their lothsome playstered skins,
Shall shew the furrowed riuels of their sins:
And now their box complexions are depos'd,   85
Their iaundise looks, and raine-bow like disclos'd,
Shall slander them with sicknes e're their time,   [C7ᵛ]
For pocket-healths, vaine vsage in their prime.
Then shall their owly consciences shun light,
And thus like Bats shall flutter in the night,   90
Asham'd that any eye should testifie,
Their now impouerish'd beauties beggary,
Nay, they so far shal be asham'd thereof,
That from themselues they shal feare cannon scoffe,
And hate to see themselues: *all glasses breake*,   95

    81 freede,] freede

By which before they taught their looks to speake:
And parly with their lusts. But I'me a foole,
Which talk to deafe eares, & dull stocks do schoole:
Me thinks the painted Pageant's out of sight,
It's time to end my lecture then: good night.   100

Satire III

Mary and gup! haue I then lost my cap?
It shall be a warning for an after-clap,
Not that I weigh the tributary due,
Of cap and courtship complements, and new
Antike salutes, I care not for th'embrace,   5
The Spanish shrug, kiss'd-hand, nor cheuerell face,
God saue you sir, good sir, and such like phrases,
Pronounc'd with lisping, and affected graces,
Moue me no more then t'heare a Parrat cry
Her by-roate lesson of like curtesie: 10   [C8]
    But this I wonder, that th'art so estrang'd,
And thy old English looks to outlandish chang'd,
Howsoe're thy selfe by English birth art freed,
Thou hast neede to haue thy looks endenized:
With thee I haue beene long time well acquainted: 15
But those beyond-sea looks haue now disioynted
Our well knit friendship, for whose sake I doubt
Th'art quite turn'd Dutch, or some outlandish lowt,
Thou hast cleane forgot thine English tong, & then
Art in no state to salute Englishmen: 20
Or else th'hast had some great sicknes of late,
Whose tiranny doth so extenuate
Thy fraile remembrance, that thou canst not claime
Thine old acquaintance, mothers tong, nor name
Giuen thee in thy baptisme: for I cannot, I,   25
Impute it vnto pride, Philosophy
Hauing so well fore-season'd thy minds caske.
    Of gulls and fooles I will no question aske,
Wherfore they looke so strange, because I know

They are but poore in wit, though rich in show.   30
Looke on *Panduris*, with whom in th'infancy
Of my then greene, now riper iudgment, I
Was well acquainted: he sir will not speake,
Thinking himselfe the better man belike
Because his father with bartring, and trucke   35
Of bad greene-sicknes wines, hath heapt vp muck,   [C8ᵛ]
And for his mother with her greedy gripes,
Hath out of neats-feet, chitterlings, and tripes,
Scrapt many a durty pound: this is he,
That lookes like *Guazzo*, or pedant grauitie,   40
Spits controuersies, prates of *Bellarmine*,
And yet perhaps nere saw of his a line.
     Then there is *Cynops*, whose grand-mother sold
Good ale and wigs, in curtesey growne cold,
Because his father with a cossening fetch,   45
Purchasd land for him, which his conscience stretch
Hath almost sworne the whole world, that the man
Is damnd, to make his sonne a gentleman.
     With them in ranck *La volto Publius*,
Who's growne a reueller ridiculous: 50
And for his dad with *Chimicke* vsurie,
Turnd yron to sterling, drosse to land and fee,
And got so by old horse-shooes, that the foole
Enterd himselfe into the dauncing schoole;
Thinks scorne to speake: especially now since   55
H'ath beene a player to a Christmas prince.
When these, & such like doe themselues estrange,
I neuer muse at theyr fantasticke change:
Because they are Phantasmas butterflies,
Inconstant, but yet witlesse *Mercuries*.   60
I know some of their humorous neere of kin,
Which scorne to speake to one which hath not bin   D

    47 that] thar

In one of these last voyages: or to one
Which hauing bin there yet (though he haue none)
Hath not a *Cades*-beard: though I dare sweare   65
That many a beardlesse chin hath marched where
They durst not for their berds come, thogh they dare
Come where they will not leaue theyr beardes one haire.
But I doe wonder what estrangeth thee,
New cast in mold of deepe philosophy: 70
Thee whom that Queene hath taught to moderate,
Thy mounting thought, nor to be eleuate
With puffingst fortunes? though (for ought I know)
Thy fortunes are none such to puffe thee so.
　　　How like a *Musherom* art thou quickly growne,   75
I knew thee when thou war'dst a thred-bare gowne:
Siz'd eighteene pence a weeke, and so did I,
As then thou wert faine of my company,
Of mine acquaintance glad; how art thou altred?
Or wherein's thine estate so bettered?   80
Thou art growne a silken dauncer, and in that
Turn'd to a caper, skipst from loue to hate,
To daunce *Ma piu*, French-galliard, or a measure,
Doost thou esteeme this cunning such a treasure?
Neuer be proud of that, for dost thou know,   85
That *Laureàt* Batchelor *Del Phrygio*?
He with a spade-beard can full mannerly,
Leade the olde measures to a company   [D₁ᵛ]
Of bare chind-boyes, and with his nimble feete,
Make our fore-wearied Counsellours to sweat: 90
For enuie at his strange actiuitie,
Because they cannot do't as well as he.
But then a simple reueller, thou art more,
Thou hast had som doings with the prince *d'Amore*
And playd a noble mans part in a play: 95

68 haire.] haire

Now out vpon thee *Fabian*, I dare say,
If *Florus* should alledge that cause of pride,
Hisse him thou wouldst to death for't: and beside,
Thou mightst haue had som doings with that prince
Which wold haue made thee lesse proude euer since.   100
      Yet art thou stately, and so stately to,
That thou forget'st thy state, and wilt not know
Them which knowe thee and it: so long thou hast
True follower beene of fashions, that at last
Thou art growne thy selfe a fashion: for to day   105
Thou art common, popular, in vse euery way
Fitting the various world, but by and by
Thou art disusde, growst stale, and too proudly
Wringst thy selfe from the humorous worlds conceit,
Now art thou like the wide breech, doublet strait,   110
But er't be long, thou wilt estranged be,
Like the French quarter slop, or the gorbelly,
The long stockt hose, or close Venetian.
Now fie vpon this pride, which makes wise men   D2
Looke like expired leases; out of doubt   115
Thou wert wise, but thy lease of wit is out:
For such fond toyes thou hast estrangde thy selfe
For vaine braue Bragardisme, and durtie pelfe,
And yet I thinke, thy pelfe with thee'le dispence
To kisse the Counter, ere twill bale thee thence.   120
      These foolish toyes haue quite disparaged
Philosophy thy Mistris, and tis said,
Thou art like to *Damasippus*, for thy hayre
Precisely cut, makes thee Philosopher,
And nothing (God wot) else. But what care I?   125
Why should I reason with thy surquedry?
I smile at thy Atturneys silken pride,
Tufttaffeta state, and make my Muse deride,
In these her scoffing rimes thy beeing strange,
And haue good pastime at thy motley change.   130

Prethee be proude still, strange still, stately still,
And with thy winde my Muses organs fill,
To sound an Antheme of thy folly foorth,
It wil be merry musicke, richly worth
The laughing at, for I will play a Iigge,   135
And thou shalt daunce, my Muse shall play the rig
Once in her dayes, but shee shall quittance thee,
For thy contemptible inconstancie.
       Well, if thou wilt speake, so, and so farewell,
       If not, I thinke thee worse foole then I'le tell.   140

Satire IV

What a scald humour is this iealous care,
Which turnes a man to a familiare?
See how *Trebatio* yonder haunts his wife,
And dares not loose sight of her for his life:
And now there's one speakes to her, mark his grace,   5
See how he basts himselfe in his owne greace:
Note what a squint askew he casts, as he
Already saw his heads hornd-armory.
Foule weather ielousie to a forward spring,
Makes weeds grow ranke, but spoyles a better thing: 10
Sowes tares (gainst haruest) in the fields of loue,
And dogged humor Dog-dayes-like doth proue:
Scorching loues glorious world with glowing tong;
A serpent by which loue to death is stung,
A fire to wast his pleasant sommer bowres,   15
Ruine his mansions, and deface his towres.
       Yonder goes *Cælius* playing fast and loose
With his wiues arme, but not for loue God knowes,
Suspition is the cause she well doth know,
Can she then loue him that doth wrong her so?   20
If she refuse to walke with him hee'le frowne,
Fore-wearied both, they rest, he on her gowne
Sits for his ease he saith, afrayd in hart,
Least sodainly she should giue him the start:
Thus doth he make her prisoner to his feare,   25
And himselfe thrall to selfe-consuming care.   D3
A male-kind sparrow once mistooke his nest,

23 he saith,] she saith,

[78]

And fled for harbour to faire *Liuias* breast:
Her husband caught him with a iealous rage,
Swearing to keepe him prisoner in a Cage: 30
       Then a poore flye dreading no netty snare,
Was caught in curled meshes of her haire,
Humming a sad note for's imprisonment;
When the mad beast, with ruder hands doth rent
That golden fleece, for hast to take the flie,   35
And straight-wayes at a window gins to prie,
Busie, sharp-sighted blind-man-hob, to know
Whether t'were male or female taken so.
       Marke how *Seuerus* frigs from roome to roome,
To see, and not to see his martirdome: 40
Peeuish disease which doth all foode distast,
But what kils health, and that's a pleasing feast:
Like Weauers shuttles which runne to and fro,
Rau'ling their owne guts with their running so.
       He which infects these with this lunacy,   45
Is an odd figgent iack called *Iealousie,*
His head is like a windmils trunk so bigge,
Wherin ten thousand thoughts runne whirligigge,
Play at barly-breake, and daunce the Irish hay
Ciuill and peacefull like the *Centaures* fray;   50
His body is so fallen away and leane,
That scarce it can his logger-head sustaine.   [D3ᵛ]
He hath as many hundred thousand eyes
As *Argus* had, like starres plac't in the skies,
Though to no purpose, for blinde loue can see   55
Hauing no eyes, farther then Iealousie.
Gulfe-brested is he, silent, and profound,
Cat-footed for slie pace, and without sound,
Porpentine backed, for he lies on thornes,
Is it not pitty such a beast wants hornes?   60

      38 taken so.] taken so, 47 bigge,] bigge. 50 fray;] fray

Is it not pitty such a beast should so,
Possesse mens thoughts, and timpanize with woe
Their bigge swolne harts? for let *Seuerus* heare,
A Cuckow sing in *Iune,* he sweats for feare:
And comming home, he whurries through the house,   65
Each hole that makes an inmate of a mouse
Is ransackt by him for the cuckold-maker,
He beates his wife, & mongst his maides doth swagger
T'extort confession from them who hath been
Familiar with his wife, wreeking his teene   70
Vpon her ruffes and iewels, burning, tearing,
Flinging and hurling, scolding, staring, swearing.
Hee's as discreet, ciuill a gentleman,
As *Harry Peasecod,* or a Bedlam man,
A drunken captaine, or a ramping whore,   75
Or swaggering blew-coate at an ale-house doore.
      What an infection's this, which thus doth fire
Mens most discreetest tempers, and doth tire   [D4]
Their soules with furie? and doth make them thirst
To carouse bolles of poyson till they burst?   80
Oh this it is to be too wise in sin,
Too well experienst, and skilld therein:
"*For false suspition of another, is,*
"*A sure condemning of our owne amisse.*
Vnlesse a man haue into practise brought   85
The *Theoricke* art of loue which *Ouid* wrote,
Vnlesse his owne lewd life haue taught him more
Then *Aretines* aduenturous wandring whore,
Vnlesse he haue an antient souldiour beene,
Brags of the markes, and shewes the scarres of   90
        sinne,
How could he be so gorgde with louing hate,
As to thinke women so insaciate?
How could he know their stratagems and shifts,

    81 in sin,] in sin.

Their politicke delayes and wilie drifts?
No no, tis true, he hath beene naught himselfe,   95
And lewdnes fathereth this wayward elfe,
    Then take this for a Maxim generall rule,
    No iealous man, but is or knaue, or foole.

Satire V

Let me alone I prethee in thys Cell,
Entice me not into the Citties hell;
Tempt me not forth this *Eden* of content,   [D4^v]
To tast of that which I shall soone repent:
Prethy excuse me, I am not alone   5
Accompanied with meditation,
And calme content, whose tast more pleaseth me
Then all the Citties lushious vanity.
I had rather be encoffin'd in this chest
Amongst these bookes and papers I protest,   10
Then free-booting abroad purchase offence,
And scandale my calme thoughts with discontents.
Heere I conuerse with those diuiner spirits,
Whose knowledge, and admire the world inherits:
Heere doth the famous profound *Stagarite*,   15
With Natures mistick harmony delight
My rauish'd contemplation: I heere see
The now-old worlds youth in an history:
Heere may I be graue *Platos* auditor;
And learning of that morrall Lecturer,   20
To temper mine affections, gallantly
Get of my selfe a glorious victory:
And then for change, as we delight in change,
(For this my study is indeede m'Exchange)
Heere may I sit, yet walke to *Westminster*   25
And heare *Fitzherbert*, *Plowden*, *Brooke*, and *Dier*
Canuas a law-case: or if my dispose

    23 change,] change.

Perswade me to a play, I'le to the *Rose*,
Or *Curtaine*, one of *Plautus* Comedies,   [D5]
Or the *Patheticke Spaniards* Tragedies: 30
If my desire doth rather wish the fields,
Some speaking Painter, some Poet straitway yeelds
A flower bespangled walk, where I may heare
Some amorous Swaine his passions declare
To his sun-burnt Loue. Thus my books little case,   35
My study, is mine All, mine euery place.
      What more variety of pleasures can
An idle Citty-walke affoord a man?
More troublesome and tedious well I know
T'will be, into the peopled streets to goe,   40
Witnes that hotch-potch of so many noyses,
Black-saunts of so many seuerall voyces,
That Chaos of rude sounds, that harmony,
And *Dyapason* of harsh *Barbary*,
Compos'd of seuerall mouthes, and seuerall cries,   45
Which to mens eares turne both their tongs & eies.
There squeaks a cart-wheele, here a tumbrel rumbles;
Heere scolds an old Bawd, there a Porter grumbles.
Heere two tough Car-men combat for the way,
There two for looks begin a coward fray,   50
Two swaggering knaues heere brable for a whore,
There brauls an Ale-knight for his fat-grown score.
      But oh purgation! yon rotten-throated slaues
Engarlanded with coney-catching knaues,
Whores, Bedles, bawdes, and Sergeants filthily   55   [D5ᵛ]
Chaunt *Kemps* Iigge, or the *Burgonians* tragedy:
But in good time, there's one hath nipt a bong,
Farewell my harts, for he hath marrd the song.
      Yet might all this, this too bad be excusd,
Were not an Ethicke soule much more abusd,   60

    39 well] will   43 Chaos] Chaons   47 rumbles;] rumbles

And her still patience choakt by vanitie,
With vnsufferable inhumanitie:
For whose gall is't that would not ouerflow,
To meete in euery streete where he shall goe,
With folly maskt in diuers semblances?   65
The Cittie is the mappe of vanities,
The marte of fooles, the *Magazin* of gulles,
The painters shop of Antickes: walke in Poules,
And but obserue the sundry kindes of shapes,
Th'wilt sweare that London is as rich in apes   70
As *Affricke Tabraca:* One wries his face.
This fellows wrie necke is his better grace.
He coynd in newer mint of fashion,
With the right Spanish shrugge shewes passion.
There comes one in a muffler of Cad'z-beard,   75
Frowning as he would make the world afeard,
With him a troupe all in gold-dawbed sutes,
Looking like *Talbots, Percies, Montacutes,*
As if their very countenaunces would sweare,
The Spanyard should conclude a peace for feare: 80
But bring them to a charge, then see the luck,   [D6]
Though but a false fire, they theyr plumes wil duck;
What maruell, since life's sweete? But see yonder,
One like the vnfrequented Theater
Walkes in darke silence, and vast solitude,   85
Suited to those blacke fancies which intrude,
Vpon possession of his troubled breast:
But for blacks sake he would looke like a ieast,
For hee's cleane out of fashion: what he?
I thinke the *Genius* of antiquitie,   90
Come to complaine of our varietie,
Of tickle fashions: then you iest I see.
Would you needs know? he is a malecontent:

     82 duck;] duck

A Papist? no, nor yet a Protestant,
But a discarded intelligencer.   95
Here's one lookes like to a king *Arthurs* fencer,
With his case of rapiers, and suted in buffe,
Is he not a Sargeant? then say's a muffe
For his furrd sattin cloake; but let him goe,
Meddle not with him, hee's a shrewd fellow.   100
      Oh what a pageant's this? what foole was I
To leaue my studie to see vanitie?
But who's in yonder coach? my lord and foole,
One that for ape tricks can put *Gue* to schoole:
Heroick spirits, true nobilitie   105
Which can make choyce of such societie.
He more perfections hath than y'would suppose,   [D6v]
He hath a wit of waxe, fresh as a rose,
He playes well on the treble Violin,
He soothes his Lord vp in his grosest sin,   110
At any rimes sprung from his Lordships head,
Such as *Elderton* would not haue fathered:
He cries, *oh rare my Lord,* he can discourse
The story of *Don Pacolet* and his horse,
(To make my Lord laugh) sweares and iest,   115
And with a *Simile non plus* the best,
(Vnlesse like *Pace* his wit be ouer-awde)
But his best part is he's a perfect Bawde,
Rare vertues; farewel they. But who's yonder
Deep mouth'd Hound, that bellows rimes like thunder; 120
He maks an earthquake throughout *Paules* churchyard,
Well fare his hart, his larum shall be heard:
Oh he's a puisne of the Innes of Court,
Come from th'Vniuersity to make sport
With his friends money heere: but see, see,   125
Heere comes *Don Fashion*, spruce formality,

95 intelligencer.] intelligencer, 120 thunder;] thunder

Neat as a Merchants ruffe, that's set in print,
New halfe-penny, skip'd forth his Laundres mint;
Oh braue! what, with a feather in his hat?
He is a dauncer you may see by that;   130
Light heeles, light head, light feather well agree.
Salute him, with th'embrace beneath the knee?
I thinke twere better let him passe along,   [D7]
He will so dawbe vs with his oyly tongue,
For thinking on some of his Mistresses   135
We shall be curried with the briske phrases,
And prick-song termes he hath premeditate,
Speake to him woe to vs, for we shall ha'te,
Then farewell he. But soft, whom haue we heare?
What braue Saint *George*, what mounted Caualiere?   140
He is all court-like, Spanish in's attyre,
He hath the right ducke, pray God he be no Frier:
Thys is the Dictionary of complements,
The Barbers mouth of new-scrapt eloquence,
Synomicke Tully for varietie,   145
And Madame Conceits gorgeous gallerie,
The exact patterne which *Castilio*
Tooke for's accomplish'd Courtier: but soft ho,
What needs that bownd, or that curuet (good sir)
There's some sweet Lady, and tis done to her,   150
That she may see his Iennets nimble force:
Why, would he haue her in loue with his horse?
Or aymes he at popish merrit, to make
Her in loue with him, for his horses sake?
    The further that we walke, more vanitie   155
Presents it selfe to prospect of mine eye,
Here sweares some Seller, though a known vntruth,
Here his wife's bated by some quick-chapt youth.
There in that window mistres minkes doth stand,   [D7^v]

148 accomplish'd] accomplish

And to some copesmate beckneth her hand,   160
In is he gone, Saint *Venus* be his speede,
For some great thing must be aduentured:
There comes a troupe of puisnes from the play,
Laughing like wanton schoole-boyes all the way.
Yon goe a knot to *Bloome* is Ordinary,   165
Friends and good fellowes all now, by and by
Thei'le be by the eares, vie stabs, exchange disgraces,
And bandie daggers at each others faces.
     Enough of these then, and enough of all,
I may thanke you for this time spent; but call   170
Henceforth I'le keepe my studie, and eschew,
The scandall of my thoughts, my follies view:
Now let vs home, I'me sure tis supper time,
The horne hath blowne, haue done my merry rime.

Satire VI

Oh that mens thoughts should so degenerate,
Being free borne, t'admit a slauish state:
They disclaime Natures manumission,
Making themselues bond to opinion:
Whose gally-slaues they are, tost on the sea   5
Of vulgar humors, which doth rage and play,
According as the various breath of change
Calmes or perturbs her smooth brow. Is't not strang   [D8]
That heau'n bred soules, discended from aboue
Should brooke such base subiection? feare reproofe   10
From her cold northerne gales, or els be merry
When her *Fanonian* praise breathes a sweet perry?
        (Rason) thou art the soules bright *Genius*,
Sent downe from *Ioues* throne to safe conduct vs
In this lifes intricate *Dædalian* maze: 15
How art thou buffuld? how comes this disgrace,
That by opinion thou art bearded so,
Thy slaue, thy shadow: nay, out-bearded too?
She earth-worme doth deriue her pedegree
From bodies durt, and sensualitie,   20
And marshald in degree fitting her birth
Is but a dwarffe, or iester to make mirth.
Thou the soules, bodies Queenes allie most neere,
The first Prince of her blood, and chiefest peere,
Nay, her protector in nonage, whilst she   25
Liues in this bodies weake minoritie,
Art yet kept vnder by that vnderling,
That dreame, that breath, nay that indeed *Nothing*.

    28 *Nothing.*] *Nothing,*

[88]

The ale-house *Ethicks,* the worlds vpside downe
Is verefied: the prince now serues the clowne.   30
If reason bandy with opinion,
Opinion winnes in the conclusion:
For if a man be once opinionate,
Millions of reasons nill extenuate   [D8ᵛ]
His fore-ceited mallice: conference   35
Cannot asswage opinions insolence.
But let opinion once lay battery
To reasons fort, she will turne heresie,
Or superstition, wily politist,
But she will winne those rampires which resist.   40
Then sith such innate discord is maintain'd
Twixt reason and opinion; what staid-brain'd,
True resolute, and philosophick head
Would by opinion be distempered?
    Opinion is as various as light change,   45
Now speaking Court-like friendly, strait-wayes strange;
She's any humours perfect parasite,
Displeas'd with her, and pleas'd with her delight,
She is the Eccho of inconstancie,
Soothing her no with nay, her I with yea.   50
    Then who would weigh this feather, or respect
The fickle censure of shallow neglect?
Shall graue *Lycurgus* straite repeale his lawes,
Because some Cobler finds fault with this clawse,
Some Ale-konner with that? or shall the state   55
Be subiect to each base-groomes arbitrate?
No, let's esteeme Opinion as she is,
Fooles bawble, innouations Mistris,
The Proteus Robin-good-fellow of change,
Smithfield of iaded fancies, and th'Exchange   60   E
Of fleeting censures, nurse of heresie,
Begot by Malice on Inconstancie:

    61 *heresie,*] *heresit*

It's but the hisse of Geese, the peoples noyse,
The tongue of humours, and phantasticke voyce
Of haire-brain'd Apprehension: it respects   65
With all due titles, and that due neglects
Euen in one instant. For in these our times
Some of Opinions gulls carpe at the rimes
Of reuerend *Chawcer*: other-some do praise them,
And vnto heau'n with wonders wings do raise them.   70
  Some say the mark is out of *Gowers* mouth,
Others, he's better then a trick of youth.
  Some blame deep *Spencer* for his grandam words,
Others protest that, in them he records
His maister-peece of cunning giuing praise,   75
And grauity to his profound-prickt layes.
  Daniel (as some holds) might mount if he list,
But others say that he's a Lucanist.
  Markham is censur'd for his want of plot,
Yet others thinke that no deepe stayning blot;   80
As *Homer* writ his Frogs-fray learnedly,
And *Virgil* his Gnats vnkind Tragedy:
So though his plot be poore, his Subiect's rich,
And his Muse soares a Falcons gallant pitch.
  Drayton's condemn'd of some for imitation,   85   [E1ᵛ]
But others say t'was the best Poets fashion,
In spight of sicke Opinions crooked doome,
Traytor to kingdome mind, true iudgments toomb,
Like to a worthy *Romaine* he hath wonne
A three-fold name affined to the *Sunne*,   90
When he is mounted in the glorious South,
And *Drayton's* iustly sirnam'd *Golden-mouth*.
  The double volum'd *Satyre* praised is,
And lik'd of diuers for his Rods in pisse,
Yet other-some, who would his credite crack   95

63 *peoples*] peoeples 70 them.] ‡hem

Haue clap'd *Reactioes* Action on his back.
    Nay, euen wits *Cæsar*, *Sidney*, for whose death
The Fates themselues lamented *Englands* scath,
And Muses wept, till of their teares did spring
Admiredly a second *Castal* spring,   100
Is not exempt for prophanation,
But censur'd for affectation.
    Thus doth Opinion play the two edg'd sword,
And vulgar iudgments both-hand playes afford,
Then who but fooles, and empty caske like minds,   105
Would be engross'd with such phantastique winds?
Let Players, Minstrels, silken Reuellers,
Light minded as their parts, their aires, their fethers,
Be slaues t'Opinion, when the people shoute
At a quaint iest, crosse-poynt, or well touch'd
         Lute,   110   E2
Let their sleight frothy minds be bubled vp,
And breake againe at a hisse, or howt, or hup.
Let *Caius* when his horse hath wone the bell,
Conceiue more ioy than his dull tongue can tell:
Or let *Lycanor* feare a tennis set   115
More then his soules losse, and for it more fret.
    Pollio me thinks is going into the Towne,
Boy, set your Maisters ruffe, and brush his gowne,
Least some spruce Taylor sitting on his stall,
Say, there goes a slouen, carelesse of all.   120
Heere comes young *Pansa*: whether away so fast?
Why, going to the Barbers in all hast,
Thy haire's all short enough: but I must craue
A little labour to be smug'd, and haue
A blessing of Rose-water, ere I goe   125
To see such and such Ladies, for you know
Thei'le flowt a man behind his backe, if he

99 Muses wept,] Muses-wept,   120 all.] all,

Be not trim furbish'd, and in decencie.
     Oh what a slauerie's this? shall a free mind
Sicke of a Cockneys Ague, feare the wind?   130
No, let's be Stoicks, resolute, and spare not
To tell the proudest Criticke that we care not
For his wooden censure, nor to mittigate
The sharp tart veriuice of his snap-haunce hate
Would change a line, a word, no not a poynt   135   [E₂ᵛ]
For his deepe mouthed scoffes, as soone disioynt
His grind-iest chaps as hurt our credites, who
Are carelesse of what he can say or do.
     Oh *Epictetus*, perfect libertine,
Who though a slaue, tyr'd daily in the mine,   140
Yet hadst as free a soule, as free a powre
To calme content as any Emperour,
Thou wert no busie *Polypragmons* thrall,
No slaue to censures, caring not at all
Which way the vulgar wind stood, negligent   145
Whether the world were angry or content.
Thy vertue-purged soule, thy *Genius*
Made all thine inclinations vertuous:
Which thou didst follow, carelesse of th'euent,
Or of the worlds applause, or discontent.   150
True patterne of a philosophick soule,
Not subiect to Mechanick mates controule,
Nor puff'd vp with the praises of each hind
Which gaue a froathy battery to thy mind.
     With such resolue, such perfect temperature   155
Should a Socratique mind her thoughts assure:
And as he taught young *Alcibiades*
Audacity to pleade, and to despise
The popular scarcrow estimation;
For that such bodies composition   160   E3

Consisted but of Brokers, Coblers, slaues,
Black-men, trap-makers, and such kind of knaues,
Whose many headed doomes he neuer weighd,
Nor of their giddy vnion was afraid:
So let all others care for vulgar breath,   165
Which neither can preserue, nor plague with death,
(Vnlesse their sent of Garlike poyson vs.)
Should I take it at hart, or for hainous,
To heare some Prentize, or some Players boy
Hath iested at my Muse, and scoff'd my ioy?   170
Or that some Chaundler slopt a mustard pot,
Or wrap'd Sope in some leaues, her petticoate?
Or perfum'd Courtiour in a peeuish scorne,
Some pages thereof, tyrant-like hath torne,
To scauenger his backe dore from the durt?   175
Which if he do (though me it shall not hurt)
May my harsh stile (the Muses I beseech)
Be but as arse-smart to his tickled breech:
Or shall I thinke my selfe t'haue better hap,
If that some weeuil, mault-worme, barly-cap,   180
Hearing my lines halfe-snorting ore his kanne,
Sweares them for good, and me a proper man?
Or shall I waxe proud if some Pedant daigne
The Epethite of Pretty for my paine?
The pox I will as soone: let others care,   185   [E3ᵛ]
Ile play the Gallant, I, the Caueleire;
Once in my dayes Ile weene, and ouer-weene,
And cry, a *Fico* for the *Criticke* spleene:
For let them praise them, or their praise deny,
My lines are still themselues, and so am I.   190

FINIS.

COMMENTARY

ABBREVIATIONS

CS   Marston, John. *Certaine Satyres . . . ,*
                            in *The Metamorphosis of Pigmalions
                            Image.* In *The Poems of John Marston,*
                            edited by Arnold Davenport. Liver-
                            pool: University Press, 1961.

Cunnington   Willett, Cecil, and Cunnington, Phillis.
                            *Handbook of English Costume in the
                            Sixteenth Century.* London: Faber and
                            Faber [1954].

Davies (ed. Howard)   Davies, Sir John. *The Poems of Sir John
                            Davies.* Edited by Clare Howard. New
                            York: Columbia University Press,
                            1941.

H. & S.   Jonson, Ben. *Ben Jonson.* Edited by
                            Charles H. Herford, Percy Simpson,
                            and Evelyn Simpson. 11 vols. Oxford:
                            Clarendon Press, 1925-52.

Harington, *Ajax*   Harington, Sir John. *A New Discourse of
                            a Stale Subject, Called The Metamor-
                            phosis of Ajax.* Edited by Elizabeth
                            Story Donno. New York: Columbia
                            University Press, 1962.

Harington, *L. & E.*   Harington, Sir John. *The Letters and Epi-
                            grams of Sir John Harington.* Edited by

Norman E. McClure. Philadelphia: University of Pennsylvania Press, 1930.

Harvey   Harvey, Gabriel. *The Works of Gabriel Harvey.* Edited by Alexander B. Grosart. 3 vols. 1884-85. Reprint. New York: AMS Press, Inc., 1966.

Linthicum   Linthicum, Marie C. *Costume in the Drama of Shakespeare and His Contemporaries.* Oxford: Clarendon Press, 1936.

Lodge, *Wks.*   Lodge, Thomas. *The Complete Works of Thomas Lodge.* 4 vols. Glasgow: Printed for the Hunterian Club, 1883.

Nashe   Nashe, Thomas. *The Works of Thomas Nashe.* Edited by Ronald B. McKerrow. Revised by F. P. Wilson. 5 vols. Oxford: B. Blackwell, 1958.

I, II, III Parnassus   Leishman, James B., ed. *The Three Parnassus Plays (1598-1601).* London: Nicholson & Watson, 1949.

Partridge   Partridge, Eric. *Shakespeare's Bawdy.* London: Routledge & Paul [1955].

Sugden   Sugden, Edward H. *A Typographical
                  Dictionary to the Works of Shake-
                  speare and His Fellow Dramatists.*
                  London: Longmans, Green & Co.,
                  1925.

SV   Marston, John. *The Scourge of Villanie.*
                  In *The Poems of John Marston,* edited
                  by Arnold Davenport. Liverpool:
                  University Press, 1961.

Tilley   Tilley, Morris P. *A Dictionary of the
                  Proverbs in England in the Sixteenth
                  and Seventeenth Centuries.* Ann Ar-
                  bor: University of Michigan Press,
                  1950.

Vd   Hall, Joseph. *Virgidemiae.* In *The Col-
                  lected Poems of Joseph Hall,* edited by
                  Arnold Davenport. Liverpool: Uni-
                  versity Press, 1949.

Abbreviations for periodicals, Shakespeare's plays, and books of reference are those commonly used. Abbreviations for other familiar works, both primary and secondary, which are used on occasion to conserve space, will present no problem to students of Elizabethan literature. "G." stands for "Everard Guilpin." All references to classical writers, unless otherwise indicated, are to the Loeb edition. Lineation to Shakespeare's works, unless otherwise indicated, is based on the Globe edition.

PRELIMINARIES

Title. SKIALETHEIA] The Greek is probably Renaissance, inspired perhaps by Chapman's *Shadow of Night*, Σκιὰ νυκτός (1594), and following the general fashion at this time for Greek titles. It apparently translates "imago veritatis," from the celebrated definiton of comedy ascribed by Evanthius to Cicero: "imitatio vitae, speculum consuetudines, imago veritatis," used by Jonson and others to describe and justify satiric comedy. *Shadowe* ("reflected image," "picture") places the work alongside the *Mirror, Glass, Speculum,* etc., works in the moral tradition. *Shadowe,* moreover, directs attention to the satirist's method and style, his use of unreal character types ("shadows") rather than substantial persons, his obscure, delusive language and allusion. Lodge, arguing the need for "Satericall Poetes nowe a dayes to penn our comedies," maintained that the "poet's wit can correct, yet not offend" if he reprove particular vices "couertly in shadowes," that is, "in the person of" Pamphilus, Davus, Gnato, etc. (*Defence of Poetry,* ed. Smith, 1:82). And satirists felt that their style should be difficult, "darksome," "duskie," like the "darkness" with which Chapman "labor[ed] to be shadowed" (Epistle, *Ovids Banquet,* ed. Bartlett, p. 49), a conception they tried more or less to embody. Finally, by drawing on the antithesis of *substance-shadow,* G. intends a mildly ironic jest at or defense of himself, saying, "What I present here is only the shadow, not the real truth."

Device.] No. 301 in McKerrow's *Printers' & Publishers' Devices* (London, 1913). The ling, says McKerrow, is "manifestly a rebus" on the publisher's name, but the "honeysuckle does not appear to have been explained" (p. 118). The rebus becomes complete if we note a pictorial anagram—*Honisocal-Nicholas*—possible with a number of variant spellings. The device appears on the early *Hamlet* quartos and on numerous other Ling publications.

I.R.] James Roberts.

To the Reader] l. 1. *Ingling*] amorous, coaxing; alluding to fashionable love poetry.

l. 2. fall to] begin, esp. eating.

  carpe thy fill] i.e., find fault. The eating metaphor is common in such dedications, and suggests some wordplay; cf. Lodge, "To the Reader," *Wits Miserie* (1596), *Wks.*, 4:5: "if you meet not Carpes in your dish, you may hap haue Gogins if you angle"; and Harington's address in *Ajax*, ed. Donno, p. 80.

EPIGRAMS

These follow the contemporary practice of imitating the form and particular epigrams of Martial. See T. K. Whipple, *Martial and the English Epigram from Sir Thomas Wyatt to Ben Jonson* (Berkeley, 1925), who discusses G. on pp. 349-53. The practice was already popularized by Harington and, esp., Davies. G.'s reliance on Martial for particular models is heavy, as will be observed, more so than Whipple indicates in his list of nine parallels. G., according to Whipple, "beyond question was a disciple of Davies," whom he follows in a number of epigrams and refers to as "Our *English Martiall*" (Ep. 20), but differs from Davies in that he "makes a larger use of conventional devices and therefore approximates more nearly to Martial." Otherwise, "his savage bitterness of temper estranged him from Martial." Davies's epigrams were probably written before 1594 and were published at various unspecified dates in the 1590s and after in the same volume with Marlowe's *Elegies*, a volume ordered burned in 1599. On Davies's publication dates see P. Simpson, *RES*, n.s. 3 (1952): 49-50 and J. M. Nosworthy, *RES*, n.s. 4 (1953): 260-61.

  Most of G.'s type-names (e.g., Nævia, Matho, Issa, Cinna, Chrestina, Cotta) are from Martial, and are not traced unless there seems reason.

Procemium. I. 1. 4. *controules*] overpowers.

l. 6. "(*As great things* . . .] Cf. Horace, *Epode* 16. 2: "Suis et ipse Roma viribus ruit"; a favorite with Elizs.; cf. Spenser, *Ruines*, ll. 76, 571, and Jonson, *Cat.* 1. 1. 531-34. G.'s line appears in *England's Parnassus* (1600), under "Greatnesse." For gnomic lines Elizs. frequently prefixed inverted commas; for quotations they often used parentheses.

l. 9. (*now mounted the full height,*)] i.e., at the peak of (natural) power, probably a metaphor from falconry.

l. 10. *confounded*] defeated utterly, perhaps confused.
      barbarismes] i.e., ignorance in general, but with special regard for rude or unpolished language (*OED* 1).

l. 12. *Engraue*] a) record, by incised letters, b) entomb.

ll. 12-14. *ciuill warres . . . mother*] Probably the current literary quarrels of Nashe-Harvey (both of Cambridge) and/or Hall-Marston. Bastard, it should be noted, has two epigrams in *Chrestoleros* (1598), *Lib.* 4, Eps. 4, 5, ed. Grosart, p. 44, on the general enmity between Oxford and Cambridge, referring to them as sisters.

To the Reader. 2. l. 1. *pedler rimes*] i.e., plain and of little worth, such as peddlers sold. Cf. *Vd* 3. Prol. 4: "*packe-staffe plaine uttring what thing they ment.*"

l. 3. *Hermaphroditize*] render effeminate. Cf., below, *Sat. Pre.* 1-2; and the similar allusion at *SV* 8. 146. Perhaps in specific allusion to B. Barnes, *Parthenophil*, Madr. 13 (ed. Victor A. Doyno [1971], p. 38): ". . . bounde / With her enfolded thighes in mine entangled, / And both in one selfe-soule plac'de, / Made a Hermaphrodite, with pleasures rauish't." But on Ovidian poetry in general note Hallett Smith: "The Hermaphrodite myth is . . . a central one in the whole movement" (*Elizabethan Poetry* [Cambridge, Mass., 1952], p. 74).

l. 5. *trim Say*] a) pretty saying or "assay"; b) possibly the frequent sense of a cloth of fine texture resembling serge, perhaps silk, but more likely, the infrequent "bucket for domestic use" (*OED sb*3), one such as an itinerant tinker might mend. With the next line cf. Tilley A4: "He swears like a tinker."

Of Titus. 3. Henry Parrot offers virtually the same epigram as his own in *Laquei Ridiculosi* (1613), *Lib.* 1, Ep. 95, D8ᵛ.

l. 2. *Blazoning*] boasting, with a punning reference to heraldic language.

To Livia. 4. T. K. Whipple justly compares this with Martial 2. 10 (*Martial and the English Epigram* [1925], p. 352). Marston has a "modest" Livia (*SV* 11. 65), who Davenport thinks "may be suggested by the dignity and quiet bearing of the Empress Livia." See, below, Satire IV. 28 for another Livia.

Of Matho. 5. A traditional "promise and payment" epigram, of which there were scores both native and classical; cf., e.g., Heywood, *Fifth Hund.*, *18*, *Sixth Hund.*, *44*, in *Wks.*, ed. Milligan (Urbana, 1956), pp. 208, 236; Davies, *In Flaccum 18*, in *Poems*, ed. Howard, p. 41; see also Marston's description of Gallus, *SV* 4. 21 ff., which is esp. close to G.: "He aunswers me, *to morrow, . . .* / Putting me of with (*morrow*) euermore. / Thus when I vrge him, with his sophistrie / He thinkes to salue his damned periurie." Among satirists "Matho" occurs frequently, usually as the type of disreputable but wealthy lawyer; cf., e.g., Martial 4. 79; 8. 42; and Juvenal 1. 32; 7. 129; *Vd* 4. 5. 1 ff., 69-70; *SV* 3. 127; and, below, Satire I. 27. Matho may be John Davies, the lawyer, as he almost certainly is in several Benjamin Rudyerd epigrams of the same time; see James L. Sanders, *RES*, n.s. 17 (1966): 241-55.

l. 3. *sophistrie*] In the logical sense here (cf., below, Satire II. 46: "logicke sophistrie"), with a play on the sense "trickery or craft" below at l. 5.

l. 6. *gaue me his word . . .*] Cf. Lat. *dare verba,* to deceive, as in Martial 2. 76. Cf. also *Volpone* 1. 4. 139-40.

Of Faber. 6. l. 1. *prouder*] With a quibble on the sense "sexually excited, swelling" (*OED* 8), as is frequent throughout the satires.

l. 2. *take him a hole lower*] Based on the proverbial "take one a button-hole lower," that is, to humiliate one.

Of a railing humour. 7. Comparisons of the satirist's impulse to the body's excretory functions are commonplace. Writers of epigrams, for Puttenham, "would and must needs utter their splenes in all ordinarie matters also or else it seemed their bowels would burst" (*Arte,* ed. Willcock and Walker, p. 54).

l. 1. *kennel wits*] i.e., "dogged," as often applied to cynical satirists. Marston, "a barking Satyrist" (*CS,* The Authour in prayse, l. 56), was esp. fond of applying canine metaphors to himself. Also "muddy" (*OED sb2,* from *cannel,* gutter).

l. 5. *embrac't*] a) undertaken, b) enclosed, with a glance at the belt brace or buckle.

To Deloney. 8. Thomas Deloney (d. 1600?), famous balladmaker, novelist, and silk-weaver. After 1596 his fortunes both literary and personal suffered a decline as a result of hard times, of his troubles with the authorities for socially inflammatory writings, and of the decline in popularity of his ballads (all of which may have turned him to writing novels in 1597). This epigram may comment on both personal and literary problems, as they were closely related. His ballad on the "want and Scarcity of Corn within the Realm" in 1596 (now lost) aroused the wrath of the Lord Mayor, ostensibly for its having Queen Elizabeth speak "in very fond and vndecent sort." Deloney escaped arrest, though others were taken, and he may have become thereby for some time a fugitive. M. Lawlis thinks the ballad was misinterpreted, which may account for G.'s "Such massacre's made of thy balladry." Perhaps the epigram alludes to warrants for his arrest and anticipates his punishment (with some exaggeration). It may, further, allude to his illness. We know nothing of his death, only that he was dead by 1600. For what little is known of his life and his troubles over the ballad, see F. O. Mann's introduction to *Works* (Oxford, 1912) and Lawlis's introduction to *Novels* (Bloomington, 1961). On its primary level the epigram is about his literary reputation. Thus there may be an allusion to *Canaans Calamitie, the Destruction of Ierusalem,* by "T. D.," thought by some, including Mann, to be Deloney's, and ent. S. R. 5 Jan. 1598. This poem (it is not a ballad) seems not to have been popular, gives extraordinary descriptions of hunger, and begins on a note G. may echo: "Like to a Mourner clad in dolefull black, / That sadly sits to heare a heauie tale, / So must my pen proceed to shew the wrack" (ed. Mann). In *Saffron Walden* (1596), Nashe says of Deloney (3:84), "since Candlemas or his Iigge of *Iohn for the King,* not one merrie Dittie will come from him."

ll. 1-2. Like to the fatall . . .] As Collier observed, these lines echo closely the first two lines of *Jew of Malta,* act 2 (first pr. 1633?, ed. H. S. Bennett): "Thus, like the sad presaging raven, that tolls / The sick man's passport in her hollow beak." And Bullen (ed., *Wks.,* 2:29) compared Marlowe with Peele's *David and Bathsabe* (ent. 1594): "Like as the fatal raven, that in his voice / Carries the dreadful summons of our death." Moreover, Dyce noted that Peele's lines were imitated from Du Bartas's *L'Arche* (see Bennett's note in his edition).

l. 3. *paper-clothed post in Poules*] Alluding to broadsheet ballads, or advertisements thereof, or title pages to books attached to posts in front of the booksellers' shops in Paul's Churchyard.

l. 5. *hempen tragedie*] Referring to the hangman's halter, and possibly to the rope used to tie the advertisement to the post. Cf.

Dekker, *Seven Deadlie Sinnes*, ed. Brett-Smith (Oxford, 1922), p. 52: "So many lamentable hempen Tragedies acted at Tiburne." There may be an allusion to some lost Deloney ballad, hangings being one of his specialties and popular.

l. 7. *Such massacre's . . .*] The ballads were either censured or else left hanging to the post, unpurchased, unread. Cf. Nashe, 1:343: *"a number of you there bee, who consider neither premisses nor conclusion, but piteouslie torment Title Pages on euerie poast, neuer reading farther of anie Booke, than Imprinted by* Simeon *such a signe."*

l. 8. *pine*] frequently simply "starve" (*OED* 4).

l. 9. Fuscus] The name *Fuscus* (Lat. "swarthy") derives either from the dramatic writer and scholar Aristius, who appears in an amusing role in Horace, *Sat.* 1. 9. 61 ff., again among his literary friends in 1. 10. 83, and to whom the famous *Integer vitae* ode is dedicated (*Carm.* 1:22); or else from Arellius Fuscus the rhetorician, who taught school and who sought to please Maecenas by quoting Virgil.

Of Paule. 9. Cf. the niggardly "Paulus" of Martial 8. 33.

l. 3. *that*] i.e., his soul.

Of Sylvio. 10. l. 3. *singularitie*] peculiarity. Cf. Lodge, *Wits Miserie* (1596), *Wks.*, 4:12: "In his study hee affecteth singularity, and is more proud in being the author of some new sect of heresie, then a good man is humble in the fulnesse of his knowledge." G. doubtless alludes to contemporary philosophical attitudes toward numbers such as that of the so-called School of Night, on which see F. Yates, *Study of "Love's Labour's Lost"* (Cambridge, 1936), pp. 96 ff., which discusses the idea that "Pythagoreans dwelt upon the opposites of odd and even numbers" and that they preferred the odd. Agrippa refers to "that frowarde contention of the *Arithmeticians*, whether the equal or unequal number is to be preferred" (*Of the Vanitie and*

Uncertaintie of Artes, trans. James Sanford [1575], p. 27).

ll. 5-6. Scaliger, / *Old* Cardan . . . *chimick wits*] Julius Caesar Scaliger (1484-1558) and Girolamo Cardano (1501-76), both famous throughout Europe as natural philosophers and physicians. Scaliger's most popular and philosophical work was the *Excercitationes* (1557), an attack upon Cardan's *De Subtilate Rerum* (1551). Cardan's work, along with his *De Varietate Rerum* (1557), displayed esp. his characteristic tendency to the mystical and occult, his belief in astrology and in the notion that inferior metals must be regarded as *conatus naturae* toward the production of gold (here *chimick=alchemic*), and his important theory that nature produces an infinite variety of species. Cf. Harvey, 2:66: "Cardans multiplied matter."

l. 9. *to make the wise men euen*] a) bring into agreement those "at odds," b) make for an "even" number of famous Wise Men. See Cicero, *Tusc. Disp.* 5. 3. 8-9 on the word "philosophy" and the Seven Wise Men.

l. 10. Nerues] sinews (Lat. *nervi*), alluding to the cosmic body; a metaphor for the four elements. The epigram may not be so innocent as it appears. Lat. *nervus* is sometimes phallus, as in Juvenal 9. 32, and philosophers were traditionally homosexual, which may be Sylvio's "oddness."

To Gue. 11. As W. Strunk, Jr., points out, *MLN* 32 (1917): 220-21, Gue was almost certainly a blind performing baboon, and thus "the chief rival in public favor of Jack of Paris Garden." Such apes made a deep impression on the populace and appear constantly in satire as symbols of imitativeness and foolishness. Strunk gives a number of references to Gue. G. refers to Gue again below at Satire V. 104 and to apes throughout.

Gue may be Gabriel Harvey, who imitated and was imitated to his own detriment. The epithet "Ape" was tossed back and forth between Harvey and Nashe, on which one should consult Davenport's notes to Marston's *SV 9*, itself based on the idea of the ape. The comparison to Gue at Satire V. 104 occurs in a passage which probably attacks Nashe. Tradition held that satirists could drive men to hang themselves; cf. Sidney, *Apology*, ed. Smith, 1:207, and Nashe, 1:285, within an attack on Harvey. The epigram may have been suggested by Martial 2. 80.

Of Cotta. 12. The first of four epigrams (13, 35, 49) that compare and contrast Cotta with a picture, three, like this, by way of ridiculing his overuse of cosmetics and gaudy dress. Epigrams on paintings, with similar points, were common, modeled after *The Greek Anthology*, 4:145, 151, 212-15 and Martial 1. 109. See also that of Rufus's picture, "The Image of this Image," in Timothy Kendall, *Flowers of Epigrammes* (1577) (Manchester, 1874), p. 120, and that by Donne (ed. Milgate, p. 53) which Jonson often quoted (*Conv.*, H. & S., 1:150): "Thy flattering picture, *Phryne*, is like thee / Onely in this, that you both painted be."

To Licus. 14. This epigram draws on a number of Martial's, primarily his several on "bellus homo," 2. 7, 1. 9, 3. 63, 12. 39. As such it compares with *To Licus. 38*, and with Eps. 26, 27, each with "fine fellow." Stressing the ironic rather than complimentary connotation of Eliz. "fine," this epigram turns in the middle from the sense "consummate in virtue or excellence" to "delicately beautiful" and "showy, smart." It may also owe something to Martial 1:41, of Caecilius, who fancies himself a wit though in truth he is a dull hack. Its final point, that he cares for his feet more than for his thoughts, perhaps after Martial 12. 45, is made (with variations) by a number of Eliz. epigrammatists.

l. 6. *doth that fine addition affoord*] i.e., bestows that a) excellent honor, b) "style" of address or title "fine."

l. 9. *dauncing, vaulting . . .*] A number of satirists give such a series of accomplishments, it being a recurrent motif with them. See, e.g., Spenser, *Mother Hubberds Tale*, l. 692; *SV* 11. 192-93; Davies, "Ignoto" sonnet (the second), and *In Cineam 23* (ed. Howard), which G. seems to follow: "I am as good a man, / And better too by many a qualitie, / For vault, and daunce, and fence, and rime I can." See also Ep. 38, below. *vaulting*, leaping, as into a saddle, with an allusion to "whoring"; cf. "vaulting house" (*Sat. Pre.* 58).

l. 12. Lucius *golden Asse*] i.e., *The Golden Ass* of Lucius Apuleius. The term was frequently applied by satirists to the rich young "gulls" of the period, those arrogant, "fortunate & vnwise"; cf. Harvey, 1:198; 2:82; Overbury, "A Golden Asse," in *Characters* (1616), ed. W. J. Paylor (Oxford, 1936), pp. 7-8.

l. 14. *shodde in Veluet, and in Naples bisse*] Fashionable footwear, single-soled shoes or "pumps," and the high-heeled shoes slipped over the pumps, the "pantoffles," worn by courtiers and often made of such fine materials as to be unfit for wear outdoors (see Linthicum, pp. 254-55). Stubbes describes them at length, and concludes: "and handsome how could they be, when they go flap, flap, up and down in the dirt, casting up the mire to the knees of the wearer" (*Anatomy*, ed. Furnivall, 1:57-58). *bisse*, a fine kind of silk, the Italian being among the best (Linthicum, pp. 94-95). Nashe has a passage closely resembling this (3:220).

ll. 15-16. *Nay then I yeeld . . .*] Based on the proverb: "who fights with durty foes must needs be soyld" (see Tilley P358, T602). Cf. Davies's epigrams of Quintus (Ep. 12, ed. Howard) whose wit is in his feet, which concludes: "Doubtlesse his wit intends not to aspire, / Which leaues his head to trauell in the mire."

Of Zeno. 15. Based on Zeno's philosophy of *apatheia*, the composure of feeling and mind taken as the *summum bonum*.

l. 7. *catch-fooles*] i.e., those who take advantage of fools; on the analogy with *catch-pole*, a petty officer who arrests for debt.

Of Rivvs. 16. An adaptation of Martial 1. 115, which concludes: "iam suspendia saeva cogitabas: si novi bene te, Procille, vives." *Riuus*, not met with elsewhere, perhaps from Lat. "stream," to suggest the mouth watering, or the proverb "e rivo flumina facere."

Of Clodius. 17. This Clodius should probably be identified with the swaggering Clodius who forgets his friends in Ep. 22, the histrionic coward in Ep. 43, and the two-faced flatterer at Satire I. 77-82, though not, it seems, with the famous adulterer of Juvenal 6. 344. The epigram resembles Davies's Eps. 27, 28, in both of which Silla fails to "answer."

Of Curio. 18. Ultimately based on Martial 3. 9, but probably after Harington's *"Against a foolish Satyrist called* Lynus" (*L. & E.*, pp. 153-54): "Helpe, friends, I feele my credit lyes a bleeding, / For *Lynus*, who to me beares hate exceeding, / I heare against me is eu'n now a breeding / A bitter Satyr all of Gall proceeding: / . . . what he writes, I take no care nor heeding, / For none of worth wil think them worth the reeding." The "Lynus" of Harington's epigrams is generally thought to be Barnabe Barnes; see Mark Eccles, "Barnabe Barnes," in C. J. Sisson, *Lodge* (Cambridge, 1933), pp. 222-29. Davenport believes the dancing courtier "Curio" (Lat. *curia*, court) often attacked in Marston to be Davies and cites this epigram in support, Davies having written epigrams. See his note to *CS* 1. 125.

Of Faustus. 19. As this epigram connects *Fuscus* with *Faustus*, there is the possibility that the *Fuscus* of Ep. 8, above, esp. in view of the echo of *Jew*, and the *Fuscus* of Ep. 24, below, is

Marlowe. *Faustus*, however, is relatively common with epigrammatists. He occurs several times in Harington, as a
poetaster (Eps. 38, 55, 112, in *L. & E.*), and in Davies, as a frequenter of bawdy houses (Eps. 7, 16, ed. Howard). Marlowe's
atheism, of course, was notorious.

l. 2. *Oh gracelesse manners! . . .*] Like Satire I. 39, below,
based on Cicero, *In Cat.* 1. 2. Martial begins 9. 70 with Cicero's
expression. *manners*, a) etiquette, b) morals.

To Candidus. 20. As he indicates, G. here imitates Davies's *Of a
Gull. 2*, which begins (ed. Howard): "Oft in my laughing rimes I
name a gull, / But this new terme will many questions breede; /
Therefore at first I will expresse at full / vvho is a true and
perfect gull indeede." Davies, in turn, was adapting Martial
3. 63, which G. also follows in Ep. 38. On the gull as literary
type, a creation of the satirists in the nineties, and his develop-
ment from crédulous simpleton to would-be gallant and wit, see
note and references in H. & S., 1:345.

l. 1. *Friend* Candidus] Cf. Martial 2. 43, of his "friend" Candidus.

l. 3. *Our* English Martiall] i.e., Davies. Richard Carew, in *The
Excellency of English* (1595-96?), ed. Smith, 2:293; Francis
Meres, *Wits Treasury* (1598), ed. Smith, 2:321; *III Parnassus*
(1601/2?), ed. Leishman, 1. 2. 257-58—all compare Davies with
Martial. Davies boasted that he had "put down" Heywood the
epigrammatist (*In Haywodum. 29*, ed. Howard). Harington
responded that Heywood "is not yet put down by any of our
countrey" (*Ajax* [1596], ed. Donno, p. 103), and moreover that
Davies's "putting down hath raised" Heywood (*L. & E.*, p. 306);
the author of *Ulysses upon Ajax* found "maister *Dauies* epigram
[to be] two bowes and a halfe short of the cloute *Haewod* stucke
in" (1596, C7v); and finally, Bastard wished that he himself
"would sing *Dauy* downe" (*Chrestoleros* [1598], *Lib.* 4, Ep. 15,

ed. Grosart, p. 22). G. is surely aware of this repartee.

l. 4. *close nips*] a) compressed rebukes or reproofs, and b) secret (with the suggestion of lewd) pinches. Puttenham, *Arte*, ed. Willcock and Walker, p. 53, refers to epigrams as *"bitter taunts, and priuy nips or witty scoffes."*

l. 5. *conceit*] a) conception, b) pun (?), -*seat* (after "set downe").

l. 6. *much receit*] large capacity (for interpretation or description; *OED Receipt* 15); perhaps with quibbles on "reception" (*OED* III), alluding to the popularity of the word, and on "recipe" (*OED* I), alluding to the variety of "ingredients."

l. 8. *Cracks his purse strings*] i.e., goes in debt ("cracks his credit"). Purses were drawn at the top by strings. With a possible second meaning, after *"Perstringere*—to nippe, taunte, or checke shortly in writinge or speakinge,"* Cooper, *Thesaurus* (1587), in *OED Nip*; cf. Eliz. "crack a jest." The gull, like Davies, writes indiscreet epigrams to be in fashion. It may be that the epigram can be turned against Davies.

l. 9. *long in taking roote*] Cf. Dekker, *Gull's Hornbook* (London, 1812), pp. 3-4: "The tree of GULLS was planted long since; but not taking root, could never bear till now." See also Job 5:3.

l. 12. *twelue dayes wonder*] As everyone knew, "the greatest wonder lasteth but nine dayes" (Greene, *Wks.*, ed. Grosart, 12:261).

l. 16. *spends vpon her score*] i.e., on her account, with the common implicit pun *tally-tail*, and a sexual quibble on *spend*.

l. 17. *commodity*] "Goods which the prodigal took as a part of the sum he wished to borrow from the usurer, and which he was to turn into cash in the best way he was able" (Dyce). On this notorious practice, see Lodge, *An Alarum against Usurers*, *Wks.*, 1:16 ff., 36-37; and Nashe, 2:95.

l. 20. *Peiseth*] weighs or balances. Cf. Sidney, *Apology*, ed. Smith, 1:160: "peyzing each sillable of each worde by iust proportion according to the dignitie of the subiect."

Of Procus. 21. For the similar motif of one who in thought and act makes a whore of his wife, see Jonson, Eps. 25, 26 (H. & S., 8:34-35, with notes to sources, 11:5), and Davies, *In Quintum 4* (ed. Howard).

l. 3. *tale of a rosted horse*] Proverbial for a nonsensical and perhaps bawdy story; cf. Tilley T44 and, below, Satire V. 113-14 with note.

l. 9. *better conceit*] i.e., estimation (of you) or thought.

l. 12. *paine*] punishment (Lat. *poena*).

To Clodius. 22. Based on Martial 3. 95, perhaps after Davies's *In Cineam 23* (ed. Howard), also from Martial, which concludes: "You keepe a whore at your own charge men tel me, / In deede friend Cineas, therein you excell me." G. constantly ridicules the arrogance of the Inns of Court men, a popular topic of the times, as in, e.g., below, Satires III and V. 119-25. See the "Amoretto" of the *Parnassus* plays, and Overbury's "A Fantasticke Innes of Court Man," whose "best grace in his behaviour, is to forget his acquaintance" (in *Characters* [1616], ed. Paylor [1936], p. 45). Clodius also appears in Eps. 17, 43, and in Satire I. 77-82.

l. 5. *Goad*] With a glance (?) at Roger Goad, Provost of King's College, Cambridge (1570-1610).

l. 6. Mounsieur Littleton] Sir Thomas Littleton (1422-81), the famous lawyer whose *Tenures*, in law-French, was the basic authority on the common law and textbook for students of the law.

l. 7. *walkt in Poules* . . .] H. & S. quote (9:444) Francis

Osborn, *Historical Memoires on the Reigns of Queen Eliz. and King Jas.* (1685), pp. 64-65: "It was then the fashion of those times . . . for the principall Gentry, Lords, Courtiers and men of all professions not merely Mechanick, to meet in Pauls Church by eleven, and walk in the middle Ile till twelve, and after dinner from three, to six, during which time some discoursed of Business, other of Newes." The "walke in Poules" was a favorite topic with satirists; cf., below, Satire V. 68.

l. 11. *swagger*] On this word see *2H4* 2. 4. 71-76; and *Achilles Shield* (1598), in Chapman's *Homer* (ed. A. Nicoll [1956], 1:548): "Swaggering is a new worde amongst them, and rounde headed custome giues it priuiledge with much imitation." G. uses it repeatedly.

Of Sextilius. 23. For a Leuca in the same embarrassment, see Davies's *In Leucam 14* (ed. Howard), to which Harington refers in *Ajax*, ed. Donno, p. 103.

l. 2. *kind hart*] a) loving disposition, b) *natural* mistress, "heart" being a term of endearment.

Of Fuscus. 24. Fuscus here may be one of three writers (given in order of likelihood):
    1. Nashe, who, after a charge from Harvey, admitted that out of need he did "follow some of these newfangled *Galiardos* and *Senior Fantasticos*, to whose amórous *Villanellas* and *Quipassas* I prostitute my pen in hope of gaine" (*Have with You* [1596], 3:31). Marston attacks one Ruscus who constantly intends to "cease for lucar to be a iering scoffe" (*SV* 4. 66), and whom Davenport takes to be Nashe. Nashe seems clearly to be the Ingenioso of *II Parnassus* who has "made wanton lines to please lewd Gullio" (5. 1. 1466) and who generally suffers from the system of patronage. Leishman adduces substantial evidence to make the identification (pp. 71-79), all of which strengthens the supposition that Fuscus here is Nashe. His *Choice of Valentines*

was the most celebrated bawdry of the period. And the last "foure acts" of the *Ile of Dogs* (1597), a play judged seditious and for which there was probably an attempt to arrest him, he claims "by the players were supplied, which bred both their trouble and mine too" (3:154). He dedicated his works to a number of potential patrons very few of whom seem ever to have been grateful.

2. Marston. So Collier thought; see his introduction to *Skialetheia* (1878). Davenport, on the basis of certain lines in *SV*, thinks the epigram may be a "not unfriendly dig at M." (p. 263). Cf. "Nay then come all, I prostitute my Muse, / For all the swarme of Idiots to abuse" (*In Lectores*, ll. 61-62); "Who can abstaine? what modest braine can hold, / But he must make his shamefac'd Muse a scold?" (2. 143-44).

3. Marlowe. He is possibly the Fuscus of Ep. 19 and may be that of Ep. 8 (see notes to these), and his "stalking" vein was widely imitated, though it would not seem to be that of a scold. G. refers, it would seem, to Nashe.

l. 5. *players, and artificers*] Both terms were depreciatory. The latter could refer to playwrights and poets, as well as the more usual "craftsmen." It may allude to Nashe's relations with the unscrupulous printer Danter, on which see Leishman, ed., *Parnassus*, p. 76.

l. 6. *Deale with*] a) associate or have business with, b) have sex with; cf. *Per.* 4. 6. 22.

Of Gnatho. 25. The description of Sloth as he proceeds through the "circle" of his day was apparently a favorite with Eliz. moralists, and is thus easily typical of their constant retreatment of traditional themes. G., as would be expected, follows closely Davies, *In Fuscum 39* (ed. Howard), which begins:

> Fuscus is free, and hath the world at will,
> Yet in the course of life that hee doth leade,
> Hees like a horse which turning round a mill,
> Doth alwaies in the selfesame circle treade:
>   First he doth rise at ten.

This epigram Harington praised and paraphrased in *A Treatise on Playe*, ca. 1597 (in *Nugae Antiquae* [London, 1804], p. 198). The same theme with a similar treatment occurs in Stubbes (see passage given in the Introduction, p. 19); in Harington, "Of a Lady early up" (no. 254 in *L. & E.*, p. 253); in Rowlands, Ep. 7, *Letting of Humours Blood* (1600), in which "gentlemen" go to plays, to brothels, drink and play at games because "To sit thus idle, is both sinne and shame" (*Wks.*, ed. 1880, 1:13); in *III Parnassus* 3. 4. 1330, where Sir Raderick is "one that goes to a play, to a whore, to his bedde in [a] Circle"); and in Davies of Hereford, Ep. 136, *"Against Tuballus his time keeping in his ill rule-keeping,"* in *Scourge of Folly* (1610/11?), *Wks.*, ed. Grosart, repr. 1967, 2:35. A cursory look at Nashe's description of Sloth in *Pierce* (1:208 ff.) will suggest that these are Eliz. versions of the medieval sin.

l. 2. *high-stomackt*] a) high-spirited, courageous, b) with a large appetite.

l. 4. *walks to*] With a quibble on the sense "to beat, drub (a person)," often for sins (*OED v2* 2).

l. 5. *fore-tyrde*] a) already dressed, b) exhausted.

l. 7. *wakes*] i.e., a) for prayer, vigil, etc. (*OED* 3), b) for pleasure, revel (*OED* 1d).

l. 10. *trot so foule a ring*] As often with Elizs., alluding to the exercise of the horse in the circular piece of ground where he went through his feats of agility. Cf. Nashe, 3:240; *SV* 11. 193. Devils, of course, danced in rings (cf. *OED Trot sb1* 3).

To Pollio. 26. Based on Martial's "bellus homo" epigrams, esp. 3. 63 and 12. 39; cf. Eps. 14, 38, and see notes to them. "Pollio" is to be associated with that of Satire VI. 117-20, below.

l. 3. *thy ingles face*] Cf. Lodge, *Wits Miserie* (1596), *Wks.*, 4:95, of one whose "whole delight is to haue a well faced boy in his company."

l. 4. *naperie*] "Personal linen" would seem redundant; thus probably "tablecloths, towels, napkins, etc." Cf. *Vd* 5. 1. 88, and see Davenport's note.

l. 5. *wagge thy head*] Lodge, in *Alarum for Usurers, Wks.*, 1:48, includes "wagging their heads" among gallants' "unseemely iestures."

l. 9. *faine*] obliged, content (under the circumstance); pun (?), *fine.*

Of the same. 27. l. 1. *my good conceit*] i.e., a) opinion, estimate, b) (poetic?) conception. Thus *fallne in* is ambiguous: "fallen into" and "declined in."

l. 3. *fatte buttocke*] Stuffing was the mode (see Linthicum, pp. 204-6).

l. 4. *french Galliard*] a lively, complicated dance (Fr. *gaillarde, merry*).

l. 6. *credits*] authorities (on which testimony is accepted, *OED* 2b).

Of Zeno. 28. Based on Martial 9.5: "Nubere vis Prisco: non miror, Paula; sapisti. / ducere te non vult Priscus; et ille sapit." Parkhurst had imitated the epigram; it is quoted and discussed in H. H. Hudson, *Epigram in the English Renaissance* (New York, 1966), pp. 96-97. "Æagle," used occasionally by Martial, suggests proverbial superiority (Tilley E1: "The Eagle does not catch flies") and singleness (E7: "Eagles fly alone"), and almost surely some topical value. The eagle is the most prominent feature of the Derby crest. Ferdinando Stanley, fifth Earl of Derby, died in 1594. In 1600 his widow Alice married Thomas Egerton, Lord Ellesmere, Lord Keeper.

Of Arion. 29. "Arion," type name for musicians, after the famous cithara player of Methymna.

l. 2. *crotchets*] quarter notes; perhaps with the usual quibble on "(perverse) whims." Most of the musical terms here have sexual overtones.

   quauers] eighth notes (half the value of crotchets).

l. 3. *sembriefe time*] Either with two beats in a bar or the time occupied by a semi breve (our "whole note").

l. 5. *well fretting of a Lute*] To "fret" is to furnish the fingerboard of stringed instruments with rings of gut or bars of wood to regulate the fingering. This refers either to the positioning of these frets or to the fingering itself. For the quibble in the next line cf. *Ham.* 3. 2. 362.

l. 8. *stops*] Either the placing of the fingers over the open holes of wind instruments or on the frets, or the holes themselves or positions on the frets. Cf. *Luc.* l. 1124: "My restless discord loves no stops nor rests."

   trumperie] a) rubbish, b) that having to do with *trump* (*trumpet*).

Of Chrysogonus. 30. Chrisogonus ("golden-born") is the name of the sinister and greedy freedman attacked by Cicero in *Pro Roscio*, and of a noted singer mentioned in Juvenal 6. 74, 7. 176. In *Histriomastix*, probably written for the Middle Temple revels of 1597/98 (see P. J. Finkelpearl, *HLQ* 29 [1966]: 223-34), he is a poet and professor thought by many to be Jonson. In *Satiromastix* (ent. 1601) Dekker portrays Jonson as ugly and desirous to frighten. G. may be thinking of Martial 3. 42.

l. 2. *Teacheth a wrinckled action*] i.e., puts on a frown, from the training of orators or players (*action*=gesture). Cf. Nashe, 1:167: "runne through an Alphabet of faces," and 3:349.

Of Torques. 31. l. 1. *indifferent liuing*] i.e., fairly large, "tolerable."

l. 2. *free of house-keeping, nor giuing*] i.e., neither liberal in hospitality nor in giving, alluding to the Lord's traditional duty of generosity to the poor. In view of the conclusion, "free of" becomes ironic for "released or exempt from" his obligations in this respect.

l. 3. Debet *booke vncrost*] A *debet* (debt) book was crossed when payment was made; cf. *Vd* 4. 1. 91-100. With the epigram cf. Davies, *In Cineam 23* (ed. Howard): "You keepe a whore at your own charge," and *In Paulum 41:* "But on the land a little gulfe there is, / Wherein he drowneth all this wealth of his."

Of Lais. 32. Suggested by the two Corinthian courtesans by the name.

l. 1. *note*] melody.

l. 3. *close nips*] a) secret (lewd) pinches, b) "clothes" pinches; for another instance of the pun see *Englands Helicon*, ed. Rollins (1935), 1:181, l. 17.
    by the rood] a) "by the cross," but also b) "rod," drawing on *nip*, reproof, censure (*OED sb*[1] 2); cf. Tilley N189: "To give him a privy nip"; c) bawdy.

l. 4. *nip will cheare her blood*] Customarily said of the sharp cold of weather.

l. 6. *weare*] a) "wear" up, b) pun *were*. A further quibble may exist. "Nip" in Eliz. underground parlance was a cutpurse (*OED* 7a); and how one wore his clothes determined the ease or difficulty with which the "nip" could be made. Moreover, the courtesan Lais seems to have been noted for stealing the purses of her lovers, on which see Deloney, *Novels*, ed. Lawlis, p. 100.

Of Orpheus. 34. l. 1. Scan *Orphëus*(?). The line may be defective.

Of Cotta. 35. Cf. Eps. 12, 13, 49, and see note to 12.

l. 1. *like*] a) please, b) make a likeness of (*OED v*[2] 1).

Of Metius. 36. l. 2. *earnest*] a) serious, b) with a quibble on "earnest money."

l. 6. *for almes*] i.e., for bribes. There may be a quibble on the legal sense, tenure by free gift of charity (*OED* 3), thus "out of charity" rather than because he knows the law.

Of the same. 37. l. 2. *of meere almes*] a) for nothing but bribes, b) perhaps "out of charity alone." Probably some play on law-Latin *jus-merum*, right as distinguished from possession.

To Licus. 38. An adaptation of Martial 3. 63, of "bellus homo," with a possible eye to l. 9. See note to Ep. 14.

l. 6. *out-spends*] exceeds (his resources) in spending.

l. 7. *piertly iets*] With this line cf. Ep. 14, l. 9, with note, and the passage from Davies's "Ignoto" sonnet (ed. Howard): "I cannot dally, caper, daunce, and sing, / Oyling my saint with supple sonnetting, / I cannot crosse my armes and sigh ay me, / . . . I cannot busse thy fist, play with thy haire," etc.

l. 9. *companying with*] a) keeping company with, b) cohabiting with (*OED* 3b).

l. 12. *Sups with his* Ingles] Satirists refer a number of times to such dinners; see, e.g., Dekker, *Plague Pamphlets*, ed. Wilson, p. 65: "The now-onely-onely-Supper-maker to Engles & Plaiers-Boyes"; *EMO* Ind. 104, 335; *Poetaster* 1. 2. 15-17.

l. 13. *gracious*] enjoying favor (Lat. *gratiosus*).

l. 14. *Iniure not my content*] a) i.e., my happiness, b) "slander not my capacity"—by the epithet "fine"; and c) the "content" of my poems? (by reciting them, they not being well-received).

l. 18. Cf. Martial 1. 9: "sed qui bellus homo est, Cotta, pusillus homo est," and 3. 63: "res pertricosa est, Cotile, bellus homo."

Of Chrestina. 39. This epigram belongs to the tradition which also includes the improper jest about Socrates, "How Xantippa caste pisse upon his heed" and his response, according to Chaucer (*WBPr*, ll. 727-32), "Er that thonder stynte, comth a reyn!" which derives from Diogenes Laertius, *Socrates*, 2. 26, and which was quite popular in the sixteenth century; cf. Harington, *Ajax*, ed. Donno, p. 153, and see note, which points to Erasmus, *Apophthegmes*, C1ᵛ and *Merry Tales, Wittie Questions and Quicke Answeres*, no. 49, in Hazlitt, *Shakespeare Jest-Books*, 1:65. Fire and water apparently served as the basis for a bawdy allusion; cf. Davies of Hereford, Ep. 380, in *Scourge of Folly* (1610/11?), *Wks.*, ed. Grosart, 2:49, which is quite crude, of one who "trafiqu'd both by water and fyre," and begins: "Luce beares fire in th'on hand and water in th'other: / But in her chaffendish beares both together." Cf. also *Vd* 4. 2. 145-46, with Davenport's note.

l. 3. *keepe my selfe from water and from fier*] i.e., the proverbial dangers (Tilley F285, F254). *fier* is intentional, to rime with *her*.

l. 6. *fired out*] Lit., "to drive (one) away from a place by fire" (*OED*); here probably "to contract a venereal disease." See commentators on Shakespeare's *Sonnet 144*.

Of Nævia. 40. This along with Eps. 41 and 42 below follow Martial 1. 79, of Attalus, the lawyer and merchant of poor behavior.

l. 2. Brooke, Fitzherbert, *and in* Dyer] All famous jurists and authors of books on common law. Sir Robert Brooke (d. 1558?), Chief Justice of the Common Pleas, held in great respect as a learned and upright judge, compiler of *La Grande Abridgement* (1568), based on Fitzherbert's earlier compilation, an abstract of the yearbooks down to his own time.

  Sir Anthony Fitzherbert (1470-1538), Justice of the Common Pleas, whose *Graunde Abridgement*, first pr. 1514, *La*

Novel Natura Brevium (1534), and *Loffice et auctoryte des Jus-tyces de peas* (1538), saw many editions and were popular textbooks.

Sir James Dyer (1512-82), Chief Justice of the Common Pleas, whose nephews, R. Farewell and James Dyer, edited a collection of cases reported by him, *Cy ensuont ascuns novel cases* (1585).

A similar list of lawyers occurs at Satire V. 26, below; in Davies, *In Publium 43* (ed. Howard), which may have suggested this; and *EMO* 2. 3. 166-67.

l. 4. *Moyling*] drudging, with the implications of wallowing, as in the mire (*OED* 3). Often occurs in the phrase "toil and moil," which G. varies (see l. 2). See *SV Proem. in libr. sec.*, ll. 19-21, for similar variation, and Davenport's note. There is, I think, some play on the *mule*, sometimes the "lawyer's moyle," which judges and sergeants of the law once rode upon (that the common people might have access to them); see H. & S., 9:435n., and Overbury, *Char.* (1616), ed. Paylor, p. 87. Martial's lawyer becomes a mule-driver in 1. 79.

Of the same. 41. Note Nashe 2:159: "Is it not a common prouerbe amongst vs, to say, Hee hath playde the Merchant with vs? But Merchants, they turne it another way, and say, He hath playd the Gentleman with them." *Merchant* was common for (contemptuous) "fellow"; cf. *Rom.* 2. 4. 142.

Of the same. 42. With this cf. Martial, *De Spectaculis*, 4, against informers, and the Harington epigram quoted in note to l. 8.

l. 4. *engrossing*] monopolizing, suggesting the illegal "engros-sing" of grain by speculators in attempts to get higher prices, against which proclamations were issued several times in 1597/98; b) the "engrossing" of legal documents.

l. 7. *busie*] busybodying.

l. 8. *Promoter*] i.e., an informer or professional accuser, rewarded with part of the fines, and complained against bitterly by the citizens. Nævius's third occupation. It seems certain that G. sharpens the point by suggesting still a fourth, that of Baud or Whoremonger. For the obscene sense of *occupy*, almost unavoidable at this time, cf. *2H4* 2. 4. 139; Jonson, *Disc.*, ll. 1545-48 (H. & S., 8:610); for *engrossing*, cf. *OED v* 9a, "to fatten the body"; for *more to do*, cf. Ep. 67, where Crocus, knowing so many whores, has "too much to do," and Partridge, under *do*; for *honesty*, the (ironic) *chastity*; and for general parallels (and a possible model), Harington's Ep. 9, *L. & E.*, p. 151:

> *Lesbia* doth laugh to heare sellers and buyers
> Cald by this name, Substantiall occupyers:
> *Lesbia*, the word was good while good folke vsd it,
> You mard it that with *Chawcers* iest abusd it:
>> But good or bad, how ere the word be made,
>> *Lesbia* is loth to leaue the trade.

Of Clodius. 43. This may owe its idea to that ascribed to Martial, 3. —*In Ponticum* (Loeb, 2:523). Clodius appears also in Eps. 17, 22 and at Satire I. 77.

l. 1. *passing big*] surpassing mighty or proud.

l. 2. Dunstons] Alluding to James Tunstall (sometimes *Dunstone*), longtime actor with the Admiral's company (Chambers, *Elizabethan Stage*, 2:347).

Allens Cutlacks *gate*] i.e., Edward Alleyn, the actor with the Admiral's company famous for his role as boistering Tamburlaine and apparently for his "stride" (*gait*), and perhaps esp. in the lead part of the lost play *Cutlack* (*Guthlac*?), revived in 1594 and again in 1599. *Cutlacks*, probably from the short broad cutting sword called variously "curtal ax," "cuttle axe," and "cutlass," became emblematic for a swashbuckler; see *Tamb.*, pt. 1, 1. 2. 238 (ed. Tucker Brooke).

l. 4. *eyes are lightning . . .*] Usual details of tyrannical types; cf. *LLL* 4. 2. 110.

l. 10. *Stalking and roaring . . .*] In addition to the "roaring devil i' the old play" (*H5* 4. 4. 69-70) in the mystery play of Job, G. seems to˙ be thinking still of the stage figure of Tamburlaine, of whom the word "stalking" was used time and again; cf. *Vd* 1. 3. 16; Middleton, *Black Booke*, ed. Bullen, 8:25; Dekker, *Plague Pamphlets*, ed. Wilson, pp. 31, 225. Moreover, the play was a byword for noise (see H. & S., 11:238n.). Note Job 1:7, 2:2.

Of Phrix. 44. Imitating Martial 12. 88: "Tongilianus habet nasum, scio, non nego. sed iam nil praeter nasum Tongilianus habet." G.'s epigram, like this and others in Martial (cf. e.g., 13. 2), and a number of the many nose-epigrams in the tradition, plays on *habere nasum*, to be critical (keen scented), and to have a large nose. Phrix is all nose, i.e., critic and nothing else. There may also be intended a comment on the effects of syphilis, and possibly on sexual impotence ("[of] no worth").

In Zelotypum. 45. Imitating Martial 9. 25, on which see Whipple, *Martial and the English Epigram* (1925), p. 352. Timothy Kendall, *Flowers of Epigrammes* (1577), ed. 1874, pp. 50-51, gives a similar rendition, which concludes: "Let *Phineas* blind, and *Oedipus*, thy guests then Apher be." Lat. *zelotypus*, a jealous man.

l. 10. *Harpers*] Cf. Tilley H175: "As blind as a harper."

Of Gellia. 46. l. 2. *skip-iack*] puppyish, foppish, perhaps hopping or jumping (*OED*).

l. 3. *so proues*] turns out to be so (i.e., a fiddler).

ll. 6-7. Sir Raderick quotes these lines in *III Parnassus* 3. 2. 1200-1203, speaking of university men lately come to London to seek preferment: "And an other made a couple of verses on my Daughter that learnes to play on the violl *de gambo*: Her violl *de gambo* is her best content, / For twixt her legges she holds her instrument." G. follows Davies's "Ignoto" sonnet (ed. Howard): "Faith (wench) I cannot court thy sprightly eyes, / With the bace viall plac'd betweene thy thyghs . . . ," or else he follows *CS* 1. 19 ff.: "Come *Briscus*, by the soule of Complement, / I'le not endure that with thine instrument / (Thy Gambo violl plac'd betwixt thy thighes, / Wherein the best part of thy courtship lyes)," etc.

l. 6. *her best content*] a) most to her liking, b) quibbling on "capacity."

To the Reader. 47. l. 2. *light lines*] i.e., a) frivolous, b) lascivious (pun?, *lines* = *loines*). Note Bastard, *Chrestoleros* (1598), ed. Grosart, p. 4: "I haue taught Epigrams to speake chastlie, besides I haue acquainted them with more grauitie of sence, and barring them of their olde libertie, not onelie forbidden them to be personall, but turned all their bitternesse rather into sharpenesse." Cf. Martial 1. 1., one of his many defenses of the epigram, which G. is probably following, esp., "lascivam verborum veritatem, id est epigrammaton linguam, excusarem, is meum esset exemplum: sic scribit Catullus, sic Marsus," etc.

To Lydia. 48. l. 1. *so mote I thee*] a) "so might I thrive," b) with a play on *mot*, "word."

l. 2. *brownetta*] Thus, as was thought, ill-favored; cf. "brown wench" (*H8* 3. 2. 295); *CS* 1. 66.

l. 6. *no faire to loose*] Cf. *Venus*, ll. 1081-83.

l. 7. None] a) "own," from "mine own," used in familiar affectionate phrases; b) "nothing" (of beauty).

ll. 8-14. *Oh th'art a mummer . . .*] The business of the masked prostitute is compared with the "dicing" of the masked mummers. Chambers discusses the association and quotes at length one of a number of contemporary complaints against "mumming" as a pretext for cheating at dice (*Elizabethan Stage*, 1: 150 ff.).

l. 10. *about*] i.e., "a bout," a throw or game of dice, but also, as common, with bawdy implication; cf. Partridge and, e.g., *1H6* 3. 2. 56.

l. 11. *box*] a) either the mummer's beggar's box (see H. & S., 10:559), or the dice box; b) bawdy.

l. 12. *cast at all*] hazard or throw for everything, a dice player's expression.

    goe not out] i.e., "do not lose," or (therefore) withdraw.

l. 13. *Nothing by mum? nay then . . .*] i.e., "silence gives consent."

To Cotta. 49. Cf. Eps. 12, 13, and 35, and see note to 12.

To Women. 50. l. 2. *prick-song-lesson without ditty*] i.e., a lesson in the written music (that "pricked") without words. Cf. Nashe, 1:285: "Whatsoeuer harpeth not of one of these two strings of praise and reproofe, is as it were a *Dirige* in pricksong without any dittie set to it, that haply may tickle the eare, but neuer edifies." For a parallel to the bawdry, cf. Nashe, *Choice of Valentines*, ll. 187 ff. (3:411).

Of Chrestina. 51. Suggested by Martial 11. 16, perhaps through Harington, Ep. 109, *L. & E.*, p. 190: "*Against* Cayus *that scorn'd his Metamorphosis*," wherein Cayus's mistress "spits" at the name of "a Iax" because her "lips doe water" in memory of an early experience there.

l. 1. *spals*] spit copiously or coarsely; occurs frequently with "spets," implying contempt, anger.

Of Pansa. 52. Based on Martial 2. 11, of Selius, disconsolate because he must dine at home, but perhaps with suggestions from Davies, Ep. 47 (ed. Howard), also based on Martial, which begins: "See yonder melancholy Gentleman, / Which hood-winck'd with his hat, alone doth sit, / Thinke what he thinkes, and tel me if you can, / What great affaires troubles his little wit," etc. Details of the Malcontent's affectation which G. draws upon were by now commonplace. For another description see, below, Satire V. 83-95.

l. 5. *Like hate-man* Timon . . .] Timon, the Athenian, is "very frequently named by Ren. writers as the embodiment of melancholy cynicism and misanthropy" (Lawrence Babb, *Elizabethan Malady* [East Lansing, 1951], p. 94). Cf. *Timon* 4. 3. 52. The opening line of Rowlands's *Melancholic Knight* (1615), *Wks.*, ed. 1880, 2:7, echoes this line: "Like Discontented *Tymon* in his Cell, / My braines with melancholy humers swell."

l. 6. *like a smoaky roome*] G. is thinking of the "smoke of sighs" (Nashe, 3:396); cf. Lyly, *Love's Meta.* 4. 1. 11-12 (ed. Bond): "my sighes couer thy Temple with a darke smoke."

l. 8. *To his sights life, his hat becomes a toombe*] One feature of the malcontent remarked by almost all was his failure to wear a hatband (his "melancholy hat") with the result that his hat fell over his eyes. Cf., among others, Harington, *Ajax*, ed. Donno, p. 67; Lodge, *Wits Miserie* (1596), *Wks.*, 4:23; Nashe, 1:169; *LLL* 3. 1. 15-16: "with your hat penthouse-like ore the shop of your eies."

l. 14. *Butterflies*] Frequent for courtiers in their finery; cf., below, Satire III. 59, and note; *SV* 4. 84-86: "troupes of gaudie Butter-flies / . . . In pie-bauld sutes, of proude Court brauerie," and Davenport's references.

l. 15. *Torch-light sommer*] i.e., "torch-lit"; cf. *SV* 7. 81: "torch-light maskeries."

l. 16. *shew good legs*] a) i.e., dance well, b) display well-shaped legs, one grace of the gentleman.

Of Cornelius. 53. Probably inspired by Martial 2. 29, which to some extent it follows; but, again, cf. Davies, *In Sillam 28* (ed. Howard), of the braggart who refuses to fight: "Who dares affirme that Silla dares not fight?", etc. Also, as Davenport points out, it shares a large number of significant details with Marston's braggart soldier Tubrio, *CS* 1. 89 ff., *SV* 7. 100 ff. See also Captain Tucca at, below, *Sat. Pre.* 29 and note.

l. 1. *sits o're the stage*] Either *upon* the stage, as was the custom with lords, or *above* the stage, as apparently in *EMO* 2. 3. 191-93: "as if he had seene 'hem stand by the fire i' the presence, or ta'ne tabacco with them, ouer the stage, i' the lords roome": probably the former.

l. 3. *braue gallant*] The epigram develops out of the two directions implicit in these terms: a) heroic, proud, b) well-dressed, fashionable—which are played against each other throughout. Cf. *EMO* 4. 6. 83 ff., where Fastidious Briske describes a duel in order to mention the clothes he was wearing at the time.

l. 4. *new printed*] i.e., newly stamped or marked with a pattern or decorative design in one or more colors.

l. 5. *Ierkin cudgeld . . .*] Jerkins were sometimes trimmed (or *laid*) with gold lace, which provided Elizs. with a number of variations on the quibble here: *laid, basted, quartered, beaten, whipped,* etc. Cf. *SV* 7. 114: "What he that's drawne, and quartered with lace?"

l. 6. *profound slop*] a) i.e., full, deep; cf. Ep. 52, l. 16; b) subtle, crafty; cf. Hosea 5:2: "the revolters are profound to make slaughter"; and, below, Satire IV. 57.

    scarce pipkin high] i.e., hardly as high as a small pot or pan. These small, skull-fitting, narrow-brimmed hats, usually made of taffeta, and called "pipkins" or "porringers" after the pots they resembled, became popular with interest in Spanish dress and were often ridiculed (see Nashe, 2:300, and Linthicum, pp. 218-19).

l. 7. *dagge cases*] i.e., pistol holsters, with a pun (?) on "tag," or boot laces (*OED Dag sb*[1] 2), alluding, it would seem, to extraordinary laces. Codpieces were *tagged*, and Nashe has a codpiece a "case for pistol" (2:223).

l. 8. Cads-*beard*] The beards worn by those who returned from the expedition against Cadiz in June 1596, and who maintained them as a symbol of their success. Essex apparently wore one. G. refers to them again in Satires III. 65 and V. 75. See also Nashe, 3:147.

l. 9. *wallows in his walk* . . .] Marston's Tubrio "in his swaggering slops / Wallowes vnbraced all along the streete" (*SV* 7. 103-4). Pun (?), *grace-grease*.

l. 11. *fashion*] with a quibble on the horse disease (Fr. *farcin*); cf. Dekker, *Gull's Hornbook*, ed. 1812, p. 42: "Fashions then was counted a disease, and horses died of it: but now, thanks to folly, it is held the only rare physick; and the purest golden asses live upon it."

l. 12. farewell sweet Captaine] Cf. Marston's Tubrio, who "Salutes each gallant he doth meete, / With *farewell sweet Captaine, kind hart, adew*" (*SV* 7. 105-6).

l. 13. *Sir* Bevis] Bevis of Hampton, legendary hero renowned for his feats of arms, celebrated in a medieval romance printed a number of times in the sixteenth century.

the fayery Knight] Marston has (*SV In Lectores*, l. 53) "Goe buy some ballad of the Faiery King, / And of the beggar wench, some rogie thing," etc., which Davenport suggests is probably the ballad listed as no. 551 in H. E. Rollins, *Analytical Index of the Ballad Entries in the S. R.*: "Description of the king of fayries." The date of entry, however, is 1634.

l. 14. *Put vp the lie*] i.e., our "put up with," submit to.

To Mira. 55. Given G.'s customary attitude toward women, and to Mira in Ep. 59, this could hardly be commendatory. The expression "Nature frame" (compose, plan) occurs typically in passages of exalted praise of some exceptional creation. Here it is used in ironic overstatement, Mira being a monstrosity, a "wonder." Cf. Lat. *miracula*, a marvelously ugly woman; "Miraculae a miris, id est monstris" (Varro, *De Ling. Lat.* 7. 64). Perhaps also "mire," as in "foule myre" of Satire I. 61.

De Ignoto. 56. Based on Martial 12. 61. Cf. Bastard's imitation in *Chrestoleros* (1598), *Lib.* 7, Ep. 24, ed. Grosart; and see, below, Ep. 60.

l. 1. *odd*] notorious.

l. 2. *lines*] Pun (?), *loins.*

Of Nigrina. 57. l. 2. *Her skins lawn's . . .*] Proverbial; cf. *Repentance of Robert Greene*, Bodley Head Quarto, p. 3: "the finest lawne the soonest staind."

l. 3. *Her tendrest poultry . . .*] i.e., her youngest feathers (of her dress)? garment of skin? (cf. *OED Pelt*). With a play on "counter" (*Poultry* being one of the noted "counters," or debtors' prisons), a derogatory word for coin or a debased coin, which will "abide the touch," i.e., pass the test as genuine. *touch* has sexual implications. Nigrina may be figured as a "poultry maid"; cf. Heywood, Ep. 15, *Fifth Hund., Wks.*, ed. Milligan, p. 207: "Iane thou sellest conies in this pultry shoppe; / But none so sweete as thy selfe, sweete conye moppe. / What is the pryce of thee?" Jonson describes a prostitute as "leane playhouse poultry" (*Bar. Fair* 2. 5. 106).

l. 4. *out-face*] brave, defy.

l. 5. *winter Cherry*] It ripens in the winter (*OED*).

l. 7. *Mulberry*] "Whensoeuer you see the Mulberie begin to spring, you may bee sure that winter is at ende" (Googe, *H. H.*,

1586, 2:92, in *OED*). Cf. also Lyly, *Euph.*, ed. Bond, 3:5, and Pliny, *H. N.* 16. 41.

l. 9. Ione] "A generic name for a female rustic" (*OED*); proverbially, "Joan is no lady"; see *LLL* 3. 1. 195; *John* 1. 1. 184.

ll. 11-12. Henry Parrot uses these lines, with slight variation, for one of his epigrams, *Laquei Ridiculosi* (1613), *Lib.* 1, Ep. 61, C8.

Of Drus. 58. Cf. the confused but resolute Drus of Satire I. 25. I see no clear connection with Marston's Drus (*SV* 4. 69; *Ad Rithmum*, 18; 11. 40), now a wastrel young man, and now an actor thought by some to be Richard Burbage. Cf. Lat. *durus*, hard, obstinate, unfortunate, etc.

l. 1. *miserable's*] i.e., a) miserly, b) unfortunate.

l. 2. *hard-head*] Belongs with both ideas, providing the play; cf. 1519 quote at *OED Hard-head*: "Some men counte them nygardis and hardheedis that wyll haue a rekenynge of expensis."

To Mira. 59. Perhaps based on a current saying ultimately from Thucydides, *Hist.* 2. 45, which Nashe renders as follows (3:121): "through his incredible praising of her, I say . . . he hath brought all the world into a perswasion that shee is as common as Rubarbe among Phisitions; since (as *Thucidides* pronounceth) shee is the honestest woman, of whose praise or dispraise is least spoken." McKerrow says that "the saying is frequently referred to."

De Ignoto. 60. Cf. Ep. 56, and see note.

Of Nigrina. 61. l. 2. *light*] lascivious, a common quibble. Cf. *LLL* 2. 1. 199: "light in the light"; and Cotgrave, *Dict.* (1611): "*Oeil*: An eye distempered cannot brooke the light; sick thoughts cannot indure the truth," and the similar idea in Satire II. 89.

Of the same. 62. 1. 3. *with one case she doth another case*] i.e., with her mask she covers (encases) her (painted) face. Cf. *Rom.* 1. 4. 29-30: "Give me a case to put my visage in: / A visor for a visor!"; and *SV* 8. 64-71. With a quibble on "predicament, plight."

Of Bassus. 63. 1. 1. *with a grace*] a) gracefully, b) with the complimentary periphrasis "your grace" (?).

To Mira. 64. Based on the proverb (Tilley F140) meaning that what one fears generally happens.

Of Nigrina. 65. 1. 4. *abide the tuch*] a) pass the test; said of coins which were genuine, not *light* (from "clipping") or debased; b) *tuch*, euphemism for sexual contact.

Of Gellia. 66. 1. 1. *good-man*] husband (who is also a "good" man here).

1. 2. *giue him the lurch*] i.e., get the better of him or cheat him (*OED* 3b).

1. 3. *witty*] ingenious.

1. 6. *ring all in*] give the final peal (of the bell before service begins); Cotgrave, *Dict.* (1611): "*Coppetur*, to ring all-in, or the last peale." For the bawdy, cf. *FQ* 3. 10. 48, and Partridge, *ring.* Cf. also Nashe, 1:124: "By the transgression of one, all are damned," from Romans 5:18.

Ad Crocum. 67. 1. 2. *many a poore man . . .*] Cf. *AYLI* 3. 5. 98-103: "So holy and so perfect is my love, / And I in such a poverty of grace, / That I shall think it a most plenteous crop / To glean the broken ears after the man / That the main harvest reaps: loose now and then / A scattered smile, and that I'll live upon."

l. 4. *too much to do*] Apparently (?) even a few harlots are too much for Crocus. This may play on the proverbial "harvest ears" of the "busy man" (one too busy to listen), on which see Tilley H186.

Of Caius. 68. An adaptation of Martial 2. 7, perhaps after a suggestion from Lodge's passages of the Flatterer who cries "Oh rare" at whatever his Lord does, in *Fig for Momus* (1595), *Wks.*, 3:9, and *Wits Miserie* (1596), 4:26, in which the description of the wit concludes with "his wit is too shallow." See also, below, Satire V. 113: "He cries, *oh rare my Lord*," etc., and note. There are a number of classical passages on the same theme; cf., e.g., Horace, *Sat.* 2. 5. 95 ff. The Caius of Satire VI. 113-14 has similar difficulty in expressing himself.

l. 2. *blackman grunt his note*] Perhaps "seller of blacking and blacking-brushes" (H. & S., 9:505). See "Turners dish of Lentten stuffe," st. 13, for the blackman's cries, in H. E. Rollins, *Pepysian Garland* (Cambridge, 1922), p. 34; and the various cries in the "Blackman" jig in C. R. Baskervill, *Elizabethan Jig* (New York, 1929), pp. 465-72. *note*, melody.

ll. 3-4. *to heare the* Irishmen . . .] Apples were cried as "pips," "pippins," and "pippe" by Irish fruitmongers. Cf. Marston, *Jacke Drum*, act 1 (*Plays*, ed. Wood, 3:191): "Hee whose throat squeakes like a treble Organ, and speakes as smal and shrill, as the Irish-men crie Pip, fine Pip."

l. 5. *Mercers chappell*] In Cheapside (north), formerly the Hospital of St. Thomas of Acon or Acre; see Stow, *Survey*, ed. 1908, pp. 269-70.

l. 6. *plaine-song*] With a play on *plaine = complain* in reference to the monotonous cry of "Pity the poor prisoners" that the prisoners gave out to solicit alms from passersby, on which see Sugden's quotations under "Ludgate."

l. 9. *cold S.* Pancras *church*] Note Norden, *Speculum Britan-niae* (1593), p. 38: "Pancras Church standeth all alone as vtterly forsaken, old and weatherbeaten."

l. 10. *scratch the elbow*] From pleasure; cf. Tilley E100, and Nashe, 3:192: "Their elbows itch for joy."

l. 18. *æquipage*] uniforms, "get up." Cf. Brome, *City Wit* 3. 1 (*Wks.*, reissued 1966, 1:318): "He is indeed my brother, and has been one of the true blew Boyes of the Hospitall; one of the sweet singers to the City Funeralls with a two penny loafe under his arme." Blue coats were worn by lower retainers.

l. 19. *a carted bawde*] Bawds were frequently carted around to various stations in London, accompanied by various officers of the law, with a sign announcing their offense, and to the sound of a beaten basin, something of a show. See the description of one such, from 1597, in H. & S., 10:27.

whore in cage] Each ward of London contained a lock-up for petty malefactors; see McKerrow, ed., Nashe, 4:131-32.

l. 20. *Gongfarmers*] i.e., a dung carter's.

ll. 24-25. Cf. *II Parnassus* 3. 1. 897-901: "*Ingenioso* I faith an excellent witt, that can poetize vpon such meane subiectes: . . . thats a rare wit that can make somthinke of nothinge." Pun (?), *rare*=*rear*.

To the Reader. 69. Suggestions come from Martial 3. 2, 11. 16, 3. 68, but it follows none of these closely.

l. 1. *wax-rubd Citty roome*] Apparently the practice then, as now. Cf. Dekker, *Gull's Hornbook*, ed. 1812, pp. 79-80, speaking of the ear: "and, because when the tunes are once gotten in, they should not too quickly slip out, all the walls of both places are plastered with yellow wax round about them."

l. 2. *salt rhume*] watery discharge from mouth or nose; with a quibble on *salt*, lecherous, and/or the more general, acutely witted, as in Gascoigne: "unless the invention have in it also *aliquid salis* . . . some good and fine divise, shewing the quicke capacitie of a writer," etc. (*Certayn Notes*, ed. Smith, 1:47).

l. 4. *ligge so lasciuiously*] Jigs "became a byword for their coarseness and obscenity" (Baskervill, *Elizabethan Jig*, p. 38; see also p. 112 and note).

l. 6. *quick* Couranto] lively dance, characterized by a running or gliding step (as distinguished from leaping); with *quick* to suggest "sharp, caustic" (*OED* 18b); cf. *LLL* 5. 1. 52: "a quick venue of wit."

ll. 7-8. *And say she keeps* Decorum . . .] Alluding to the Renaissance doctrine that style should conform to matter and to the audience addressed. Cf. Harington, *Ajax*, ed. Donno, p. 72: "let them pardon me, that sought but to keepe *decorum*, in speaking of a slovenly matter, and of slovenly men somewhat slovenly." Marston expresses the same idea in several places; see, e.g., *CS* Authour in prayse, ll. 7-8; *SV Prom. in lib. sec.*, l. 8; 5. 18: "Rude limping lines fits this leud halting age." The *loose gown* hung shapeless from the neck to the ground, and was constantly associated with "loose" women (see Linthicum, p. 183). Note Lat. *toga*, prostitute; *togata*, Roman comedies; and see Ep. 70, l. 16, along with the note.

l. 9. *humorous pleasance*] a) whimsy, b) moist lawn or gauze.

ll. 10-14. With these lines cf. *Wives* 4. 2. 90-93: "We'll leave a proof, by that which we will do, / Wives may be merry, and yet honest too: / We do not act that often jest and laugh; / 'Tis old, but true,—Still swine eats all the draff." Hart in his edition suggests that there was a song based on these lines (or, we may presume, the lines themselves are the song), and he quotes the song in the Halliwell-Phillips MS (from the late seventeenth century, he says): "We merry wives of Windsor, Whereof you make your play; and act us on your stages In London day be day: Alass, it doth not hurt us, We care not what you do, for all you scoff, we'll sing and laugh, And yet be honest too." *Wives* is thought written between 1597 and 1599.

Conclusion to the Reader. 70. 1. 2. *swaggers as in her ruffe*] i.e., in her pride, or fury (*OED sb*5, *sb*6). Whores, it seems, wore big ruffs; see *2H4* 2. 4. 136, and Dekker and Middleton, *Roaring Girl* 5. 1. 314 (ed. Bowers), where Moll says, "How many are whores, in small ruffes and still lookes?" (implying the answer "none").

1. 3. Cf. Martial 13. 2. 8 (speaking of his book): "nos haec novimus esse nihil."

ll. 5-6. *to th'Apotheta, / To wrap Sope in . . .*] Such was frequently referred to as the final use of poor paper and contemptible books; cf., below, ll. 11-12 and Satire VI. 170-78 with note. Cf. also Horace, *Ep.* 2. 1. 269-70; Martial 3. 2. 3-5; 4. 86. 8; Persius 1. 93; Nashe, 1:196, 239, 300, etc. Perhaps *Apotheca* (?), apothecary's shop, from Lat., storehouse, esp. (late Lat.) for drugs.

Assifœtida] our asafetida, a resin used in medicine; rendered thus for the scatological pun. Cf. similar "Os foetidum" in Nashe, 1:189; 3:277.

1. 8. *bastards of my* Muse] Conventional denigration by the satirist of his own work, not a judgment as to their form, as in, e.g., Marston, *SV* To those that seeme: "Tearming all Satyres (bastard) which are not palpable darke."

1. 10. The rime *lines-rimes* is "vnsauory." For other such depreciatory descriptions of their verses by satirists, see, e.g., *Vd* Defiance to *Envie*, l. 76; 1. 1. 23; 3. Prol.; Nashe, 1:285.

1. 12. For a fuller example of the traditional medicinal function of satire and epigram see *Sat. Pre.* 65 ff.

ll. 13-15. Literature, esp. satire, as enema is commonplace, with its one poison driving out another; see, e.g., Lodge, *Defence*, ed. Smith, 1:66; *AYLI* 2. 7. 58-61: "*Jaq.* . . . give me leave / To speak my mind, and I will through and through / Cleanse the foul body of th'infected world, / If they will patiently receive my medicine."

    beray] a) reveal, expose, b) soil, defile.

ll. 16-18. *And keepe* Decorum . . .] Satire, like comedy, with which it was traditionally associated, was understood to "make men see and shame at their owne faults" (Harington, *Brief Apology*, ed. Smith, 2:210). Epigrams were "comicall" writings (Webbe, *Of English Poetry*, ed. Smith, 1:249). On decorum in general, see Puttenham, *Arte*, ed. Willcock and Walker, bk. 3, chap. 23, esp., "how pleasant speeches and sauoring some skurrillity and vnshamefastnes haue now and then a certaine decencie, . . . as when the speaker himselfe is knowne to be a common iester or buffon, such as take vpon them to make princes merry" (pp. 267-68).

    There may be a general allusion to the critical concern over the mingling of clowns and kings in drama, or to the criticism of the "scoffing Scurrilitie" of comedy, as in Spenser's *Teares* (ll. 211 ff.). But the lines sound quite specific, probably in reference to some current saying, tale, or play. In *Merry Tales* (Hazlitt, *Shakespeare Jest-Books*, 1:37), "Lowes of Fraunce" has a "lowce" plucked from him by a servant, "a plaine meanynge felowe," but this seems a little wide of the mark. Perhaps the lines refer to "Chester" (playing on his name), the same of *Sat. Pre.* 86, a railer against those in high places, and whom Nashe calls "foule mouthde" (1:190-91).

l. 20. *lean*] After "moral," hinting at Pharoah's lean kine, a) emblematically, malicious, spiteful; cf. *2H6* 3. 2. 315: "leanfac'd Envy," and b) of style, severe, unelaborate; cf. *Lycidas*, ll. 123-24: "their lean and flashy songs / Grate on their scrannel Pipes of wretched straw."

l. 22. *my pen, my Rapier*] Cf. Lat. *stilus*, pen and weapon, and
Horace, *Sat.* 2. 1. 39-40. Cf. also *EMO* Ind. 16-17 (Asper): "But
(with an armed, and resolued hand) / Ile strip the ragged follies
of the time," etc., and Marston, *CS* Authour in prayse, ll. 35 ff.;
III Parnassus 3. 4. 1352-53: "*Furor* Ile shake his heart vpon my
verses poynte, / Rip out his gutts with riming ponyard," etc. A
common attitude with satirists, and one much ridiculed.

l. 23. Momes] God of mockery and censure; the carping critic.
    convince] overpower (Lat. *convinco*).

Alden took the "SA-" to be other than catch-letters and con-
sequently assumed a possible separate author for the epigrams
(*Rise of Formal Satire*, p. 149).

Satyre Preludium

For the general content of this introductory satire G. follows both Persius and Juvenal who attack in opening satires the
poetic tastes of their day and defend satire as a form they are
compelled to write. Hall had imitated the two in bk. 1 of *Vd*
(1597), and judging from the number of parallels, G. seems to
have had Hall in front of him. Another probably guide (depend-
ing upon an answer to the question of influence) was Marston's
SV 6, which attacks in similar form various types of poets and
with which there are specific affinities. For the sentiment G. required no direction other than objections to poetry already
much in the current. How typical his attitude is can quickly be
seen by a comparison with a passage in which Sidney summarizes part of Gosson's objections (*School of Abuse* [1597]), a
passage which gives an outline and certain phrases to the first
half of G.'s satire: "Their third [charge] is, how much it abuseth
mens wit, trayning it to wanton sinfulnes and lustfull loue: for

indeed that is the principall, if not the onely abuse I can heare alledged. They say the Lirick is larded with passionate Sonnets: The Elegiack weepes the want of his mistresse: And that euen to the Heroical *Cupid* hath ambitiously climed" (*Apology*, ed. Smith, 1:186). The types of poetry and the order of presentation are more or less traditional; cf., e.g., Puttenham's categories and arrangement (*Arte*, ed. Willcock and Walker, p. 25).

ll. 1-5. Here G. relies on the ancient formulation, frequent in contemporary descriptions of poetic styles, of two contrasting ethical modes of music: "that Dorian [frequently *Doricke*] inspired men to be disciplined, martial and courageous . . . while Lydian music had the demoralizing effect of making a man effeminate and unfit for political and military discipline" (F. W. Sternfeld, *Music in Shakespearean Tragedy* [London, 1963], pp. 83-84). If G. has a model (which would not be necessary) it may be Harvey (2:95): "awaye with these scribling paltryes: there is another Sparta in hande, that indeede requireth Spartan Temperance, Spartan Frugality, . . . and hath no wanton leasure for the Comedyes of Athens; nor anye bawdy howers for the songes of Priapus, or the rymes of Nashe."

l. 2. Hermaphrodites] "unmanly things," as often; cf. Ep. 2, and see note.

ll. 3-4. *touch, whose* Semphony, */ And dauncing aire*] *Semphony* probably alludes to rime, as in Puttenham, *Arte*, ed. Willcock and Walker, p. 76: "*Of Proportion in Concord, called Symphonie or rime*"; in which case *dauncing aire* signifies meter, as in "measure" (*Arte*, p. 5). Cf. *SV Ad Rithmum*, ll. 1-4: "Come prettie pleasing symphonie of words, / Yee wel-match'd twins (whose like-tun'd tongs affords / Such musicall delight,) come willingly / And daunce Leuoltoes in my poesie."
    touch, i.e., strain of music.

l. 5. *light vaulting spirits and capering*] Dancing terms with

bawdy references: *light*, lascivious; *vaulting*, leaping, forni-
cating; *capering*, beating the feet together in the air, lustful (via
Lat. *caper*, goat, a lascivious beast).

l. 6. *Woo* Alexander . . .] Alluding to the well-known episode
which Dryden celebrates in "Alexander's Feast."

ll. 7-8 *Bid* Haniball . . .] Another stock type of manliness re-
duced by lechery to effeminacy. R. W. Bond, in commenting on
a similar account in Lyly, *Euphues and His England* (ed., *Wks.*,
2:112), which does not, however, mention "Tamyras" or any
particular woman, notes a) that Antonio de Guevara, in North's
Diall of Princes (1568), chap. 10, lists "Anibal with Tamira"
among famous men ensnared by women, but that otherwise
there seems no classical authority for the name; b) that the
"fiction is . . . deduced from the loss of *morale* among his
troops at Capua and after Cannae"—sight of his annihilating
defeat of the Romans; and c) that "*Cannas* seems carelessly
adopted from some Latin translation of Plutarch." Salapia, the
ancient seaport of Apulia, revolted to Hannibal after Cannae.

l. 9. *lines*] With possible plays on a) fiddle-strings, and b) baited
fishing lines.

l. 13. *marre* Resolutions *ruffe*] Because of their size and complexity ruffs were easily spoiled by food or dampness, which is
the case here. Cf. "larded" in the Sidney quote in the headnote,
and see Linthicum, p. 160.

l. 14. *melt true valour with lewd ballad stuffe*] *melt*, weaken;
lewd, a) worthless, b) lascivious; *stuffe*, literary contents. Alluding, apparently, to the notorious practice among milliners of
combining good cloth (*valour*, value—*OED* 2) with inferior—
"boiled stuff." Stubbes describes the process of combination,
Anatomy, ed. Furnivall, pt. 2, p. 24. Cf. also *Timon* 4. 3.
270-73. For the bawdry, see *mar*, *ruff*, *melt*, and *stuff* in
Partridge; for "boil'd stuff" as persons who have undergone

sweating treatment for venereal disease, see *Cymb.* 1. 7. 125-26, with J. M. Nosworthy's note (New Arden).

With this passage cf. that of Marston's Tubrio, *CS* 1. 89-124, the *Miles Gloriosus* identified by A. Davenport in a long note (*q.v.*) with Captain Tucca, whom G. here describes a few lines below (ll. 29-34). Davenport notes the similarity between G.'s opening lines and those of *SV* 8.

ll. 15 ff. While G. probably has specific authors in mind in the following attacks, I am unable to indentify them completely. His dominant concern is with the types, and his grievances are typical of other satiric attacks. McKerrow has trouble identifying those authors Nashe tasks in the *Anatomie* (1589-90; 4:7 ff.), and Davenport finds Marston's lines in *SV* 6, which resemble G.'s, "applicable to so many Eliz. poets that it is impossible to say whom he had in mind, if he had any one in particular" (pp. 323-24). The first section (ll. 15-20), e.g., R. E. Bennett thinks "might easily apply" to Donne's elegies: "His Picture," "On his Mistress," and "Loues Warre" (*RES* 15 [1939]: 71); Philip J. Finkelpearl, however, finds the passage "too general to be applicable to Donne alone" (*RES,* n.s. 14 [1963]: 166).

l. 17. Mutio] Suggested by Mutius Scaevola, who burned off his right hand in Porsena's camp to show his courage, referred to in Persius, 1. 115, Juvenal, 1. 154 and 8. 264.

l. 22. *Pigsney*] darling or pet (from "pig's eye").

l. 23. *puisne Lucius in a simpathy*] i.e., junior student or novice (from Fr. *puis né*). A similar lover named *Lucian* occurs in *CS* 3. 51 ff. Cf. S. Nicholson, *Acolastus' After-witte* (1600), D2: "The showres which daily from mine eyes are raining, / Draw the dum creatures to a sympathie," and *Rom.* 3. 3. 84 ff.

l. 24. *Laundres*] Either washerwoman or, specifically, the caretaker of the rooms in the Inns of Court, probably the latter.

Both were regarded as of dubious virtue. See McKerrow, ed., Nashe, 4:411; H. & S., 11:4.

l. 25. *roundly*] directly, with downright frankness. *Roundly* occurs in a crucial place in the second of Davies's widely cir- culated though unpublished "Ignoto Sonnets" (ed. Howard), though there seems to be no specific allusion to the sonnet. Most of it should be quoted, however, as G. not only here but else- where draws on it:

> I cannot whine in puling Elegies,
> Intombing Cupid with sad obsequies,
> I am not fashiond for these amorous times,
> To court thy beawtie with lasciuious rimes:
> I cannot dally, caper, daunce, and sing,
> Oyling my saint with supple sonnetting.
> I cannot crosse my armes or sigh ay me,
> Ay me forlorne? egregious foppery,
> I cannot busse thy fist, play with thy haire,
> Swearing by Iove thou art most debonaire:
>> Not I by God, but shal I tell thee roundly,
>> Harke in thine eare, Zoundes I can ——— thee
>> soundly.

l. 27. Cat and fidle] A reference to the famous nonsense rhyme; overlooked by Iona and Peter Opie, eds., *Oxford Dict. of Nursery Rhymes* (Oxford, 1952), who note that it appeared in print ca. 1765 and give as evidence of its existence long before references from Preston's *Cambises* (pr. 1569) and Montgom- erie's *Cherry and the Slae* (1597), neither of which applies here. *Cat and fidle*, according to Sugden, was the sign of a London or- dinary, which may add some point to the allusion.

ll. 29-34. This Captain Tucca is to be identified with that of Jonson's *Poetaster* and Dekker's *Satiromastix* as well as with the Tubrio of Marston's *CS* 1. 89-124 (see above, note to l. 14) and the Capro of *SV* 6. 73 ff. According to Dekker (Intro. Ep.) the portrait is drawn from impressions of Captain Jack Hannam, a member of Drake's company; certain details, moreover, seem based on Barnabe Barnes's famous activities and on traits of the typical *Miles Gloriosus*. By all accounts Tucca is a sometimes soldier, swearer, swaggerer, and frequenter of bawdy houses. For full discussions of him, see H. & S., 9:535, and esp. Davenport, ed., Marston, pp. 223-26. G.'s Tucca is close to Marston's Capro:

> These that doe praise my loose lasciuious rime. . . .
> *Capro* reads, sweares, scrubs, and sweares againe,
> Now by my soule an admirable straine,
> Strokes vp his haire, cryes passing passing good,
> Oh, there's a line incends his lustfull blood.

Both G. and Marston are probably sources for the following lines in *III Parnassus* 3. 2. 1211-19:

> *Recorder*   This scorne of knights is too egregious.
>   But how should these young coltes proue amblers,
>   When the old heauy gated iades do trot?
>   There shall you see a puny boy start vp,
>   And make a theame gainst common lawyers:
>   Then th'old vnweldy Camels gin to dance,
>   This fiddling boy playing a fit of mirth:
>   The gray beards scrubbe and laugh and cry,
>   Good, good,
>   To them againe, boy, scurdge th'barbarians.

And for the following lines in *Satiromastix* (perf. 1601, ed. Bowers): (Tucca to Horace) "A gentleman or an honest Citizen, shall not Sit in your pennie-bench Theaters, with his Squirrel by his side cracking nuttes; not sneake into a Tauerne with his Mermaid; but he shall be Satyr'd, and Epigram'd vpon, and his humour must run vpo' the Stage." These last two passages gather details from G.'s next few lines (35-50).

l. 31. *discourse discours'd*] i.e., thought narrated, with a probable play on Lat. *discurre*, "running to and fro," and perhaps with the same crude quibble which is in Harington's title, *A New Discourse upon a Stale Subject.*

l. 33. *Cock-sparrow*] i.e., lecherous, like the (male) sparrow, the type of lechery; cf. Tilley S715.

l. 34. *shrug*] A gesture of joy or self-satisfaction (?). Cf. Donne, *Sat.* 1. 73-74 (ed. Milgate): "He them to him with amorous smiles allures, / And grins, smacks, shrugs, and such an itch endures."

sweet sinne] i.e., lechery.

l. 36. Thalia *to the back, nay back and all*] The function of the line is clearer with the help of some or all of the following: a) *to the back* is proverbial for "thoroughly, completely"; cf. Tilley S842, and *Titus* 4. 3. 47: "But metal, Marcus, steel to the very back"; b) *back and all* plays on *bacchanal*; and *back* has bawdy connotations for Elizs. Cf. the similar "deflouring" of the muses in *Vd* 1. 2; c) the "fall back" or "back-trick" was a motion in the dance (cf. *Twelfth* 1. 3. 115), which here anticipates the next line. Cf. Chapman, *Hymnus in Nocte,* in *Shadow of Night,* ll. 187-89 (ed. Bartlett): "Now backe, now forwarde, now lockt arme in arme, / . . . like loose froes at Bacchanalean feasts." Baskervill (*Elizabethan Jig,* pp. 112, 143-44) takes this passage (ll. 35-42) to be an accurate description of the indecent jigs that followed the performances at the Curtain theater. Robert Gittings regards it as a "not-so-veiled allusion to Shakespeare" (*Shakespeare's Rival* [London, 1960], p. 18); d) this seems the first of a number of details (to be pointed out) which taken together suggest the Roman Bacchanalia and the orgiastic mystic cult, reserved for women, called Bona Dea. *"to the back,"* e.g., recalls the "ite profane" of Juvenal's description (2. 89). The whole passage was perhaps suggested by Spenser's *Teares of the Muses,* ll. 175-234, wherein Thalia (muse of comedy) mourns the banishment of "the sweete delights of learnings treasure."

l. 37. *salt*] a) leaping or dancing (Lat. *saltus*), b) lecherous.
    La volto] lively dance for two (It. "the turn").

l. 38. *Edgeth some blunted teeth, and fires the brest*] For the
irony, cf. Jonson's translation of *Ars Poet.*, 401-3 (8:327): "Next
these great *Homer* and *Tyrtaeus* set / On edge the Masculine
spirits, and did whet / Their minds to Warres, with rimes they
did rehearse."

l. 40. Medea *like . . .*] Alluding to her restoration of Aeson, the
father of Jason. The rejuvenation idea here seems to follow from
association with the Bona Dea as Juvenal presents it (6. 324-26),
which Dryden translates: "Nothing is feign'd, in this Venereal
strife; / 'Tis downright Lust, and Acted to the Life. / So full, so
fierce, so vigorous, and so strong; / That, looking on, wou'd
make old *Nestor* young." The old man may be the white-haired
old priest who presides over the Bona Dea in Juvenal (2. 111-
16); and he may in part refer to the Roman proverb "saltat
senex," elaborately explained by Erasmus in *Adagia*, 2. 1. 40
(1558, col. 742) as referring to the old man who preserves the
religious rite by continuing to dance when all others have
stopped. Here he continues by moving on to the adjacent bawdy
house. Drayton uses this line as a basis for his in *Idea* (1599), no.
44: "MEDEA-like, I make thee young again."

l. 42. *some odde garden noted house of sinne*] *some*, a certain;
odde, a) out of the way, b) notorious; *garden*, Paris Garden in
the theater district, site of the amphitheater erected for bull- and
bear-baiting and closely associated in the Eliz. mind with illicit
sex; see H. & S., 8:209, and *SV In Lect.*, ll. 44-45: "Goe read
each post, view what is plaid to day. / Then to *Priapus* gar-
dens." *noted*, a) illustrious, b) branded, stigmatized.

ll. 43-50. G. here may attack not merely a type but particularly
Nashe's *Choice of Valentines*, the pornographic description of a
visit to a brothel. Harvey had attacked it (2:91): "I will not

heere decipher thy vnprinted packet of bawdye, and filthy
Rymes, in the nastiest kind: there is a fitter place for that dis-
couery of thy foulest shame, & the whole ruffianisme of thy
brothell Muse, if she still prostitute her obscene ballatts, and will
needes be a young Curtisan of ould knauery." So had Hall, *Vd*
1. 9. 33-36:

> . . . Artes of Whoring: stories of the Stewes,
> Ye Muses can ye brooke, and may refuse?
> Nay let the Diuell, and Saint *Valentine*,
> Be gossips to those ribald rymes of thine.

l. 43. *Capritcious humor*] i.e., a) witty, b) lecherous; a phrase
first used by Harvey (2:54; see H. & S., 9:318), who also intro-
duced the word *capritious*.

l. 45. *prophane Clodian pen*] Alluding to Publius Clodius Pul-
cher, the profligate who profaned the rites of Bona Dea by
appearing as a female lutist and who carried on an adulterous
affair with Caesar's wife Pompeia; also related to the proverbial
and ironic "Clodius accuset moechos" (see Juvenal 2. 27).

l. 46. (*Like connicatching*)] Alluding to Greene's group of pamphlets in general, with a hint at the usual charge of hypocrisy; if
specific, then perhaps to *A Disputation betweene a Hee Conny-
Catcher, and a Shee Conny-Catcher* (1592), which sets forth
"what a preiudice ensues by haunting of whorehouses, what
danger grows by dallying with common harlottes, what in-
conuenience followes the inordinate pleasures of vnchast Liber-
tines" (Bodley Head Quarto, p. 3).

Orgia] Lat. neut. pl., as common; trisyllabic.

l. 47. *prouost Martiall*] The officer and the epigrammatist.

l. 49. *Midwife* Albert] Albertus Magnus, whose popular *The
booke of secretes* (a translation) saw a number of editions after
its first before 1560 (STC 260 et seq.), and whose *De Secretis
Mulierum*, published early 1495, though apparently untrans-

lated, was certainly well known. The author of *Tyros Roring Megge* (1598), considers being "*Acute*, and *Graue*, and *Circumflex* / In the deepe dealings of the *female sex*" to be in the manner of Albertus's *Secreta mulierum* (Ep. 1. 3, B₁).

the womans booke] *The byrth of mankynde, otherwise named the Womans booke*, trans. from Lat. of E. Roesslin by R. Jonas, of which there were numerous editions before 1598 (STC 21153 et seq.). It contains seventeen illustrations of children *in utero*.

l. 50. *anatomize*] Probably intended to enlarge the reference to include such works as Stubbes's *Anatomie* (1583), and Nashe's *Anatomie of Absurditie* (1589-90?).

ll. 51-54. Rabelais (frequently dissyllabic, as here) and Pietro Aretino were commonly linked as instances of licentious if brilliant writers and teachers of bawdry, although how well Rabelais was known is difficult to assess. Note Harvey (1:272): "the two monstrous wittes of their languages"; Lodge, *Wits Miserie*, *Wks.*, 4:94-95; Harington, *Ajax*, ed. Donno, p. 200; Huntington Brown, *Rabelais in English Literature* (Cambridge, Mass., 1933), pp. 52, 55, and on Aretino esp. David C. McPherson, *PMLA* 84 (1969): 1551-58.

durtie mouth discourse] i.e., "dirty-mouth discourse."

l. 54. *the errant arrant whore*] Alluding to *La Puttana Errante ovvero tra Maddalena e Giulia* ascribed to Aretino; originally a poem by Lorenzo Veniero, afterward prose, with the same title, perhaps by Niccolò Franco—both of whom were disciples of Aretino. See David Foxon, *Libertine Literature in England* (New York, 1965), pp. 27-28. *errant*, wandering, a frequent variant of *arrant* (see H. & S., 9:555) meaning "out-and-out"; the repetition is for the quibble and intensification.

l. 55. *speaking painters*] i.e., poets, a variation on the "poem as a speaking painting"; for a discussion of the commonplace see Smith, ed., *Eliz. Crit. Ess.*, 1:386n.

l. 56. Ioues *loues*] A favorite theme with Titian; alluding, it would seem, to his *Rape of Europa*, with Jove in the guise of a bull ("Elephanticke"?), to his *Prado Venus*, which has Jove as a satyr surprising Antiope ("elfantic"?), and/or to his *Danae*, on which see the account in Vasari, *Lives*, Everyman ed., 4:206-7.

Elephanticke] Perhaps in description of the forms; certainly in allusion to Elephantis, the Greek poetess who wrote lascivious poems on the various postures of love, referred to in Martial 12. 43, and Suet., *Tiberius*, 43. Note *Alch*. 2. 2. 42-44, where Mammon will have his room "Fill'd with such pictures as Tiberius tooke / From *Elephantis*, and dull Aretine / But coldly imitated."

l. 58. Circes] Analogies to the Circe (*Circes* was common) and Siren (l. 60) episodes are stock in Eliz. attacks on licentious poetry.

l. 59. *transformd to Goates lasciuiously*] On degrees of drunkenness, note Nashe, 1:207-8: "the third is Swine drunk, heauy, lumpish, and sleepie, and cries for a little more drinke, and fewe more cloathes. . . . the seuenth is Goate drunke, when, in his drunkennes, he hath no minde but on Lechery."

l. 60. *Filthing chast eares . . .*] i.e., defiling, a variation on the usual "filling . . .," as is, e.g., "Witching chast eares," in Greene, *Groatsworth*, Bodley Head Quarto, p. 17; *eares* puns a) *ars* (art) and b) *arse* (?); *pens* plays on *penis*.

ll. 61-64. A common complaint against such romantic epics as the two *Orlando* poems and the *Faerie Queene*, based on Sidney (quoted in headnote): "euen to the Heroical Cupid hath ambitiously climed," which Harington repeated (*Brief Apology*, ed. Smith, 2:209).

l. 61. *stateliest*] i.e., elevated, dignified, as is frequent in descriptions of Heroic Poetry; see, e.g., *Eliz. Crit. Ess.*, ed. Smith, 1:226n., and 2:43.

generous] a) copious, full of gravity, b) high-born.

l. 66. *Concisde*] a) brief, b) trimmed, cut away (?) (by diet; cf. Lat. *concido*).

sharpe] a) harsh, severe, b) "emaciated, thin" (?) (*OED* 9f). The description which follows in ll. 65-90 is built out of traditional comparisons: satire and epigram as proper diet, as medicine, and as physical punishment for sins. Of Eliz. satire, says M. C. Randolph (*SP* 38 [1941]: 137), "all critical definitions of the genre and all critical methods, and exegetical statements concerning its functions, methods, and essential nature are couched almost exclusively in terms of the medical concept." Her article should be seen for references.

l. 69. *censures*] judgments, criticisms.

Critticke] censorious.

spleenes] Seat of laughter and melancholy, and therefore identified with scornful laughter, ridicule, and hatred; cf. Persius 1. 11-12: "(nolo . . . sed sum petulanti splene) cachinno"; and *Vd* 4. 1. 74.

l. 71. *They heale with lashing . . .*] Cf. *III Parnassus* 1. 1. 86-89: "I, Iuuenall: thy ierking hand is good, / Not gently laying on, but fetching bloud; / So, surgean-like, thou dost with cutting heale, / Where nought but lanching can the wound auayle." *luxuriousnes,* a) excess, as in a "growth," b) as usual at this time, sensual pleasure.

l. 72. *Philosophicke true* Cantharides] A preparation of Spanish flies or dried beetles used by doctors as a rubefacient to gall the skin, which, figuratively, is one effect of satire. *Philosophicke,* in contrast to its usual function as an aphrodisiac (*OED* 2).

l. 74. *popish displing*] Cf. *FQ* 1. 10. 27; and *CS* The Authour in prayse, ll. 35-38: "Now by the whyps of *Epigramatists,* / Ile not be lasht for my dissembling shifts. / And therefore I vse Popelings discipline, / Lay ope my faults to *Mastigophoros* eyne."

ll. 75-76. *A plaine dealing lad . . . calls a iade, a iade*] Based on the old proverb for using plain speech (Tilley S699). *iade*, a) poor or vicious horse, b) whore.

ll. 77-78. The incident is doubtless available in *Les Apothegmes du S. Gaulard*, pr. in *Les Bigarrures du Seigneur des Accords* (1591). It appears on p. 17 of the edition of a late seventeenth-century manuscript, *The Pleasant and Witlesse . . . Speeches of the Lord Gaulard* (Glasgow, 1884). Gaulard was a proverbial fool of the Gotham kind.

l. 78. *meat*] Epigrams were frequently inscribed or carved on food-trenchers.

ll. 79-80. Based on the proverbs "What is sweet in the mouth is oft sour in the stomach" (Tilley M1265) and "Sweet meat must have sour sauce" (M839). Cf. *Rom.* 2. 4. 80-81: "Thy wit is a very bitter sweeting; it is a most sharp sauce. ——— And is it not then well served in to a sweet goose?" *cates* puns *cats*, i.e., whores (*OED* 2b).

l. 82. *Strappado*] An instrument of punishment that draws the victim up by a cord fastened to his arms and then lets him down suddenly with a jerk (It. *strappare*).

   paine] punishment, retribution (Lat. *poena*).

ll. 83-84. *Bridewell, / Some whipping cheere*] The prison on the west side of Fleet Ditch. *whipping cheere*, a) the proverbial "banquet" of lashes (Tilley W308, *2H4* 5. 4. 5); the recognized punishment for whores in Bridewell; cf. T. Heywood, *Royal King* 2. 2. 350, ed. Tibbals (Philadelphia, 1906): "Send him to Bridewell ordinary; whipping cheer is best for him," b) perhaps a euphemism for sex (here ironic), as in Whetstone, *Promos and Cass.*, pt. 1, 4. 1. 2 (1578, E$_1$^{v}): "She fearde of late, of whipping cheere to swell."

l. 85. *dwarfe Kings scurrill grace*] Difficult. Perhaps in reference to Oberon, King of Fairies, who appears in Greene's *James the*

Fourth (1591), and *Midsummer Night's Dream* (1595), and about whom some play probably existed as stock-in-trade for the traveling companies, a play that may have served as the basis for *MND*, and perhaps for this allusion. See H. & S., 10:526, and *MND*, ed. Quiller-Couch and Wilson (Cambridge, 1924), p. 94. Cf. Jonson's *Oberon*, ll. 62-63: "*Satyres*, he doth fill with grace, / Euery season, eu'ry place." Fairies were popularly thought to have special powers of benediction, which notion the Catholic church sought to dispel; see Chaucer's *WBT*, and *MND* 5. 1. 404-9.

l. 86. *Chester*] Charles Chester, called by Nashe (1. 190) "an odde foule mouthde knaue," often mentioned by contemporaries for his open and persistent attacks on abuses, esp. in high places, for which he was frequently punished by the authorities; see H. & S.'s long note, 10:405-6; and Donno, ed., *Ajax*, p. 254n. Jonson's Carlo Buffono is thought modeled on Chester. Apparently much of his attack was against women; see, below, Satire II. 43-45, and *Ulysses upon Ajax* (1596), E6^r: "or to use (*Charles Chesters* iest, because you are faced like *Platina*)." Pun (?), chastener.

l. 87. *bone-ach*] An effect of venereal disease.

l. 88. *Acolastus*] Alluding to the Prodigal Son play by the Dutch scholar Gulielmus Gnapheus (Wm. Fullonius), trans. in 1540 by John Palsgrave, which as a school text was very popular in the sixteenth century.

l. 89. *the scourge, the* Tamberlaine *of vice*] "*Tamb*. I that am term'd the Scourge and Wrath of God" (pt. 1, 3. 3. 1142, ed. Tucker Brooke), an epithet frequent in the two plays and in contemporary allusion. The *scourge* or beadle was responsible for the public flogging of criminals.

l. 90. *three square Tyborne*] The structure for hangings, built on three legs and thus triangular. Satire, like Tyborn, is the measure or standard (*OED Square sb* 2) of sins.

l. 91. *neere*] nearer.

l. 92. (*oh scuruey*) *to a Lenten rime*] i.e., poor, contemptible; cf. *Ham.* 2. 2. 314: "lenten entertainment" and *Twelfth* 1. 5. 8; as in "Lenten stuff," provisions suitable for Lent, usually fish, which enforces the associations set off by *scuruey*, the skin disease that is the result of an inadequate diet, and, because salty, lecherous. G. thus continues the disease-food-sex cluster of images.

l. 95. *Itch farther yet, yet nerer to them*] Cf. Nashe, 2:207: "Iost a little neere to the matter & purpose"; and *Merchant* 3. 2. 22-23: "I speak too long; but 'tis to peize the time, / to eke [ich *F*] it and to draw it out in length." Perhaps related originally to directions for back scratching; cf. Lyly (*Wks.*, 3:394, with Bond's note): "itch a little further for a good fellow?"

l. 96. *got my Muse with Tympanie*] i.e., with a "distension of the abdomen by gas or air in the intestine, etc., or the uterus" (*OED*). It functions a) to continue the sex-disease metaphor—cf. the proverbial "tympany with two legs" (Tilley T648), and Jonson, *Magn. Lady* 2. 3. 19-22; b) to suggest the uncontrollable urge in the satirist to attack, which is like the longing of the pregnant woman; cf. "with child" in *OED sb* 17c; and perhaps c) to call up the traditional image of the satyr with drum (tympany=drum); cf. *SV In Lect.* l. 38: "a Satyres dreadfull sounding drum"; and Nashe, 1:313: "the very timpanie of his Tarltonizing wit."

l. 97. *loose tayld penns*] a) i.e., styles without moral constraint, lecherous; cf. *OED* 10, which quotes (1598): "loose-taild gossips which first intic't her to folly," and b) with a play on *loose tail-pens* (feathers), out of which quills were made, which, being sharp pointed, deflate the timpany.

    to let it loose] set free from disease or clear the stomach; cf. *LLL* 3. 1. 120-21: "be my purgation, and let me loose"; *to* may be a misprint for *do*, in which case the line would require heavier punctuation at the end.

l. 98. *Syring to a Hampshire Goose*] Cf. Davies of Hereford, *Papers Complaint* (*Wks.*, ed. Grosart, 2:75): "An other comes with Wit, too costiue then, making a Glister[clyster]-pipe of his rare pen." *Hampshire Goose* is a whore. With *Syring*, related to *syrinx*, pipe, tube, etc., G. may be thinking of the pipe normally identified with Pan and the satyrs.

l. 99. *critique*] censorious.

nettle vanitie] With a play on needle, thus "deflate emptiness"; note Nashe, 1. 18: "theyr needles are nettles."

l. 101. *hangingst brow*] a) gloomiest, b) "most eager to hang"; cf. *Wives* 4. 2. 35: "hanging look."

l. 104. *reason haue . . .*] Varying the proverb (Tilley R98).

l. 108. *haue place*] i.e., rank or position.

l. 109. *his night-cap's ouer awde*] Probably "he's made a fool"; cf. Chaucer, *Gen. Prol.*, l. 586: "sette hir aller cappe"; *Tell-Troth's N. Y. Gift* (1593), p. 37: "They say that ouerawing makes fooles"; and below, Satire V. 117. *night-cap* suggests venereal disease, since they were frequently worn to conceal loss of hair (from "falling sickness"), which the satirist would expose.

Alterius qui fert . . .] "By tolerating vices a man makes them his own." Untraced.

Satire I

l. 1. *mych*] shrink from view, used contemptuously, as, e.g., of a schoolboy playing truant.

giue ayme] encourage. Cf. Juvenal's opening (1. 1): "Semper ego auditor tantum? numquamne reponam."

l. 4. *priuate*] personal, with the added sense of special.

ll. 6-7. The idea of vice disguised pervades satire of the time; cf., e.g., Nashe, 1:10: "and vice [would] no longer maske vnder the visard of vertue," and *Vd* 1 Prol. It is possible that G. here and in the next several lines remembers the Greene-Nashe attitude toward the common players; the possible pun *leapered* = *leopard* above suggests "Tygers hart wrapt in a Players hyde."

l. 8. *the* Prester Iohn *of wit*] Alluding to the famous mythical Christian ("Priest") king of the Far East or Ethopia. G.'s version of the epithet "Monarchy of wit," on which see Harvey, 2:271, and Sidney, *Apology*, ed. Smith, 1:172. Philip J. Finkelpearl suggests that this may allude to Donne (vis à vis Hall), whose satires while unpublished were well known to G. (*RES*, n.s. 14 [1963]: 167).

l. 11. *controule*] overpower.

l. 12. *cucking-stoole*] ducking-stool, a chair in which female scolds were fastened and then ducked in a pond. Marston twice refers to his Muse as a scold (*SV* 2. 96-97, 142-43).

ll. 13-16. This particular facet of the satirist's persona, his rallying cry of outrage, derives ultimately from Juvenal, esp. his first satire ("facit indignatio versum," 1. 79), with support from ll. 30-31: "Difficile est Satyram non scribere nam quis iniquae / tam patiens urbis, tam ferreus, et teneat se. Cf. *SV* 2. 1-5:

> I Cannot hold, I cannot I endure
> To view a big womb'd foggie clowde immure
> The radiant tresses of the quickning sunne.
> Let Custards quake, my rage must freely runne.
> Preach not the Stoickes patience to me, etc.,

and *SV Proem. in lib. prim.*, ll. 16-17: "Blacke Cypresse crowne me whilst I vp do plow / The hidden entrailes of ranke villanie." Marston's passage is parodied in *III Parnassus* 4. 2. 1521-25:

> *Furor* The great proiector of the Thunderbolts,
> He that is wont to pisse whole clouds of raine
> Into the earthes vast gaping vrinall,
> Which that one ey'd subsizer of the skie,
> *Don Phoebus*, empties by caliditie.

Asper uses much the same language in the opening of *EMO* (1600), and Marston mimics Asper, and thus himself, in Lampatho in *What You Will* 3. 1, prod. 1601 (*Plays*, ed. Wood, 2:266). The tone and imagery (war, tempest, and purge) became the hallmark of the Eliz. satirist.

l. 15. *foggie clowde*] Juvenal's *erroris nebula* (10. 4), and the cloud of battle. *foggie*, a) murky, b) bloated.

ll. 17-18. *Tell Gyant greatnes . . .*] i.e., "Tell Giant Greatness (Pride, Presumption) that an even greater one (than he, or than his creator) constructed the imaginative (with the added sense of *image*) Colossus of the same (Greatness)"—alluding to the famous Colossus of Rhodes which tumbled down. Query, *same=fame*? Pliny comments at length on the construction of the various colossi (*H. N.* 34. 18 ff.). Cf. Castiglione: princes and ignoble characters "are (in my judgment) like the Colosses that were made in Rome . . . which outwardly declared a likeness of great men and . . . inwardly were full of towe and ragges" (*Courtier*, trans. Hoby, Everyman ed., p. 263); Hall's "old Colossian imageries" (*Vd* 6. 1. 16), for him symbols of wrath; Marston's *"to be huge, is to be deadly sick"* (*SV* 2. 118), and "Ile make greatnesse quake; Ile tawe the hide / Of thick-skind Hugenes" (*What You Will* 3. 1); and Isa. 10:33.

l. 21. Athos] Holy mountain on the peninsula of Chalcidice in Macedonia; chosen to suggest "Atheos": a godless man.

   frozen zeale] a variation of the usual "cold charity"; Matt. 24:12.

l. 23. *iniure*] slander. The suggestion for these two lines probably comes from Lodge, *Fig* (1595), Sat. 1, *Wks.*, 3:11-12: "Find me a niggard that doth want the shift, / To call his cursed auarice good thrift?"

l. 27. Matho] Related to the hypocritical, bribe-taking lawyer referred to often by this name. See Ep. 5, above, and note.

l. 29. *aduisement*] warning.

l. 30. *rancke*] downright, but possibly also (ironic) "stout and strong" (*OED* 2).

ll. 33-34. *Like the old morrall . . .*] Alluding to R. Wilson's *Three Ladies of London*, pr. 1584, in which Lucar (common for *lucre*) is a character.

l. 38. *trick of youth*] i.e., youthful characteristic, and thus to be excused. The phrase occurs as a euphemism for sex in *Greene's News*, ed. McKerrow (London, 1911), p. 35.

l. 39. *Oh world, oh time*] Based on Cicero's expression; see also Ep. 19.

l. 40. *hipocrisie*] With a play on *hippocras, vinum Hippocraticum*, a cordial drink of spiced wine, anticipating the next image.

ll. 41-42. Based on the fact that one "carouses a health," a contradiction satirists made much of. See *Sat. Pre.* 57-58 and, below, Satire IV. 80. Cf. Nashe, 1:187: "let vs haue lesse carousing to your health in poison." The equation of wine with poison (*vinum quasi venenum*) is old and frequent; see McKerrow's note and sources, ed., Nashe, 4:434.

l. 44. *from brawling to a blubbering passion*] Cf. *SV* 5. 103-4: "Fie how my wit flaggs, how heauily / Me thinks I vent dull sprightlesse poetrie"; *SV* 9. 54: "I am too mild. Reach me my scourge againe."

l. 46. *winde instrument*] a) pipe, b) podex.

l. 48. *Satyre-footed*] i.e., with goat's feet, light of foot.

l. 49. *whirlygigging*] i.e., making rapid circling movements, probably with the implication of giddiness and inconstancy. John Peter, *Complaint and Satire* (Oxford, 1956), p. 39, notes that the concept of the world as a rolling wheel is a staple ingredient of the medieval complaint—"*volubilis et variabilis ac ruibundus*" (Barnard).

ll. 50-53. This style-as-explosive conceit is bandied about by
Nashe and Harvey and picked up by almost all the satirists. See,
e.g., Harvey, 1:204, 206, 2:71, etc.; Nashe, 1:195; 3:122, etc.
Leishman devotes a long note to the conceit, ed., *Parnassus*,
p. 296. Jonson ridicules it, *EMO* 1. 2. 214 ff.: " 'ware how you
offend him, he carries oile and fire in his pen, will scald where it
drops: his spirit's like powder, quick, violent: hee'le blow a man
vp with a jest." Cf. also, below, ll. 143-44.

l. 53. *anticke*] grotesque, ludicrous. See note to l. 94, below.
    complements] "external shows," formal courtesies.

l. 57. *pole-head*] tadpole. Cf. Marston, *What You Will* 2. 1:
"Why thou *Pole-head*, thou *Ianus*"; *CS* 1. 4:- "Yee vizarded-
bifronted-Ianian rout."

l. 60. *forkt*] equivocal, ambiguous (*OED* 5).
    oyle] essence.

l. 61. *bereyde*] befouled.

l. 62. *naked truth*] Proverbial (Tilley T561, T589); Nashe,
1:382: "Truth is euer drawne and painted naked."

ll. 63-76. As G. B. Harrison first pointed out (*TLS*, 15 Oct. 1931,
p. 802), this passage is based on the description of Bolingbroke's
"popular courses" in *R2* 1. 4. 23-36 (perf. 1595?, pr. 1597, etc.),
and thus, like it, should be taken as an allusion to Essex (Q$_1$597,
C$_2$^{v}):

> King. Our selfe and Bushie,
>   Obserued his courtship to the common people,
>   How he did seem to diue into their harts
>   With humble and familiar courtesie,
>   What reuerence he did throw away on slaues,
>   Wooing poor craftsmen with the craft of smiles,
>   And patient under-bearing of his fortune,
>   As twere to banish their affects with him,
>   Off goes his bonnet to an oysterwench,
>   A brace of draimen bid God speed him well,

And had the tribute of his supple knee,
With thankes my countreymen my loving friendes,
As were our England in reversion his,
And he our subiects next degree in hope.

Harrison takes G.'s passage as evidence that Bolingbroke would have been identified with Essex by contemporaries, and this months before J. Haywood's history of Henry IV (Feb. 1599) caused reference to Richard II to be regarded as treasonable. For the relevant passage as Haywood treats it and a discussion of the whole question see E. M. Albright, *PMLA* 42 (1927), esp. p. 713, and Harrison, *TLS*, 13 Nov., 20 Nov. 1930. Harrison thinks Shakespeare's passage added to *R2* in 1597, in reference to Essex's activities in the autumn after his return from the unsuccessful "Islands Voyages," and finds it remarkable as one of the few hostile criticisms of Essex's conduct to be printed before his fall. He confirms its topical nature by quoting from an anonymous attack on Raleigh from the end of 1603, in *Poet. Misc.*, ed. J. O. Halliwell, Percy Soc. no. 15 (London, 1845), p. 17:

Renouned Essex, as he past the streets,
    Would vaile his bonnett to an oyster wife,
And with a kinde of humble congie greete
    The vulgar sorte that did admire his life:
And now sith he hath spent his liuinge breath,
    They will not cease yet to lament his death.

He might also have noted Marston's passage, *CS* 2. 87-104:

But see who's yonder, true Humility
The perfect image of Curtesie.
See, he doth daine to be in seruitude
Where he hath no promotions liuelihood.
Marke, he doth curtsie, and salutes a block,
Will seeme to wonder at a wethercock. . . .
O is not this a curteous minded man?
No foole, no, a damn'd Machevelian.
Holds candle to the deuill for a while,
That he the better may the world beguile
That's fed with shows. He hopes thogh som repine,

> When sunne is set, the lesser starres will shine:
> He is within a haughty malecontent,
> Though he doe vse such humble blandishment.
> But bold-fac'd Satyre, straine not ouer hie,
> But laugh and chuck at meaner gullery.

If he imitates Marston, then G. has this passage in mind, as well as Shakespeare's. The account seems to draw details from Marlowe, *Ed.2* 1. 2. 224 ff. (ed. Tucker Brooke); from Nashe's description of the devils and particularly of Ambition, which Fœlix is the type of, at 1:210 ff., esp. 227-29, and 2:81-92; and from *1H4* 3. 2. (ent. 26 Feb. 1598). *Fœlix,* sarcastically, the favored or fortunate one. For another allusion to the Devereux see Satire VI. 79-84 with note.

l. 64. *vayleth*] lowers, in token of obedience, with a possible allusion ("passing through") to the lowering of topsails or colors of merchant or other inferior ships before the king's ship; see H. & S., 9:55, and *Merchant* 1. 1. 28-29.

l. 66. *truage*] homage.

l. 70. Cf. Nashe, 1:210: "they delight to see him shine in armour. . . . That is the course he that will be popular must take."

l. 71. *Swartrutters hose*] i.e., "Dutch hose," the baggy "slops" or breeches, noted for their fullness. A swartrutter was one of a class of irregular troopers in the Low Countries who wore black dress and armor and a blackened face. Cf. *CS* The Authour in prayse, l. 23: "Yet puffie as Dutch hose they are within."

l. 73. *mumming trick*] i.e., in disguise and silent. *OED* Mummers, 1648 quote: "Like mummers in a mask, make a fair shew, but speak nothing."

l. 74. *T'entrench himselfe in popularitie*] Cf. *1H4* 3. 2. 69: "Enfeoffed himself to popularity," i.e., low company, common people.

l. 75. *writhen face, and bodies moue*] i.e., with oratorical or dramatic gestures, continuing the metaphor of "mumming trick." *bodies moue*, bow (?).

l. 77. This Clodius is perhaps the erstwhile friend who has pretensions to place in Ep. 22, but not apparently the braggart of Eps. 17, 43. The Clodius of *Vd* 5. 1. 87, which may have given G. the hint for the name, is rather the suppliant in the predicament.

l. 78. *angling for repute*] Cf. "fish for honour and high dignity," *CS* 1. 74; "fish for liuings," *III Parnassus* 2. 5. 740. The collocation suggests, too, "oil of angels" and thus bribery as a part of Clodius's method.

l. 79. *entertaine*] receive (as guest), with implication of "take into service." Here as elsewhere G. alludes to the difficulty young university men have finding positions.

l. 81. *turnes the word*] i.e., (ironically) fashions artistically or gracefully.

ll. 83-84. Large sleeves ("armes"), called "trunk sleeves," were frequently used as pockets. Hall (*Vd* 5. 1. 85-87) and Nashe (1:159) use similar images in attacks on tight-fisted patrons, which may be what G. has in mind here. For the image itself, cf. *Errors* 1. 2. 97: "full of cozenage," and Donne's verse letter to G., l. 8 (ed. Milgate): "Our Theaters are fill'd with emptines."

l. 85. An identity between this *Fabius*, that of Marston, and/or G.'s *Fabian*, on which see headnote to Sat. 3, which is not unlikely, cannot be established with certainty.

l. 89. Balthazer] Perhaps suggested by *The Courtier of Count Balthazar Castilio* (cf. below, Satire V. 147 and note), and/or the duplicitous Balthazar of *The Spanish Tragedy*.

l. 92. *goe by*] i.e., go unregarded. The reference to Balthazar suggests that G. remembers the famous passage in *The Spanish Tragedy* 3. 12. 27-31:

> *Hiero.* Iustice, o iustice to *Hieronimo.*
> *Lor.* Back, seest thou not the King is busie?
> *Hiero.* O, is he so.
> *King.* Who is he that interrupts our business?
> *Hiero.* Not I, *Hieronimo* beware, goe by, goe by.

"Perhaps no single passage in Eliz. drama became so notorious as this. It is quoted over and over again, as the stock phrase to imply impatience of anything disagreeable, inconvenient, or old-fashioned" (Boas, ed., Kyd, *Wks.*, p. 406).

l. 93. *actions*] acts, with the added sense of gestures.

l. 94. *anticke*] "Originally applied to grotesques in art; then to absurdities in shape or gesture; so clown, merry andrew, and finally a clownish dance" (H. & S., 10:177); Baskervill explains that "jig" and "antick" were used interchangeably (*Elizabethan Jig*, p. 148).

l. 95. *motley fac'd Dissimulation*] In *Three Ladies of London* (1584), ed. 1911, Dissimulation has motley hair and beard (2. *s.d.*); in *FQ* 3. 12. 14, a painted face and "borrowed haire."

ll. 98-99. *all-buttockt, and no-bellied . . .*] Describes the full hose and the "strait," form-fitted doublet. For an account of trends in fashions which agrees with G. as to the shifts in padding, see Linthicum, pp. 197-99, 205.

ll. 103-6. A reference to a painted tapestry, perhaps well known in London, which was based on a detail from Esther 7:8. Jonson describes such a tapestry to Drummond (*Conv.* ll. 476-80, H. & S., 1:145): "He saw a picture painted by a bad painter of Easter, Haman & Assuerus, Haman courting Esther jn a Bed after the fashion of ours, was only seen by one Leg, assuerus back was turned with this verse over him & wilt thou Haman be so malitious as to lye wt myne owne wife jn myne house."

l. 106. *print*] With a quibble on what is "in print," referring to fastidious and precise dress.

painted cloth] "hanging for a room painted or worked with figures, mottoes, or texts; tapestry" (*OED*); with a glance at highly decorated clothes.

ll. 107-10. Alluding to the practice of appending updated or otherwise misleading title pages for purposes of advertisement. "The Lord of Lorn and The False Steward" (Child no. 271), a popular ballad sung to the tune of "Green Sleeves," was registered on 6 Oct. 1580. It may have been old at that time, or that impression may have been reissued under false pretenses in the late nineties.

l. 108 *in King* Harries *dayes*] Need not be taken literally, as it seems to have been proverbial; cf. Tilley H468: "This was a hill in King Harry's days."

l. 111. A traditional topic; cf. Tilley T199; Lodge, *Fig* (1595), Ec. 3, *Wks.*, 3:25: "They are not as they seeme, in outward face."

l. 116. *borne in wits dearths deerest yeere*] The idea is proverbial (Tilley W574). *deerest* seems (?) purposefully ambiguous: a) "most cherished," b) "direst" (to or for "wit's dearth"), and thus one of "wit's plenty." Cf. *Ham.* 1. 2. 182: "my dearest foe."

ll. 117-18. Zopirus *iudging by his face . . .*] Cicero recounts this story of the celebrated physiognomist, *De Fato* 10. 10, *Tusc.* 4. 37. 80, as does Nashe, 1:371.

l. 119. *false larumd-seeming*] A conflation of *false-alarumed* (*larumd*, an aphetic form) and *false seeming*, another name for Dissimulation.

l. 122. G. probably has something specific in mind, some honorific title or title page. But his concern is partly with aureate diction or extreme conceits, which Elizs. often spoke of as "minted." Marston complains of "new-minted Epithets," attacking incidentally the word *"Real"* (*SV* To those that seeme,

ll. 15-16); see Jonson also on *real* (H. & S., 3:472). For general
parallels to the passage see Lodge, *Wm. Longbeard, Wks.*, 2:4,
and *Measure* 2. 4. 12-17. For the proverb, cf. Guazzo, *Ciuile
Conv.*, ed. 1925, 1:76: "[Flatterers] playe their parts so wel that
they make them ["great personages"] beleeve, according to the
Proverbe, that gloe worms are lanternes"; Tilley S988.

ll. 123-36. Among many such descriptions before G., the Lying
Traveler can be found in Lodge, *Wits Miserie, Wks.*, 4:41;
Harington, *Ajax*, ed. Donno, p. 70; Nashe, 2:300-302; *Vd*
5. 6. 59-81; and *CS* 2. 127-56. G. is closest to Nashe, 3:18.

l. 123. *foisting*] a) lying, b) stinking, "breaking wind" (*OED* v^3),
c) with a possible quibble on *foist*, a small boat (sb^1), in ironic
anticipation of the traveler's pretensions.

l. 124. *face out many a lie*] i.e., carry through by effrontery.
When "given the lie," Bardolph "faces it out, but fights not" (*H5*
3. 2. 32).

ll. 129-30. *The straights of* Gibraltare . . .] Cf. Donne, "Hymne
to God my God, in my sicknesse," ll. 18-19: "Anyan, and Ma-
gellan, and Gibraltare / All streights, and none but streights,"
with Gardner's note (ed., *Divine Poems*, p. 108): "The 'Streto de
Anian' appeared first on a map of 1566, as a narrow strait sepa-
rating America from Eastern Asia. 'Anian,' placed on the west
coast of America, was Marco Polo's Anica or Anin, modern
Annam."
    The lines refer presumably to London localities, like the
"Streights, or the Bermuda's" of *Bar. Fair* 3. 6. 26-27, about
which Gifford commented (1816): "These *Streights* consisted of
a nest of obscure courts, alleys, and avenues, running between
the bottom of St. Martin's Land, Half-moon [i.e., Bedford
Street], and Chandos Street. In Justice Overdo's time they were
the receptacles of fraudulent debtors, thieves, and prostitutes"
(in H. & S., 10:195). The couplet requires heavier punctuation
after *Magellane* and constitutes a two-line quotation from the
Traveler.

l. 130 *hard by*] a) near by, b) playing on the difficulty of passage.

l. 132. *Came neuer neere him* . . .] Both figurative and literal in view of the quibble: *crake,* a) boast, b) break wind.

l. 133. *layd his head*] risked his head, as in a wager; with the usual hint of the brothel.

ll. 135-36. *th'infinity / Of* Anaxarchus *worlds*] The philosopher of Abdera (fl. 340 B.C.) was a follower of Democritus, who believed in an infinite number of worlds; see Diog. Laert. 9. 44. For the idea in the Renaissance see, e.g., *FQ* 2. Prol. 3; Drayton, *Mort.*, ll. 2850-51 (*Wks.*, ed. Hebel, 1:390); and F. R. Johnson, *Astronomical Thought in Renaissance England* (Baltimore, 1937), pp. 146-47, 163, 181. Johnson reports that in 1588 the question "An sint plures mundi?" was disputed at Oxford.

ll. 136-42. Lodge's description is similar, though the details are different (see Introduction, p. 20). G. may have noticed that Lodge joined Antiquary and Traveler in the character of Lying (*Wks.*, 4. 41). Rowlands's description, largely based on Lodge, demonstrates the continuity of treatment (*Letting*, Sat. 1, *Wks.*, ed. 1880, 1:48):

> His tongues-end is betipt with forged chat,
> Vttring rare lyes to be admired at,
> Heele tell you of a tree that he doth know,
> Vpon the which Rapiers and Daggers grow,
> As good as Fleetstreete hath in any shoppe;
> Which being ripe, downe into scabbards droppe.
> He hath a very peece of that same Chaire,
> In which *Caesar* was stabb'd: Is it not rare?
> He with his feete vpon the stones did tread,
> That *Sathan* brought, & bad *Christ* make the bread.
> His wondrous trauels challenge such renowne,
> That *Sir Iohn Maundiuell* is quite put downe.

ll. 138-39. In Greek mythology, Aegeus, legendary king of

Athens, places his sword and sandals under a great rock which his son Theseus (by Aethra), when of age, removes and uses as tokens in his trip to Athens.

l. 138. *blacke-iack*] a drinking vessel, that, like the shoe, was of tarred leather and was frequently in the shape of a shoe.

ll. 143-52. G. recalls Nashe, 1:242: "We want an *Aretine* here among vs, that might strip these golden asses out of their gaie trappings. . . . I hope hele repaire his whip, and vse it against our English Peacockes." And, on Aretino's style, 2:264: "If out of so base a thing as inke there may bee extracted a spirite, hee writ with nought but the spirite of inke, and his stile was the spiritualitie of artes, and nothing else; . . . His pen was sharp pointed lyke a poinyard; no leafe he wrote on but was lyke a burning glasse to set on fire all his readers. With more than musket shot did he charge his quill, where hee meant to inueigh."

l. 143. *the whip of fooles*] Probably based on *Il Flagello de principi*, one of Aretino's honorary titles. See Nashe, 2:265, with McKerrow's note, 4:279.

ll. 146-48. Cf. *Errors* 2. 2. 192-94: "We talk with goblins, elves and sprites, / If we obey them not, this will ensue— / They'll suck our breath, or pinch us black and blue." In Hall, *Hermae* (ed. Davenport), l. 27, "*Gobelins*" has three syllables, as it probably should here.

ll. 149-52. G. refers to the satirist's "crabbed" style (sour-tempered, peevish, harsh, difficult), using a culinary metaphor (*sauce-goose*). *varges* or *verjuice* is the acid juice "wrung" from crab apples, formed into a liquor, and used for cooking or medicinal purposes (*OED*). Cf. *SV* To those that seeme, ll. 33-35: "yet I dare defend my plainnes gainst the veriuyce face, of the crabb'st Satyrist that euer stuttered."

l. 149. *blacke*] morose and bitter, alluding to ink and gunpowder.

l. 151. *touch*] spicy taste, feeling; *Poet.* 1. 2. 113-15: "I would haue him vse some such wordes now; they haue some touch, some taste of the law. Hee should make himselfe a style out of these."

l. 152. *two-neckt goose, this falshood checkt*] Referring to the proverbial two faces of hypocrisy, perhaps an instance of the common inexact equation of *neck*=*head* (*OED sb*[1] 1d). The basic metaphor is from chess, in which a *neck* is a move to cover *check*; cf. Surrey, *Tottels Misc.*, ed. Rollins, 1:20: "Although I had a check, / To geue the mate is hard, / For I haue found a neck / To kepe my men in gard." Goose of course is prostitute; cf. *1H6* 1. 3. 53: "Winchester goose! I cry, 'a rope! a rope!'"

l. 153. The next few lines are based on Nashe, 1:197: "Me thinks I see thee stand quiuering and quaking, and euen now lift vp thy hands to heauen, as thanking God my choler is somewhat as-suag'd: but thou art deceiued, for how euer I let fall my stile a little, to talke in reason with thee that hast none, I do not meane to let thee scape so." *pie-bald*, said of animals (recalling "mot-ley," l. 95).

l. 156. *rouse him from*] startle him out of, a metaphor from hunting: to drive from the lair.

ll. 156-57. *shaking / Feauer*] i.e., palsy, a set phrase.

l. 158. *lash at euery word*] Lashes were probably applied to a voice count; cf. *Ham.* 3. 1. 50: "How smart a lash that speech doth give my conscience."

l. 160. *Cramp-fish*] The electric ray or torpedo, also called *cramp-ray* and *numb-fish*.

l. 164. *fayery elfe*] malicious imp or demon. While the idea for the "turn" against himself is not unusual, G. may have Nashe still before him (2:87): "Euen in thys dilatement against Am-bition, the deuill seekes to sette in a foote of affected applause

and popular fames Ambition in my stile, so as hee incited a number of Phylosophers . . . to prosecute theyr ambition of glory in
writing of glories contemptiblenesse. I resist it and abhorre it: if
any thing be here penned that may peirce or profite, heauenly
Christ (not I) haue the prayse."

l. 170. Quoted in *England's Parnassus*, under "Dissimulation";
and in Bodenham's *Belvedére* (1600), ed. 1875, under "Of Flat-
terie and Dissimulation."

SATIRE II

Like the numerous other Eliz. attacks on women's attire and
on their use of cosmetics in particular, this satire belongs in a
long tradition that goes back to Isaiah 3, Juvenal 16, Tertullian,
De cultu feminarum, and so on, a tradition that received full expression in the denunciations of contemporary satirists and
Puritan reformers, for whom it was a favorite topic. Stubbes,
after giving the views of Ambrose and Cyprian, assures us that
he can "show . . . the sharp Inuections and grounded reasons of
many moe, as of *Augustine, Hierome, Chrisostome, Gregorie,
Caluin, Peter Martyr, Gualter,* and of an infinite number moe;
yea, of all generally since the beginning of the world, against the
whorish and brothellous painting and colouring of faces; but to
auoid *prolixitie,* [he] will omit them" (*Anatomy,* ed. Furnivall
[1877], 1:65-66). Stubbes argues, as do the others, that cosmetics
disgrace God's handiwork, entice to sins, ruin complexions,
bring on disease and early death, and lead to ultimate damnation
(1:63-89). His treatment is typical, as is that of Nashe, 2:136-44,
and gives a useful parallel.

Carroll Camden provides the best and fullest discussion of
Eliz. attitudes toward cosmetics, giving descriptions of each, the
arguments for and against them, and relevant sources, in *The
Elizabethan Woman* (Houston, 1952), pp. 173-215. His excellent

account makes extensive commentary here unnecessary. H. & S. list contemporary sources for information about cosmetics, recipes, etc., in their comment on Wittipol's lengthy catalogue in *Devil Is An Ass* 4. 4 (10:245). And John Peter briefly sketches the medieval treatment of the theme to indicate the continuity of the tradition in *Complaint and Satire* (Oxford, 1956), pp. 99-103. G.'s arguments, images, and general structure are thoroughly traditional. Certain details, phraseology, etc., parallel Marston, and are noted. There is not, to my knowledge, another Eliz. verse satire devoted completely to an attack on cosmetics before G.

ll. 1-4. This opening and other ideas general and specific are very similar to *SV* 7. 160 ff.:

> *Peace* Cynick, *see what yonder doth approach,*
> A cart, a tumbrell? *no a Badged coach.*
> What's in't? some man. *No, nor yet woman kinde,*
> *But a celestiall Angell, faire refinde.*
> The deuill as soone. Her maske so hinders mee
> I cannot see her beauties deitie.
> Now that is off, shee is so vizarded,
> So steep'd in Lemons-iuyce, so surphuled
> I cannot see her face . . .
>   her bright spangled crown . . .
> Is all that makes her thus angelicall. . . .
>   Out on these puppets, painted Images,
> Haberdashers shops, torch-light maskeries,
> Perfuming pans, Duch antients, Glowe wormes bright
> That soile our soules, and dampe our reasons light:
> Away, away, hence Coach-man, goe inshrine
> Thy new glas'd puppet in port Esqueline. Etc.

In G.'s opening one youth (later identified as Publius) exchanges remarks with others. He renders ll. 1-2, the latter part of 3, the first part of 4, and he in turn is addressed by the satirist in line 5.

l. 1. The coach, relatively new on the London scene and still the cause of some amazement, was often attacked by satirists for its gaudiness and contribution to venery. Note Rowlands, *Letting,* Sat. 7, ed. 1880, 1:84: "Then is there a notorious bawdie Feend, / Nam'd Letcherie; who all his time doth spend, / In two-wheel'd Coatch." For the idea of the pageant cf. Dekker's *Seven Deadly Sinnes* (1606), which has each sin pass by in a coach.

l. 2. *blazing starres*] Like comets, centers of admiration, with reference to the brilliant show of the prostitute. Nashe calls prostitutes "falling starres" (1:216), and Marston refers to "Lais starrie front" (*SV* 8. 74).

l. 6. *harper from a shilling . . .*] "Elizabeth . . . caus'd indeed some Irish Shillings (call'd Harpers . . .) to be made of a baser kind than the English, so that they usually pass'd for Ninepence here" (1699 quote, *OED*). Playing on the fabulous monsters having "virgin faces, and vultures talents" (Gosson, *School,* ed. Arber [1868], p. 10), which, like falling stars, boded ill; cf. *FQ* 2. 12. 36.

l. 8. *errors sinne*] Probably with plays: a) "wandering," as in stars and/or the dance (cf. "wandering passages"), b) =*eros;* also *sinne = sign* (?).

l. 9. *S. Martins stuffe*] Proverbially counterfeit; cf. Tilley 648: "Saint Martin's ware"; probably copper instead of gold.

l. 11. *Idols, Puppets, Exchange babies*] All terms for *dolls* (itself first used in 1700, *OED*), suggesting tawdry imitation, the fairs where they were sold, and where puppet shows were performed. Often contemptuous for women. *Exchange babies* alludes a) to the proverbial "to look babies," or lovers' glances, and b) to the doubtful reputation of the women who ran the shops in the Exchange.

l. 12. *goodly Ladies*] Frequently ironic; cf. *Wint.* 2. 1. 65-68.

ll. 13-14. "The vertue conteined within the bodie of an harlot . . . may be beheld with great admiration. For hir eie in-
fecteth, entiseth, and (if I maie so saie) bewitcheth them manie
times, which thinke themselves well armed against such maner
of people." "Manie writers agree with *Virgil* and *Theocritus* in
the effect of witching eies" (Reginald Scot, *Discoverie of Witchcraft* [Carbondale, 1964], pp. 256, 399).

l. 15. *Beane flowre*] either a) the pulverulent form of the bean or
b) the distilled water of the aromatic flower (*OED Bean* 7). Both
"beanes broken in pieces & mondified" and "water of beane
blossoms" occur in recipes for cosmetics—probably the former;
see *The Secretes of the reverend Maister Alexis of Piemont. The
First Part*, trans. Wm. Warde (1562), Ki, Jiii. Stress *cómpound*.

l. 16. Acrasias] Suggested by *FQ* 2. 1. 51, the Aristotelian
ἀχραοία or intemperance, with features of the Homeric Circe.
Acratia is also the enchantress in Trissino's *L'Italia Liberata dai
Gotti*. With these lines cf. the famous passage on the power of
the "juice" of the flower in *MND* 2. 1. 169-72, a play to which
Meres in 1598 is the first reference.

l. 17. ff. The name and many of the same points are in *SV*
8. 84-117:

> *Publius* hates vainely to idolatries,
> And laughs that Papists honor Images,
> And yet (o madnes) these mine eyes did see
> Him melt in mouing plaints. . . .
> Vsing inchauntments, exorcismes, charmes. . . .
> Vnto the picture of a painted lasse. . . .
>   vow peasant seruitude
> Vnto a painted puppet, to her eyes. . . .
> O can it be the spirits function,
> The soule not subiect to dimension,
> Should be made slaue to reprehension
> Of craftie natures paint? . . .

Davenport suggests (p. 431) that as the personal name of Ovid

Publius is suitable for the amorist. *Publius* occurs again at Satire III. 49 as the son of a prosperous ironmonger.

ll. 21-22. *toad-housing sculs . . .*] Imagery traditional in descriptions of prostitutes and hypocrites; cf., e.g., Matt. 22:27. Othello will not have his skull kept after death "as a cistern for foul toads / To knot and gender in!" (4. 2. 63-64). To Elizs. toads were despicable and poisonous; *Oth.* 3. 3. 270; *Mac.* 4. 1. 6, with notes (New Arden).

l. 24. *pencils*] a) paint brushes, b) with a pun (?) on *pencel* (*pennoncel*), the pennon or streamer on a knight's lance; cf. *LLL* 5. 2. 43, with note (New Arden).

      graces] pun (?) = *greases*.

l. 26. *deaw-figs, hens dung, & the beane*] Sources for the ingredients of cosmetics, and as such occur frequently in, e.g., *Secretes of . . . Alexis* (ref. at note to l. 15), esp. Book Four, passim. The unfamiliar dew-figs are probably the "greene figges," "lytle figges that bee not rype," "yonge figges," etc. (K1v, Kiiv). Hen's dung apparently provided the required quicklime. Fig and bean (metaphorically, the ancestry) were proverbial for the worthless (Tilley F211, B118).

ll. 27-28. Cf. Dekker, *Seven Deadly Sinnes*, ed. Brett-Smith (1922), pp. 4, 25: "[They] haue basely compeld it [a book] either like a bastard, to call a great many father (And to goe vnder all their names) or else (like a common fellow at Sessions) to put himself . . . vpon twelue godfathers"; "*Truth* had euer but one *Father*, but *Lyes* are a thousand mens *Bastards*, and are begotten euery where."

      faires] a) beauties; cf. *LLL* 5. 2. 37; b) fairies.

l. 29. *effronted*] Probably "shameless" or "unblushing," though this is the first occurrence in *OED*.

l. 34. *pippins*] apples. Proverbial for a glossy surface with a rotten substance. "ffor what a vailes the gorgious shows / of

Apples outward skynn, / Yf the internall frute conteyne / not pleasing taste therein?" (Fr. Thynne, *Emblemes and Epigrams*, ed. Furnivall [1876], p. 23); cf. *CS* 3. 84-85. Perhaps an aside to venereal disease, the so-called Spanish pip, on which see quotes at *OED Pip sb*1.

ll. 35-36. Cf. Nashe, 2:137: "Why ensparkle they theyr eyes with spiritualiz'd distillations?" "The quack referred to in *The Malecontent* was good at 'spright'ning the eyes,' we remember, which must have meant to make them sparkling. Belladonna was used to produce this illusion by making the eyes appear large and glistening" (Camden, *Elizabethan Woman*, p. 189).

l. 37. *skaine of silke*] the band worn about the face to prevent sunburning (see Linthicum, p. 168).

l. 38. *philterd waters*] a) *filtered*: most recipes for cosmetics required that the water be passed through a fine linen cloth, b) perfumes that serve as love-charms or love-potions (*OED Philter*).

   asses milke] "water of the whites of egs: Take the whites of new egs about twelue, fine cinnamon an ounce and asses milke twelue ounces, distil all in a glasse stillitory: this water maketh a woman looke gay and freshe, as if she were but fifteene yeeres old." (Estienne and Liebault, *Mason Rustique, or the Countrie Farme* [1600], trans. Richard Surglet, in H. & S., 10:245).

l. 40. *Boras*] i.e., borax. With this and the next lines cf. the description of the Somonour in the *Gen. Prol.*, ll. 629-32.

l. 41. *gaules*] "*Another maner to make the face fayre*. Take the gall of a Hare, of a Cocke or Henne, and Eeles, temper them with Honnye." In *Secretes of . . . Alexis*, trans. Wm. Warde (1595, f. 71b).

l. 42. *morphew, scurffs & scauls*] All diseases of the skin.

l. 43. *quirke, quidlit case*] Alluding to the "quirks and quillets" of lawyers, which expresses the "sharp turns" and fine distinctions of the lawyer's case. *case,* a quibble on covering, as of cosmetics.

l. 45. Chester] See note to *Sat. Pre.* 86.

ll. 47-48. The repainting of such posts is alluded to time and again. See, e.g., Dekker, *Gull's Hornbook,* ed. 1812, p. 79; *Cyn. Rev.* 1. 4. 101. Apparently they, like the lady, were red and white: "their cheeks suger-candied and cherry blusht as sweetly, after the colour of a newe Lord Mayors postes" (Nashe, 1:180).

ll. 49 ff. For borrowings here from Marston, see passages quoted at notes to ll. 1-4 and l. 17. Nashe, describing the sons and daughters of Pride (2:136), is similar: "Lyke Idols, not men, they apparraile themselues. Blocks and stones by the Panims & Infidels are ouer-gilden, to be honored and worshipped: so ouergilde they themselues, to bee more honored and worshipped."

l. 53. *Ethnicks*] heathens.

l. 55. *ouer-fleeting brittle . . .*] i.e., a) overflowing, as a vessel, b) unstable, fickle (*OED Fleeting*), a sense which *brittle* also carries. Cf. Giovanni Paolo Lomazzo, "To the Reader," in *A Tracte Containing the Artes of Curious Paintinge,* trans. R[ichard] H[aydocke] (Oxford, 1598): "But because this corporall memory cannot containe all things (because it is like a vessel, which after it is ful spilleth whatsoeuer by ouerplus is poured into it) it hath neede likewise of some other helpe; and principally of the most Noble art of Painting."

l. 59. *to plague their sinne*] to punish (originally as in divine retribution) them for their sin; cf. *John* 2. 1. 183-87.

l. 60. *counterfaits*] a) shams, b) "portraits," continuing the previous idea.

l. 61. *Quickly discouers*] i.e., reveals, with possible sense "pain-fully"; cf. *OED Quickly*. Note also *Quick* 5: "of the com-plexion: Having the freshness of life." With the general idea cf. Is. 3:17.

ll. 61-62. *and to shadowes too . . .*] i.e., "shades," as of de-parted spirits, the ultimate plague of sins. Alluding to venereal disease; cf. Greene, *Wks.*, ed. Grosart, 3:74: "then they are like Cornelius shadowes, which seemed like men that were nere." And, perhaps, shadows in the sense of parasite; cf. *Cyn. Rev.* 5. 3. 19-20: "welcome *Beauties,* and your kind *Shadowes,*" re-ferring to their lovers. The idea is a variation of the proverb "Mulier umbra viri," which usually describes the fickleness of woman, though it was a common topic of poetic debate. Cf. Plautus, *Miles,* 624.

ll. 63-68. The comparison of a woman to a counterfeit coin (*slip*) was well worn.

l. 65. *copper guilt*] alluding to the copper used in counterfeiting and in cosmetics.

l. 66. *touch as slippery*] trust as deceitful, as hazardous. A meta-phor from the testing of metal, as in "touchstone." For the bawdy, see Partridge, and *Wint.* 1. 2. 273: "My wife is slip-pery."

ll. 69-70. *a whore-house signe*] Cf. ll. 47-48. There may have been specific signs. Note Dekker, *Seven Deadly Sinnes,* ed. Brett-Smith (1922), p. 27: "You commit Sinne together, euen in those houses that haue paynted posts standing at the Gates," al-though Dekker would seem to have respectable houses in mind. Taverns often served as brothels.

l. 71. *Sophisticate*] adulterated.

l. 72. *dudgin dagger*] one with a wooden or dudgeon handle, and thus inferior or worthless; a traditional association, as in

Harington, *L. & E.*, p. 257: "A gilden blade hath oft a dudgeon haft."

l. 73. *sute*] compare.

l. 74. *fane*] a) temple, b) weathercock (*vane*); both of which turn with the winds of change, the latter proverbially (Tilley W223).

l. 75. *gloriously*] boastfully (Lat. *gloriose*).

ll. 77 ff. On this fundamental Puritan objection to cosmetics see the list of references in M. P. Tilley, *RES* 5 (1929): 312-17, on *Ham.* 3. 1. 142-43: "I have heard of your paintings too, well enough. God hath given you one face and you make yourselves another."

l. 77. *natures stamp*] Continues the coin metaphor, referring now both to design and mold, the female pudendum. Nashe makes the same point (2:150, 149): "The Alcumist of Quicksiluer makes gold. These, (our openers to all commers,) with quickning & conceiuing, get gold. . . . Those that haue beene daily Fornicatresses and yet are vnfruitfull, hee shall accuse of ten thousand murders, by confusion of seedes and barrayning theyr wombes by drugges. There is no such murderer on the face of the earth as a whore. Not onely shall she be araigned and impeached of defeating an infinite number of Gods images; but of defacing and destroying the moulde, wherin he hath appointed them to be cast."

"Those skin-playstring Painters . . . doe not so much alter Gods image, (by artificiall ouer-beautifying theyr bodies,) as these doe, by debasing themselues to euery one that bringes coyne."

ll. 82-88. Camden, *Elizabethan Woman*, pp. 202-4, discusses contemporary views of the harmful nature of cosmetics, quoting among others Vives: "The tender skynne wyll riuyll the more soone, and all the fauour of the face waxeth old and the breath stynketh, and the tethe rusten, and an yuel aire all the bodye ouer, bothe by reason of the ceruse, & quicke siluer," etc.

l. 88. *pocket-healths, vaine vsage in their prime*] Probably, as Grosart suggested (based on Halliwell), the drinking of large or excessive *healths*, from Kentish "pocket," a measure of hops, from "pocket," a half sack of wool. Such excess would result in jaundice (cf. "greene-sicknes wines," Satire III. 36). G. plays on "health derived from the pocket (i.e., the cosmetic box)," and *pocked* (pitted, as a result of pox). The entire line suggests, through quibbles implied in the Nashe passages in the note to ll. 77 ff., the misuse of the female reproductive organs: "For the vain (Lat. *vanus*, empty) use of the healthy pocket (womb; cf. "pocketinge queane," *II Parnassus* 5. 1. 1424) in their prime (i.e., lechery; cf. "as prime as goats," *Oth.* 3. 3. 407)."

l. 89. *owly*] wakeful, with the usual suggestion of drunkenness. Owl and bat (of the next line) frequently occur together as symbols of shame and secrecy. See, e.g., *Vd* 4. 2. 68. Note Tilley L274: "The light is nought for sore eyes."

l. 94. . . . *cannon scoffe*] i.e., loud and boisterous derision, a play on *cannon shot*. Like the author of *I Parnassus* 1., ll. 90-91, G. thinks of painted women as "faire rotten painted walls," and the consequent association is similar to Jonson's (*EMO* 1. 2. 216-17): "I feare him worse than a rotten wall do's the cannon." But the play may be complex. *cannon shot* is appropriate to "beggary" and the tavern reckoning, and thus, through submerged metaphor, extends the idea of drunkenness. Cf. Dekker, *Gull's Hornbook,* 1812 ed., p. 162: "But, in such a deluge of drink, take heed that no man . . . free his purse from the danger of the shot." Also, a possible association, "pestilentiall shot" in the groin describes the plague (*Plague Pamphlets*, ed. Wilson, p. 109). Finally, the general idea is proverbial; Tilley S144: "A scoffe is the reward of Shamefast and pusillanimous persons."

ll. 97-100. An ending characteristic of Marston; cf. *SV* 4. 167-70: "But I forget; why sweat I out my braine, / In deepe designes, to gay boyes lewd, and vaine? / These notes were better sung, mong better sort, / But to my pamphlet, few saue fooles resort."

SATIRE III

This satire against inconstant, fashion-mongering friends takes its unity from an attack against one particular former friend, the "Fabian," apparently, addressed in l. 96. G.'s method of personal attack, the special intensity of his antagonism toward Fabian, and the general correspondence of this profligate philosopher-dancer with Marston's "Fabian," the philosopher much exercised over "habits" (*SV* 4. 93-103), and his "Fabius," of the "perpetuall golden coate . . . / [who] Hath beene at feasts, and led the measuring / At Court, and in each marriage reueling" (*SV* 1. 67-69, and see ll. 18)—all make probable Finkelpearl's remark that "anyone in the right circles [could] have identified Fabian" (*Marston* [1969], p. 89). The name *Fabian* need not necessarily contain a clue as to identity as it occurs elsewhere in Eliz. contexts to imply swashbuckler, swaggerer, perhaps champion, in such phrases as "flattering Fabian," "flaunting fabian," etc. Deriving ultimately, it is suggested, from the Fabian priests who presided over the license of the Lupercalia (see Wilson's note in Nashe, 5. 59, and *OED*) and suggesting the ancient patrician family of Rome (*Fabii*), it aptly suits the special context here of Christmas revels and "a noble mans part" (l. 95).

There is, however, a contemporary Fabian who agrees with G.'s account in several striking particulars. The record of the ecclesiastical court of the Archdeaconry of Essex contains the following unusual proceeding for 14 Jan. 1596/97: "*Magistrum Johannem Fabian, rectorem ecclesie, parochialis de Warley Magna.*—Notatur publica fama, that on Sunday at night the

second of January last he did to the scandall of his calling and offence of good Christians behave himselfe very dissolutely and
wantonly in the parish of Kelvedon etc. in taking upon him to be
a lord of misrule or Christmas lorde etc. emongest certein yonge-
linges etc. *** [*Suspended.*]—D/AEA 17, f. 244" (in Wm. H.
Hale's *Precedents* [1847], p. 213). If the two men are not the
same, the coincidence is remarkable. John Fabian matriculated
pensioner from Trinity College, Cambridge, in Lent, 1581/82
and took his B.A. on the same day, apparently having already
been in residence four years; he took an M.A. from Balliol College, Oxford, in 1585. He was appointed rector of Sapcote,
Leics., 1588, of Great Warley Essex, 1589, and of Houghton
Regis, Beds., 1591 (Venn, *Al. Cant.*, 2:115; Foster, *Al. Ox.*,
2:480). At Great Warley he succeeded William Fulke, the noted
Margaret Professor of Cambridge, which would indicate that he
was well thought of. (See R. Newcort's *Repert. Eccl. Par. Lond.*,
2:641.) He vacated his benefice at Great Warley some time
before 10 Aug. 1600 (Cooper, *Ath. Cant.*, 2:288; *Cal. Proc.
Chanc. temp. Eliz.*, 2:289). His son John, who matriculated pensioner from Pembroke College, Cambridge, in 1618, is listed as
of Great Warley.

Beyond this there is little available about Fabian. Why he
should participate in festivities at Kelvedon, perhaps some entertainment at Felix Hall, is difficult to know, although a number of
Fabians resided in the immediate area. We can only imagine
what "he did to the scandall of his calling," perhaps participation
itself, since the visitations annually warned against such fri-
volity. G. could easily have known him at Cambridge. I find,
however, no direct evidence that he was a member of any of the
Inns of Court, although he may well have been associated with
them. It may be to the Middle Temple revels of 1597/98 that G.
refers here, the principals of which (Davies, Martin, Hoskyns,
etc.) Fabian may well have been acquainted with at Oxford. He
doubtless had some reputation as a reveler. His name does not
appear in Benjamin Rudyerd's abbreviated account of the events

(*Le Prince d'Amour* [1600]); nor does any particular part that was clearly his emerge from Finkelpearl's excellent analysis of the events (based on Rudyerd—*Marston* [1969], pp. 45-61). Surely he was there. Moreover, he may have served as the basis for the enigmatic "Signiour Fabian" of *Twelfth Night*, who bears such an unexplained grudge against Malvolio. A connection, which is hard to resist, should encourage the occasional tendency to view the play as earlier than 1600/1601 or else a revision of an earlier play.

There remains the possibility that "Fabian"—in either or both of the associations we have mentioned—is a cover for John Davies, whose precipitate assault on Richard Martin (the Prince d'Amour) for some unspecified insult was notorious and the cause of considerable inconvenience to him. Davies, according to Finkelpearl, seems to have been the butt of a number of jests during the revels, some of which had to do with his "waddling gait," and he played the part of Essex ("a noble mans part"). While there is no evidence that he himself danced more than another, his dancing may have been ludicrous given his walk, and he had written *Orchestra* (ent. 1594; extant copy pub. 1596). And he may have already turned his attention to the philosophy that would result in *Nosce Teipsum* (1599, but perhaps in circulation as early as 1592; see McKerrow, ed. Nashe, 4:157). Davies seems to have inspired antagonism among a number of his contemporaries, perhaps because he was already a published and popular poet, and a barrister. A number of additional details might suggest Davies.

But it seems unlikely that G. knew Davies when he wore "a thread-bare gown" (l. 76) as they attended different universities at different times. Nor does Davies appear to have been a needy student. Also, for Marston, who seems to have had a special aversion to Davies, it is not *Fabian-Fabius*, Davenport thinks (ed., p. 308), but rather *Curio* who is Davies (*CS* 1. 125; *SV Ad Rithmum*, l. 5; 6. 1.; 8, ded. to "Inamorato Curio"; 11. 15, 34). Accordingly, if G. has a cover for Davies it would be the epi-

grammatist Curio of Ep. 18. And G.'s one explicit reference to
Davies (Ep. 20) seems complimentary, although it may be two-
handed. It may be that G. telescoped the John Fabian incident
and current connotations of "Fabian" so as to make an attack on
Davies less subject to reproof; or else that he intended an attack
on John Fabian alone; or finally that he capitalized on the
coincident disgraces to attack both at once. At present we can
only speculate.

ll. 1-2. In these difficult lines it may be that the speaker feints at
removing his cap in salutation, but does not, claiming to have
lost it, in order to rouse the wrath of his foppish friend and set
himself off into a discussion of fashionable manners. Cf. Davies,
In Cineam 23 (ed. Howard):

> When Cineas comes amongst his frinds in morning,
> He slily lookes who first his Cap doth mooue,
> Him he salutes, the rest so grimly scorning,
> As if for euer they had lost his loue:
>> I knowing how it doth the humour fit,
>> Of this fond gull to be saluted first,
>> Catch at my Cap, but mooue it not a whit[,]
>> Which perceiuing he seems for spite to burst:
> But Cineas, why expect you more of me,
> Then I of you?

The loss of one's cap leads to parental retribution ("after-clap").
Mary and gup!, an exclamation of surprise; for suggestions as to
its origin and meaning, see H. & S., 10:183. From the last couplet of the satire we know his friend refuses to speak to him.

l. 4. *complements*] manners. This description of affected salutations of foreign style (of "cap and knee") is typical of many. Cf.,
e.g., Barnabe Rich, *Faultes Faults* (1616), p. 8: "if at his returne
he hath but some few foolish phrases in the *French, Spanish*, or
Italian language, with the *Baselos manos*, the *Ducke*, the *Mump*,
and the shrugge, it is enough."

l. 5. *Antike*] With a play on *antique* (contrast "new," l. 4).

l. 6. *Spanish shrug*] Apparently the raising (and contraction) of the shoulders, esp. to express disdain, indifference, etc. (*OED*). The precise shrug of each nationality, and several occur, is difficult to arrive at (see H. & S., 9:509 n.).

cheuerell face] i.e., one that stretches into various expressions. *Cheverel,* made from the skin of the kid of the wild goat, was proverbial for its stretching capacity and frequent among poets in comparisons with wit and conscience.

l. 11. *estrang'd*] alienated, "removed" (as foreign).

l. 18. *Dutch*] generic for anyone native to the German continent.

l. 20. *state*] a) condition in general, b) political boundary. With this passage cf. *AYLI* 4. 1. 30-33: "*Ros.* Farewell, Monsieur Traveller; look you lisp and wear strange suits; disable all the benefits of your own country; be out of love with your nativity, and almost chide God for making you that countenance you are," etc.

l. 22. *extenuate*] attenuate (a medical term), fig. for "to weaken the force of."

l. 25. *I cannot, I*] With a probable pun on *Ay,* pronounced the same way and often spelled *I.*

l. 27. Cf. the proverb, "With that liquor a vessel is first seasoned, it will long keep the scent of it" (Tilley L333), usually relating to the training up of children.

ll. 28 ff. This and the next several accounts (digressions) seem indebted for details to Nashe's description of *"pesants sprung vp of nothing"*; "[who] from turning spit in the chimney corner, are on the sodaine hoised vp from the Kitchin into the waiting chamber, or made Barons of the bieues, and Marquesses of the Marybones: some by corrupt water, as gnats, to which we may liken Brewers, that, by retayling filthy *Thames* water, come in few yeares to bee worth fortie or fiftie thousand pound: others by dead wine, as little flying wormes; and so the Vintners in like

case: others by slime, as frogs, which may be alluded to Mother
Bunches slimie ale, that hath made her and some other of her
fil-pot facultie so wealthie: others by dirt," etc. (1:173-74). With
the first description (ll. 31-42), G. has an eye on Hall's account
of Lolio's son (itself probably influenced by Nashe), *Vd* 4. 2.
51-60:

> When *Lolio* feasteth in his reueling fit,
> Some sterued Pullen scoures the rusted spitt.
> For else how should his sonne maintained bee,
> At Ins of Court or of the Chancerie:
> There to learne Law, and courtly carriage,
> To make amendes for his meane parentage,
> Where he vnknowne and ruffling as he can,
> Goes currant each-where for a Gentleman?
> While yet he rousteth at some vncouth signe
> Nor neuer red his Tenures second line.

l. 30. *poore in wit, . . .*] proverbial; cf. *CS* 3. 24: "*Faire outward show, and little wit within.*"

ll. 31 ff. I am unable to identify *Panduris.* He seems unrelated to
the famous procurer; ll. 32 and 36 would suggest someone
named *Green.*

l. 33. i.e., "he 'sir' will not speak" (?).

l. 36. *greene-sicknes wines*] i.e., weak, thin wines. *Green-
sickness* was "an anaemic disease which mostly affects young
women about the age of puberty and gives a pale or greenish
tinge to the complexion" (*OED*). Nashe, quoted above at ll. 28
ff., has "dead wine." This refers as well to the effects of drinking
such, which is the case at *2H4* 4. 3. 90-92: "for thin drink doth
so over-cool their blood . . . that they fall into a kind of male
green-sickness."

   muck] dung, dirt, fig. for money; "Muck and money go together" (Tilley M1297).

l. 39. *pound*] a) weight measure, b) monetary unit.

Commentary

l. 40. Guazzo . . .] Alluding to Guazzo's *Ciuile Conversation,* trans. Geo. Pettie (1581), and, the last book, B. Young (1586), a popular courtesy book designed for such aspirants to gentility as Panduris. In the first sentence Guazzo describes his work as one of "formal gravitie" (ed. Sullivan [1925], 1:7). Soon thereafter he exhorts his readers to an unabashed display of their learning: "Therefore (Gentlemen) never deny your selves to be Schollers, never be ashamed to shewe your learnying. . . . confesse it, professe it, imbrace it, honor it. For it is it which honoureth you, it is onely it which maketh you men, it is onely it whiche maketh you Gentlemen. . . . it is Learning which accomplisheth a Gentleman."

l. 41. Bellarmine] The famous Jesuit controversialist whose lectures at the Roman College caused special chairs to be founded in Germany and England to provide replies. G. may recall the curious circumstances whereby John Rainolds, of Corpus Christi, Oxford, through the agency of intelligencers in Rome and the post, attacked Bellarmine point for point before he was in print. See Fuller's account in *Abel Redevivus* (London, 1867), 2:225 ff. It may be of some value to note that Nashe, 1:174, in the midst of his discussion of "These whelpes of the first Litter of Gentilitie, these Exhalations, drawne vp to the heauen of honor from the dunghill of abiect fortune" mentions "*Raynold,* the Fox." G. probably thinks of Nashe's attack while alluding to someone else.

l. 43. Cynops] Not met with elsewhere. Perhaps an anagram for *Hopkins* or *Hoskins,* which would suit the brewery. *Cynops* is Lat. for a plant, dog's eye; from the Greek, dog-faced, shameless; cf. *Iliad* 1. 159.

ll. 43-44. *grandmother sold / Good ale*] Cf. *Two Gent.* 3. 1. 296-97: " 'Item: She brews good ale.'—And thereof comes the proverb: 'Blessing of your heart, you brew good ale.' " See Tilley B450.

l. 45. *fetch*] To suggest "fetch a pedigree."

l. 46. *Purchasd*] acquired otherwise than by inheritance or descent (Law). Cf. *Ant.* 1. 4. 13-14: "hereditary, / Rather than purchas'd"; *2H4* 4. 5. 200-201.

ll. 49-56. R. E. Bennett, *RES* 15 (1939): 70-71, suggested that Publius is "almost certainly John Donne," whose father was a rich ironmonger, who had been on one of the recent voyages, and who was earlier, we know from the verse letter, G.'s friend. Philip J. Finkelpearl, however, in *RES*, n.s. 14 (1963): 166-67, disagreed, arguing that Publius's father has become wealthy only recently (Donne's died in about 1576), that the reference to the Cadiz expedition applies not to Publius but rather to the next topic (Martialists), and finally that this section refers not to former friends (?) but rather to "gulls and fooles" in general. I am unable to identify Publius. A clue may be "in ranck" = "Rankin(s)." Publius occurs again as an amorist, dancer, and young Inns of Court man in Satire II. 17. There may be an auditory allusion in l. 49 to "Ovid Publius."

l. 49. *in ranck*] a) in status, b) in place for the dance. *Rank* had the connotation of luxuriance, rottenness, and intemperance.

l. 51. Chimicke] alchemic. As an ironmonger, Publius's father (fig.) transmutes base metal into gold. Cf. the proverb "Iron with use grows bright" (Tilley I93).

l. 59. *Phantasmas butterflies*] Cf. Ep. 52, above. Marston refers to a dancing courtier as a *"Fantasma"* (*SV In Lectores*, l. 21).

l. 60. *yet*] still, to contrast with *Inconstant*.
  Mercuries] Cf. Greene, *Wks.*, 2:225: "So that the inconstancie of such mutable Mercurialistes, and courtly copesmates as you bee, is growne to such a custom." Besides flightiness and deceit, Mercury was identified with the arts, with the ready wit, thus *witlesse*. Cf. Cotgrave, *Dict.* (1611): *"Mercuralizer,* . . . to be humorous, fantasticall, new-fangled." Discussions of professions usually treat Mercurists and Martialists together, the two

representing desirable aspects of the accomplished courtier (*tam Marti quam Mercurio*).

l. 63. *these last voyages*] Either the Cadiz expedition of 1596 or, which is more likely, the Islands expedition of 1597.

ll. 65-68. The Martialists are brave only in facing the dangers of the bawdy house, where they lose their hair through venereal disease. Cf. "to swear by one's beard"; see Partridge, *come.*

l. 73. (*for ought I know*)] With a quibble (?): "for debt I know."

l. 75. Musherom . . .] Proverbial, *EMO* 1. 2. 162-63: "these mushrompe gentlemen, / That shoot vp in a night to place, and worship"; Tilley M1319.

l. 77. *Siz'd eighteene pence a weeke*] See note to Ep. 22, l. 3. The average ordinary dinner cost six to nine pence.

l. 82. *caper*] with a pun on Lat. "goat" (i.e., transformed to).
    skipst] Dancing is "the skipping art" (*SV* 11. 27).

l. 83. Ma piu] Probably the general name for some Italian dance, or else the opening words of some well-known song. Musical for "still more," with *piu* indicating an intensification of the adjective it precedes.
    French-galliard] See note to Ep. 27, l. 4.
    measure] "Measures (when spoken of technically) were dances of a grave and dignified kind, performed at Court and at public entertainments at the Temple, Inns of Court, etc." (H. & S., 9:512).

l. 84. *cunning*] skill, with a pun on *coining*; cf. *Troil.* 4. 4. 104: "some with cunning gild their copper crowns." Cf. also Tilley M805: "Measure is treasure."

ll. 85-92. This may allude to Thomas Lodge, although definite assignment cannot be made. The "Phrigio" of *SV* 8. 122, "That wish'd he were his Mistres dog," is clearly Lodge, as Marston

quotes from Lodge (see Davenport's note). Moreover, Lodge
was unmarried as yet, and a "Batchelor" in the academic sense,
having been refused the M.A. for reasons that are unclear, perhaps for recusancy. *Laureat* may be a play on "Goldey," Daniel's
anagram for *Lodge*. Lodge lived at Lincoln's Inn for years after
1587 and could well have written for and participated in the
revels, although there is no record of his special dexterity as a
dancer. Also, he seems to have been recognized for his gay life
and debts, if we can, following Fleay (see McKerrow, ed. Nashe,
4:100), take Nashe's description as an allusion (1:170-71): "A
yoong Heyre or Cockney, that is his Mothers Darling, if hee
haue playde the waste-good at the Innes of the Court or about
London." Fungoso of *EMO* and Asotus of *Cyn. Rev.* were
thought by Fleay and Penniman (*Biog. Chron.* [1891], 1:363,
2:131; *War of Theatres* [1897], pp. 55-56, 85-89) to be Lodge.

   Del Phrygio may allude to the hero of a lost play. It is mentioned by Greene, who has the player Roberto in *Groatsworth*
say "I am as famous for Delphrigus, & the King of Fairies, as
euer was any of my time" (Bodley Head Quarto, p. 34); and by
Nashe, who speaks of gentlemen writers without whom players
could not have "antickt it vntill this time vp and downe the
Countrey with the King of Fairies, and dine euery day at the
pease porredge ordinary with *Delfrigus*" (Preface to Greene's
Menaphon, 3:324). Harbage (*Annals* [1964]) dates the play
ca. 1570, with the moral interludes. Lodge's biographers insist he
was no common player. The epithet may, on the other hand, be
suggested by the musical mode; cf. Florio, *Worlde* (1598):
"*Phrigio*, a melodie, a musicke or tune, wherein seemed to be a
diuine furie." It is thought that Lodge departed for Avignon
sometime in 1597.

   It should not go unnoticed that G. seems to hint at sexual
perversion, particularly homosexuality, "a kinde of harlatry,
not to be recited," according to Harvey (1:290). Note, e.g., in
the next lines: *proud*, said of an animal in heat, or swollen, perhaps joined with a pun on *Batch*elor; *Phrygio*, as in *SV*

3. 78-79: "Before some pedant-tutor, in his bed / Should use my frie, like Phrigian Ganimede"; *spade*, spayed; *mannerly*, (caught) "with or in the manner or act," legal terminology but involving a bawdy play based on Numbers 5:13, cf. *LLL* 1. 1. 199-201; *olde measures*, i.e., Chaucer's "old dance," but cf. Nashe, 2:310, where "measures" is flagellation and probably more; *bare-chind boyes*, etc. *Skialetheia*, we should not forget, was burned by the authorities and criticized severely by "W. I." for its extreme bawdry.

l. 87. *spade-beard*] spade-shaped beard, as a pointed or broad spade-blade. A fashionable cut; see McKerrow, ed., Nashe, 4:99, and H. & S., 10:189, who quote Greene: "broad pendant lyke a spade."

l. 88. *olde measures*] Cf. *SV* 11. 35-36: *"Yee gracious orbs, keepe the old measuring, / All's spoyld if once yee fall to capering."*

l. 89. *feete*] Pun (?), *feat*.

l. 91. *actiuitie*] A special term for feats of gymnastics, tumbling, and dancing, associated with the mummers' play, according to R. J. E. Tiddy, *Mummers' Play* (1923), pp. 86-87, who quotes: "Room, room, brave gallants, room! . . . /I come to show activity / This merry Christmas time. / Activity of youth, activity of age, / Was never such activity / Shown upon Christmas stage."

ll. 93-100. See headnote to this satire.

l. 94. *doings*] Bawdy (*OED* 1b). For dance sense cf. *H5* 3. 7. 96 (in dance context): "Doing is activity, and he will still be doing."

l. 97. Florus] I am unable to identify. Lyly? Florio? Francis Flower? Perhaps suggested by the Julius Florius to whom Horace dedicates Ep. 1. 3 and 2. 2, one of his young literary friends whom he encourages not to neglect philosophy.

l. 106. *common, popular*] Cf. *H5* 4. 1. 38-39: "art thou base, common and popular? *K. Hen.* I am a gentleman of a company."

l. 107. *various*] changeful, fickle.

ll. 108-9. Fabian, like a fashion, will become unpopular and must, with his pride, remove himself from the whimsical world's fancy or favor. Cf. Nashe, 2:95: "wrunge himselfe into the Worlds good opinion." Metaphorically, Fabian seems to be full (*proudly*), stuffed breeches, slightly soiled (*stale*=*urine*), and thus to be wrested off the world's wet (*humorous*) seat (con*ceit*). Cf. *SV* 8. 58-60: "He's but a spunge, and shortly needs must leese / His wrong got iuyce, when greatnes fist shal squeese / His liquor out."

l. 110. *wide breech*] large, usually baggy but occasionally bombasted, bellows-shaped hose, popular after 1595 (see Linthicum, p. 211).

    doublet strait] narrow, without stuffing, doublet; cf. Satire I. 98-99.

l. 111. *er't be long*] *long* plays on length in styles. Cf. Harington, *L. & E.*, p. 168: "Ere long Ill make thee sware they be too long."

l. 112. *French quarter slop*] wide or baggy breeches (not stuffed) of thigh length.

    gorbelly] The "great-bellied" doublet, stuffed, called the "Peascod" or "Dutch," fashionable in the seventies and eighties (see Linthicum, p. 198).

l. 113. *long stockt hose*] consisting of breeches and long tailored stockings sewn together to form a single garment, demodé after 1570s (see Cunnington, p. 114; Linthicum, p. 260).

    close Venetian] close-fitting breeches. "Three styles of Venetians were worn: the close fitting, 1560-70; the bombasted, 1570-95; the pleated or bellows-shaped mode to about 1620" (Linthicum, p. 211).

Commentary [189]

l. 115. *leases*] Pun (?), *laces.*

l. 116. *but thy lease of wit is out*] Cf. the many proverbs with the idea that "Bought wit is best" (Tilley W545, 546, 565, 567).

l. 117. *fond toyes*] Pun (?), *ties*, i.e., connections, relations.

l. 118. *pelfe*] Cf. Puttenham, *Arte*, ed. Willcock and Walker, p. 274: "pelfe is properly the scrappes or shreds of taylors and of skinners."

ll. 119-20. "Your trumpery will 'excuse you' to go to debtor's prison (called the Counter) before it (money) will bail you out." *dispence* is ironic, based on the legal sense of pardon, excuse, exempt from the law. Cf. Tilley C416: "To kiss the counter"; also, *counter = tally = tail* (?).

l. 121. *disparaged*] disgraced, but also under the influence of the sense "to degrade by marrying to one of inferior rank" (*OED* 1). Again, *toyes = ties.*

ll. 123-24. Damasippus is the bankrupt merchant and Stoic philosopher whom Stertinius advised to grow a beard (which, usually untrimmed, signified the philosopher) and whom Horace (*Sat.* 2. 3) ridicules and wishes a barber upon. There may be an allusion to another commonplace gibe of antiquity, that all philosophers were homosexual, here inverted; Juvenal 2. 14-15 may have provided the suggestion.

l. 126. *surquedry*] arrogance.

l. 132. *winde*] a) metaphoric for his pretensions or boasts; cf. Tilley W410; and b) to suggest the *wind* or turn of the dance; cf. *Orch.*, st. 69 (ed. Howard): "For everywhere he wantonly must range / And turn and wind with unexpected change."

Muses organs] a) mental faculties, "the organs of her fantasy" (*Wives* 5. 5. 49); b) her instrument, "winde instrument" (*podex*).

l. 134. *merry musicke*] "A new song is better to him than a new jacket, especially if bawdy, which he calls merry" (Earle, *Micro.*, ed. 1723, p. 53).

l. 136. *rig*] wanton, strumpet. Cf. the proverbs Tilley A392: "To dance attendance"; E522: "I will not dance to every Fool's pipe." Cf. Harington's epigram on Davies's *Orch.*, *L. & E.*, p. 242: "Vnto his Auditory thus he vaunts, / To make all Saints after his pipe to daunce."

l. 137. *Once in her dayes*] The expression can apply, syntactically, both to preceding and to following ideas. Cf. Nashe, 3:79: "once in our dayes there is none of vs but have plaid the ideots"; and Harvey, 1:18: "I must needes be euen with you once in my dayes."

ll. 139-40. Cf. Martial, 5. 66: "Saepe salutatus numquam prior ipse salutas. / sic erit; aeternum, Pontiliane, vale."

Satire IV

G.'s character portrait of the Jealous Husband draws on attitudes and images associated with sexual jealousy in the Elizabethan imagination. Typically the Jealous Husband is given to delusions, tortures himself and his wife, breaks out into fits of violent rage, is, by most accounts, himself guilty, and finally a fool. His overall features are those which characterize Suspicion, Envy, and Anger, and are symptomatic of the melancholy he suffers from. Jealousy itself is disease or plague, monster, beast (serpent, cat), fire, hell, poison, covered over with eyes, sleeping and walking on needles, and so on, as G. describes it. These attitudes were informed primarily by the Italian literature of jealousy rather than the native tradition, especially by the *novelle*, from which the commonplace Jealous Husband was carried over into the prose of Painter, Fenton, Whetstone, Pettie, and Greene, and by the several jealous characters of

Ariosto's *Orlando*, which influenced Spenser, and in particular
by Ariosto's complaint against jealousy (31. 1-6), which was
translated three times (by Gascoigne, *Master F. J.*; Florio, *First
Fruits;* and Harington). During the late nineties the Jealous
Husband became a stock "humour" character in the vogue ini-
tiated by *Merry Wives* (1597?), Chapman's *An Humorous Day's
Mirth* (1597), and *Every Man In His Humour*. In *EMI*—acted at
least as early as 20 Sept. 1598—Jonson refers to jealousy three
times as the "new disease," which may allude in part to this
satire. The fullest contemporary descriptions of jealousy are
Tell-Trothes New-Yeares Gift (1593), Robert Tofte's *Blazon of
Iealousie* (1615), and Burton's *Anatomy*, pt. 3, sec. 3. A useful
survey of relevant materials is R. J. Trienens's "The Green-Eyed
Monster" (Ph.D. diss., Northwestern University, 1951). The
commentary here, by no means exhaustive, should indicate that
the details in the satire are representative.

l. 3. Trebatio] Apparently suggested by the Roman jurist C.
Trebatius Testa, contemporary and friend of Cicero, to whom
Horace dedicated *Sat.* 2. 1. Perhaps, after *familiare* in the preceding line, influenced by Cicero's *ad Familiares*, 7. 6-22 of
which are to Trebatius. There is some connection between Trebatius and jealousy such as that suggested by Burton in a passage
on the causes of jealousy which I have not traced (*Anatomy*,
pt. 3, sec. 3, ed. Shillitoe, 3:306): "Impotency first, when a man
is not able of himself to perform those dues which he ought unto
his wife: for though he be an honest liver, hurt no man, yet
Trebatius the lawyer may make a question, *an suum cuique
tribuat*, whether he give every one their own," etc. The impotent
man, Burton goes on, is suspicious of his demanding wife when
she is quiet.

l. 6. *basts himselfe in his owne greace*] Cf. *WBPr*, ll. 487-88: "in
his owene grece I made him frye / For angre, and for verray
jalousye," and Tilley, C433. G. may think of the "oylie sweat of
jealousie," as in "His Parting from Her," l. 43 (ed. Gardner),

attr. by some to Donne. *Greace* hints at lust or indecency, as at *SV* 3. 79: "greasie Aretine," and thus anticipates the revelation in the end of the Jealous Husband's lust, as do a number of the details.

l. 7. *a squint askew . . .*] Proverbial, Tilley L498: "Love, being jealous, makes a good eye look asquint." Cf. *FQ* 1. 4. 24: "whally eies (the signe of gelosy)."

l. 8. *hornd-armory*] the cuckold's horns. With a pun (?) on *amour*, as at *Ant.* 4. 4. 1: "Eros! mine armour, Eros!"

ll. 9-16. Quoted in *England's Parnassus*, under "Iealousie," with some variations. Apparently an imitation of Ariosto's poem which begins "Sì come a primavera è dato il verno, / così compagna è Gelosia d'Amore, / lui in paradiso è lei nata in inferno," etc. (Capitoli 25, *Opere Minore* [Milan, (1954)], pp. 217-18).

l. 10. ranke] in excess, regarding amount or smell; used to suggest lasciviousness.

l. 11. tares] Pun, *teares*; cf. Nashe, 2:183: "the heauie penance my poore Teares here haue endured to turne them cleane vnto tares."

l. 12. dogged] envious, as is common in Eliz. English.

l. 13. glowing tong] Pun, *tongue*, and thus "lying tongue"; cf. the proverbial "blistered tongue" of "Report" (Tilley R84).

ll. 18-19. *playing fast and loose / With his wiues arme*] i.e., constantly taking his wife's arm, losing it, and taking it again. *Fast and loose* was a cheating game in which a leather belt was folded up, the victim having to thrust a skewer through the middle. The belt was "fast" or "loose" at the wish of the holder, who had only to move the ends to change the middle. Unlike other instances, where it merely means "cheating" (see Tilley P401), the metaphor here is quite graphic and useful. Reginald Scot gives two forms of the game in *Discoverie of Witchcraft* (Carbondale, 1964), pp. 281 ff.

ll. 22-23. *he on her gowne / Sits*] Cf. the proverbial "to sit on one's skirts," meaning to annoy, injure, and perhaps deal heavily with. Explained in Puttenham, *Arte,* ed. Willcock and Walker, p. 302.

l. 24. *giue him the start*] i.e., presumably, "put distance between them," as in racing. Cf. Tilley S828. For possible bawdy, cf. *Errors* 2. 1. 30: "How if your husband start some other where?"

l. 26. *selfe-consuming care*] Proverbial; *FQ* 2. 7. 25: "selfe-consuming care"; *Errors* 2. 1. 102: "Self-harming jealousy!"

l. 27. *male-kind sparrow*] i.e., cock-sparrow, associated with lechery. This incident is reminiscent of those in the medieval *Laustic,* a lay by Marie de France, and *The Owl and the Nightingale,* in which jealous husbands wreak their spite on nightingales which have comforted their wives.

l. 28. *fled*] an occasional past form of *fly.*

ll. 31-32. Based on the frequent conceit of the lover ensnared by the lady's hair. Cf. Du Bartas, in Thos. Tuke, *A Treatise against Paint[i]ng* (1616, B2^v): "What should I doe with such a wanton wife, / Which night and day would cruciate my life / With Ieloux pangs / sith euery way shee sets / Her borrowed snares, not her own haires, for nets, / To catch her cuckows with aloof, light attires," etc. The net is either the hair itself or the caul, a close-fitting net of gold or silver. *Flye,* like the sparrow, is a symbol of lechery.

l. 33. *note*] melody.

l. 34. *ruder*] i.e., brutal, the comparative for intensification.

l. 37. *Busie*] meddling or busybodying.
     blind-man-hob] a variation of the game "Hobman's Blind," presumably "Blind-man's-buff," in which one player is blindfolded and tries to catch and identify any of the others.

l. 39. Seuerus] Intended to suggest the Roman emperor Alexan-

der Severus (222-235) who for Eliz. moralists was the type of the
strict and upright magistrate intent on harsh measures against
lax morals. See the account of the "Severus legend" and references in J. W. Lever's introduction to the New Arden *Measure
for Measure*, pp. xliv-li.

    frigs] stirs, moves about restlessly.

l. 40. *To see, and not to see his martirdome*] Always the Jealous
Man's enigma; cf., e.g., Earle, *Micro.*, ed. 1733, "A suspicious
or jealous Man," p. 163; Donne, "The Storme," ll. 49-50, with
which Milgate (ed., *Satires*, p. 205) compares Paradox 6: "that
ridling humour of Jealousie, which seekes and would not finde,
which requires and repents his knowledge," and (from Grierson), Ovid, *Amores* 2. 2. 51-60: e.g., "Verderit ipse licet, credat
tamen ipse neganti." *martirdome* was a favorite term for the
torment of jealousy.

ll. 41-42. Based on a medical commonplace, and almost always
present in accounts of jealousy. Cf., e.g., *Arcadia* (1593), bk. 2
(ed. 1922, 2:9); Greene, *Vision, Wks.*, ed. Grosart, 12:257; and
Harington, trans., *Orlando*, ed. Hough, 32. 102 (of Brada-
mante): "Fell jealousie bard her of all delight, / Her stomacke so
distempring, and her tast, / She tooke no pleasure of that sweet
repast."

l. 41. disease] a) vexation, b) sickness.
    distast] render distasteful.

l. 46. *figgent jack*] fidgety or restless (first entry in *OED*) knave
or busybody. Possibly to suggest the drinking vessel ("black
jack") and/or the "Jack-o'-the-Green" (on which see *OED Jack
sb*[1]), both of which images G. has in mind throughout this passage.

ll. 47-48. Windmills were noisy and often unsteady, and became
proverbial as a metaphor for harebrained projects. Cf. *Epic.*
5. 3. 61-63: "My very house turnes round with the tumult! I

dwell in a windmill!" Tilley W455: "He has windmills in his head."

l. 48. *whirligigge*] See note to l. 49. Nashe, 1:86: "a whirlegig in his braine."

l. 49. *barly-breake*] A game much like Prisoners' Base in which two players who occupy a prescribed area (called "Hell") try to capture others who run through from opposite ends, with those captured replacing or reinforcing them in the center. Cf. *Changeling* 5. 3. 164-65 (ed. Bullen): "Yes, and the while I coupled with your mate / At barley-break now we are left in hell"; Suckling (ed. Thompson [1910], p. 20): "Love, Reason, Hate did once bespeak / Three mates to play at barley-break."

daunce the Irish hay] The *hay* was "a country dance, having a winding or serpentine nature, or being of the nature of a reel" (*OED*). "To dance the hay became a proverbial expression signifying to twist about or wind in and out without making any advance" (Chappell's *Orchesography* [1859], in R. Davis's note to *LLL* 5. 1. 149, New Arden). Cf. Dekker, *Strange Horse-Race* (1613), *Wks.*, ed. Grosart, 3:365; Day, *Law Tricks* (1608), 4. 2., ed. Bullen, p. 179: "a company of bottlenos'd devils dauncing the Irish hay." Drunkenness is important to the metaphor.

l. 50. *Ciuill*] With the same irony found in "civil butchery" (*1H4* 1. 1. 13) and "civil monster" (*Oth.* 4. 1. 64).

Centaures fray] Alluding to the battle between the drunken Centaurs and the Lapithae which took place at the marriage of Pirithous and Hippodamia; see Ovid, *Met.* 13. 210 ff.

l. 51. Cf. Tilley M96: "An envious man grows lean."

l. 52. *logger-head*] i.e., with a head out of proportion to the body (first entry in this sense in *OED*), implying sluggishness. Note Florio, *Montaigne*, ed. J. I. M. Stewart (New York, 1933), pp. 786-87: "The drowsie beast [jealousy] rouzed himselfe and suddenly started up. *One hath often the worst bargaines at the hands of such sluggish logger-heads.*"

ll. 53-56. Descriptions of jealousy almost invariably contain this allusion to Argus's futile eyes; cf., e.g., *MerT*, ll. 2111-14; *WBPr*, ll. 357-61; *FQ* 3. 9. 7; Daniel, *Rosamond*, l. 500. Allegorical figures of Suspicion present him with eyes all over; see various commentators to *1H4* 5. 2. 8: "Suspicion all our lives shall be stuck full of eyes"; and cf. Tilley S1017, E254, as well as L506: "Love is blind."

l. 57. *Gulfe-brested*] i.e., having a breast as deep as a gulf. Suggesting a large-breasted preying animal, like the cat of the next line, and one with a voracious appetite (*OED Gulf* 3b). *Lucrece*, l. 557, in the description of a vulture which follows immediately that of a cat, relies on the sense of whirlpool: "A swallowing gulf that even in plenty wanteth." Note also *OED Breast* 5: "the repository of consciousness, designs, and secrets."
    profound] implying crafty; see note to Ep. 53, l. 6.

l. 58. *Cat-footed*] The "green-ey'd monster" of *Oth.* is basically a cat-and-mouse image. Cf. also the similar image in *Luc.*, l. 554, with its "foul night-waking cat," and F. T. Prince's note (New Arden).

l. 59. *Porpentine backed . . .*] The porcupine; cf. Gascoigne, *Master F. J., Wks.*, ed. Cunliffe (1907), 1:424, where the jealous Ferdinando sleeps on "Porpentine quilles"; and Tilley T239: "To sit upon thornes."

l. 60. Is it not pitty such a beast wants hornes?] From *Astrophel* 78 (ed. Ringler, 1962) which provides other suggestions:
        Oh HOW the pleasant aires of true love be
            Infected by those vapours, which arise
            From out that noysome gulf, which gaping lies
            Between the jaws of hellish Jealousie.
        A monster, other's harme, self-miserie,
            Beautie's plague, Virtue's scourge, succour of lies;
            Who his owne joy to his owne hurt applies,
            And onely cherish doth with injurie;

> Who since he hath, by Nature's special grace,
>> So piercing pawes as spoil when they embrace,
>> So nimble feet as stirre still, though on thornes:
> So manie eyes ay seeking their owne woe,
>> So ample ears as never good newes know:
> Is it not evill that such a Devil wants hornes?

The line occurs in *England's Parnassus*, under "Iealousy," with credit to Sidney; Withers gives a similar expression in Sat. 7, "Iealousie," *Abuses Stript*, in *Juvenilia* (Manchester, 1871), pt. 1, p. 108: *"And pitty 'twere they had horned him, / Were't not a greater pittie so to sinne."* Cf. also *Titus* 2. 3. 71: " 'Tis pity they should take him for a stag."

l. 62. *Possesse mens thoughts . . .*] Cf. *Orlando*, trans. Harington, ed. Hough, 31. 6: "Jealousy is a plague that quickly doth infect / All lovers hearts, and doth possesse their thought." For *timpanize* see note to *Sat. Pre.* 96, and cf. *FQ* 3. 10. 18: "his hart with gealosy did swell."

l. 64. *A Cuckow sing in* Iune] "The cuckoo . . . Mocks married men" (*LLL* 5. 2. 894-95); Tilley A309: "In April the cuckoo can sing her song by rote; in June, out of tune, she cannot sing a note."

l. 65. *whurries*] variation of whirry, to move rapidly, with great commotion (*OED*).

ll. 66-67. *Each hole that makes an inmate of a mouse . . .*] Like the Avaricious Man, the Jealous Man traditionally looks about for the hidden mouse. Cf. Withers, "Iealousie," *Abuses Stript*, p. 108; and the "mouse-hunt" in *Rom.* 4. 4. 11-13. *Mouse* was common as a term of endearment. For the bawdy of *hole* see Partridge. *inmate*, lodger or foreigner, with a suggestion of contempt.

l. 70. *Familiar with his wife*] Cf. *Oth.* 1. 3. 386-90: "*Iago*. . . . Let's see: / After some time, to abuse Othello's ear, / That he is too familiar with his wife."

l. 72. *staring, swearing*] The two words frequently occur in conjunction, with *staring*, according to McKerrow (ed. Nashe, 4:100), meaning little more than to swagger, to behave in an overbearing and offensive manner. See Nashe, 1:170; 2:220; *Wives* 5. 5. 153; and Greene, *Wks.*, ed. Grosart, 11:11. Severus's activities at home resemble those of the swaggerer in the bawdy house.

l. 74. Harry Peasecod] Not met with elsewhere, although Nashe, 3:129, has "Cod-pisse Kinko" and *MND* 3. 1. 173, "Master Peasecod." Fools wore remarkable codpieces.

l. 75. *drunken captaine*] Alluding to the boisterers and swaggerers, bogus "Captains" of the London streets, taverns, and brothels. Cf. *2H4* 2. 4. 130 ff.

    ramping] fierce and unrestrained; cf. *John* 3. 1. 122: "A ramping fool, to brag, and stamp, and swear."

l. 76. *blew-coate*] Servants wore liveries of blue.

ll. 77-80. Traditional as a figure for Wrath. Cf. Lodge, *Wits Miserie* (1596), *Wks.*, 4:82: "Wrath by the schoolemen . . . is compared to a burning fever, which as it hath two accidents . . . continuall heat, and great thirst; so a wrathfull man vpon euery froward word in gesture, words, and lookes, is drawne into a great heat, and afterward is seased with a great thirst of revenge." The disease is dropsie. G.'s expression may have come from Lodge (*Wounds*, 3:322): "fowle ambitious thoughts, / That fires mens harts and makes them thirst for Euel."

ll. 77-78. *fire / Mens most discreetest tempers*] i.e., produce a *hot temper* through an excess of choler (hot and dry). A man's discretion depended upon the mixture (or *temper*) of the four humors.

l. 80. *carouse bolles of poyson*] Cf. Satire I. 39-42, and see note.

ll. 81-end. This final exposure of the Jealous Man as himself guilty has place in accounts of jealousy, as well as, in a more general form, in the proverbial lore of England. Withers, e.g., thus concludes his satire on jealousy (*Abuses Stript*, p. 112): "For none's so iealous I durst pawn my life, / As he that hath defil'd another's wife." Both Tofte and Burton quote these lines, adding two: "And for that he himself hath gone astray, / He straight way thinks his wife will tread that way" (*Blazon of Iealousie* [1615], ed. H. M. Henderson [Ph.D. diss., University of North Carolina, 1956], p. 23; *Anatomy*, pt. 3, sec. 3, ed. Shillitoe, 3:312). Donne has in "The Anagram," l. 38 (ed. Gardner), "thy past sinnes have taught thee jealousie!" For proverbs of the sort "mala mens, malus animus," see Tilley D432, F107, F117.

ll. 83-84. Quoted in *England's Parnassus*, under "Suspition," and in Bodenham's *Belvedére*, under "Of Iealousie."

ll. 85-86. Alluding to *Ars Amatoria*. *Practice* and *Theoric* (= *Theoretical*) frequently were used as divisions of sciences; cf. Hoby's *Theorique and Practice of Warre* (1597), and Barret's *Theorike and Practice of Modern Warres* (1598). *Practice* here has the added derogatory sense of craft or machination.

l. 88. Aretines *aduenturous wandring whore*] See note to *Sat. Pre.* 54.

l. 91. *louing hate*] Jealousy was often recognized as a product of extreme love. Cf., e.g., *FQ* 3. 10. 22: "loves extremity, / That is the father of fowle gealosy."

l. 92. *women so insaciate?*] Possibly influenced by the opening line of Drayton's *Mortimeriados*, 1596: "Pale Jealousy, child of insatiate love"; Drayton's passage is quoted in Tofte, *Blazon* (ed. Henderson, p. 12), where it is attributed to Thos. Watson; in Burton, *Anatomy*, pt. 3, sec. 3 (ed. Shillitoe, 3:305); and in *England's Parnassus*, under "Iealousie."

l. 93. *shifts*] tricks, evasions, with possible quibble on changes of clothing.

l. 95. *he hath been naught himselfe*] Along with the other causes for jealousy among men, Burton includes that "they have beene formerly naught themselves" (*Anatomy*, pt. 3, sec. 3 [ed. Shillitoe], 3:306).

l. 97. *a Maxim generall rule*] Apparently tautological, perhaps requiring punctuation. Cf. Harvey, 2:260: "the wise man . . . might easily haue bene entreated, to haue set it downe for a souerain Maxim, or generall rule; *Asinorum plena sunt omnia.*"

Satire V

Here the satirist describes the various forms of vanity to be met in the teeming city streets of London. Enticed from the quiet meditation of his study into the noisy press of Vanity Fair, he is outraged by the grotesque apes that parade in many shapes before him—Fashion-monger, Swaggering Soldiers, Malcontent, Parasite, Inns of Court Man, Fantastic, Gallant, Lying Chapman, Prostitute, and Crew of Rowdies—all types familiar in contemporary satire. In the end he returns disgusted to the peace of his study, determined never again to venture forth.

For the structural device of the city walk, the satire is partly indebted to Horace, 1. 10, "Ibam forte Via Sacra," but for other and more obvious aspects it is indebted to Juvenal, 3, with its framing device in praise of the country and its attack on the evils of Rome, including the noise, dangers, parasites, etc. Satirists have always been attracted to crowded·scenes, and used some such means to arrange and point out details. More immediately, the satire seems to have been inspired by Donne's first (1593?), the beginning of which, as Alden first noted (*Rise of Formal Satire*, p. 153), G. imitates closely (ed. Milgate):

> Away thou fondling motley humorist,
> Leave mee, and in this standing woodden chest,
> Consorted with these few bookes, let me lye

> In prison, and here be coffin'd, when I dye;
> Here are Gods conduits, grave Divines; and here
> Natures Secretary, the Philosopher;
> And jolly Statesmen, which teach how to tie
> The sinewes of a cities mistique bodie;
> Here gathering Chroniclers, and by them stand
> Giddie fantastique Poets of each land.
> Shall I leave all this constant company,
> And follow headlong, wild uncertaine thee? Etc.

l. 9. *chest*] i.e., chamber. *Chest* often meant "coffin," hence "en-coffin'd."

l. 11. *freè-booting abroad purchase offence*] Punning on *free-boot*, to plunder, said esp. of pirates. *purchase* implies illegally; cf. *H5* 3. 2. 40-41: "They will steal anything and call it purchase"; Nashe, 3:180: "Voiages of purchase."

l. 12. *scandale*] a) disgrace, b) disturb; cf. Cotgrave, *Dict.* (1611), "*Scandale* . . . sturre, tumult." Cf. Lat. *scandalum*, stumbling-stone. Suggested by the common Eliz. association of *scandale* and *offence*, after Romans 9:31-33 and 1 Peter 2:8. For another example see Lodge, *Wits Miserie, Wks.*, 4:24.

    discontents] With the added sense of "the discontented" or "malcontents," as at *1H4* 5. 1. 76. The author of *I Parnassus* (1598/99?) may have this satire in mind (and Donne's) when he has Stupido say (3, ll. 326-29): "And now not hauing anie serious business to goe aboute, leaste the bad disposed people should corrupte and contaminate my pure thoughtes by there vngodlie conversations, I am goinge abroad."

l. 13. *diuiner spirits*] Elizs. used the comparative in such contexts; cf. Lodge, *Fig, Wks.*, 3:43: "Diviner *Plato.*"

l. 14. *admire the world inherits*] *admire*, admiration (*OED sb*); *inherits* contrasts with *purchase* (l. 11): "to obtain otherwise than by inheritance" (*OED* 5).

l. 15. Stagarite] Aristotle, from his being born at Stagira.

l. 22. *Get of my selfe a glorious victory*] Plato, *Leges*, 1. 626E: "Self-conquest is the first and finest of all victories." *Of* is frequent for *over*.

l. 23. *we delight in change*] Proverbial (Tilley C229). Cf., esp. along with what follows below, the lines by Sir William Cornwallis the essayist in a verse letter in Bodleian MS. *Tanner 306* addressed "To my ever to be respeckted freand Mr John Done Secretary to my Lorde Keeper," quoted by Milgate, ed., *Satires*, p. 216; (printed in full by Grierson, ed., *Donne*, 2:171-72): "If then for change, of howers you seem careles / Agree wth me to loose them at the playes" (ll. 15-16).

l. 24. *my study . . . m'Exchange*] Cf. Dekker, *Gull's Hornbook*, ed. 1812, p. 131: "The theater is your Poet's Royal Exchange."

l. 26. Fitzherbert, Plowden, Brooke, *and* Dier] All famous jurists and authors of textbooks the Common Lawyer would use. For Fitzherbert, Brooke, and Dier, see note to Ep. 40, l. 2. Edmund Plowden (1518-85), noted for his honesty, diligence as a student of law, and esp. for *Les comentaries, ou les reportes de Edmunde Plowden* (1571), which ranked with Littleton's *Tenures* in importance as a text.

l. 27. *dispose*] temperament, perhaps "determined attitude"; cf. *Troil.* 2. 3. 159.

l. 30. Patheticke Spaniards *Tragedies*] i.e., Seneca, born at Corduba, Spain. *Patheticke*, emotionally moving in a general sense.

l. 32. *speaking Painter*] i.e., poet; see note to *Sat. Pre.* 55.

   yeelds] grants, bestows. G. probably has no particular poet in mind, or poem, but it should be noted that Marlowe's "Passionate Shepherd to his Love" uses the same rime in the opening stanza: "That valleys, groves, hills, and fields / Woods or steepy mountain yields."

l. 35. *sun-burnt*] a) ill-favored (?), sun-burn being considered a blemish; b) "addled" (?).

case] a) bookcase or container, which becomes figurative for the walls of the study; cf. *East. Hoe* 5. 3. 19: "My Case . . . is stone walles"; b) law-case or situation (plot).

l. 36. *study . . .*] i.e., a) chamber, b) application to learning. With the idea cf. Donne, "The Good-morrow," l. 11 (ed. Gardner): "And makes a little roome, an every where."

l. 41. *hotch-potch*] or "hodge-podge," a confused mixture; in vogue in contexts referring to a mixture of languages, primarily what G. has in mind. Cf., e.g., E. K.'s Dedicatory Epistle to *Shep. Cal.*: "so how they have made our English tongue a gallimaufray or hadgepodge of al other speeches"; and Guazzo, *Civile Conv.*, ed. 1925, 1:145. The word is either of legal origin (perhaps suggested by *Witnes* here) or of culinary, on which note *III Parnassus* 4. 2. 1544 ff., with Leishman's note.

l. 42. *Black-saunts*] i.e., "Black sanctus," a burlesque hymn or anthem; "rough music" (*OED*).

seuerall voyces] different voices, with a quibble on the musical *voice*. Cf. *Epic.* 2. 6. 36-37: "it will be an excellent *comoedy* of affliction, so many seuerall noyses." The city's discord contrasts with the "mistick harmony" of the study.

l. 44. Barbary] General name for N. Africa along the Mediterranean, a source of trade and home base of pirates, by this time synonymous with barbarity. G. is still thinking of language mixtures as well as of noise generally.

l. 49. *Car-men combat for the way*] Cf. *EMI* 3. 2. 67-69: "[we'll go] serue out the remnant of our daies in *Thames*-street, or at *Custome*-house key, in a ciuill warre, against the car-men." On the violence which often resulted from attempts to get passage see H. & S., 9:371n.

l. 52. *Ale-knight*] a votary of the ale-house, a tippler.

ll. 53-58. In these lines G. has in mind the jigs at the ends of plays, participated in by the populace and notorious for their disorder. Baskervill (*Elizabethan Jig*, p. 116) quotes from "An Order for suppressinge of Jigges att the ende of Playes" of 1 Oct. 1612 that "divers cutt-purses and other lewde and ill disposed persons in greate multitudes doe resorte thither at th'end of euerye playe many tymes causinge tumultes and outrages where-bye His Majesties peace is often broke and much mischiefe like to ensue therby." Cf. Davies's *In Cosmum 17* (ed. Howard): "For as we see at all the play house doores, / When ended is the play, the daunce, and song, / A thousand townsmen, gentlemen, and whores, / Porters and seruingmen togither throng," etc. The theater district was famous for its noise; see *Epic.* 4. 5. 15.

ll. 53-54. *slaues / Engarlanded*] i.e., surrounded or "crowned," as if waiting for their sacrificial slaughter.

l. 56. Kemps *Iigge, or the* Burgonians *tragedy*] There were many ballads about Kemp's exploits, including "Kemp's Newe Jygge betwixt a souldiour and a Miser and Sym the clown," ent. S.R. 21 Oct. 1595, although he himself complained, in *Nine Daies Wonder* (1600), D2ᵛ, Bodley Head Quarto, p. 28, that he was not responsible for them. Their popularity is also attested to by references in *SV* 11. 31 (which includes mention of "the *Burgonians* ward," l. 63) and *III Parnassus* 4. 4. 1796 ff. See also Baskervill, *Elizabethan Jig*, pp. 109-10, and passim.

"*Burgonians* tragedy" alludes to some ballad of immediate topical interest. Among the executions for July 1598, Stow records the following (*Annales* [1605], p. 1308): "*Iohn Barrose* a *Burgonian* by nation, and a Fensor by Profession, that lately was come ouer and had chalenged all the Fencers of England, was hanged without Ludgate, for killing of an officer of the Citie which had arrested him for debt." For other references see *SV* 11. 63; Marston, *Jacke Drum* II (*Plays*, ed. Wood, 3:200); *EMI* 4. 4. 17; Dekker, *Satiromastix*, preface (ed. Bowers, 1:309).

l. 57. *in good time*] *à la bonne heure*, with a quibble on musical time. Cf. *Wives* 1. 3. 23-25: "his thefts were too open; his filching was like an unskillful singer; he kept not time."

nipt a bong] cut a purse (*bung*). Cf. the relevant "One ill condition mars all the good" (Tilley C585, and the similar S308, W240).

l. 61. *her still patience choakt by vanitie*] i.e., "her silent patience (itself) silenced by vanity"; she is forced to speak out. Patience characteristically "chokes" anger, grief, etc. Cf. Greene, *Wks.*, 12:261: "chokt Fortune with patience." With a probable play on Lat. *vanitas*, emptiness: to choke with emptiness.

l. 68. *Antickes*] grotesque images; cf. Florio, *Worlde* (1598): "*Grottesca*, a kind of rugged unpolished painters work, anticke work."

walke in Poules] See note to Ep. 22, l. 7.

l. 71. Tabraca] A city of Numidia on the coast of the Mediterranean, now Tabarca. Probably suggested by Juvenal 10. 194.

l. 72. *wrie necke*] A common affectation; cf. Harvey, 1:84; Nashe, 1:361; Hall *Vd* 4. 2. 85-89, quoted below at note to l. 132.

l. 74. *Spanish shrugge*] See note to Satire III. 6.

l. 75. *Cad'z-beard*] See Ep. 53, l. 8 with note, and Satire III. 65.

l. 77. *gold-dawbed sutes*] i.e., ornamented ("smeared") with gold lace; on which see Linthicum, pp. 133 ff., and cf. *CS* The Authour in prayse, l. 21.

l. 78. Talbots, Percies, Montacutes] Alluding to the stage presences of representatives of these individuals or families noted for their ferocity, and thus ironic. Of Talbot, note *1H6* 2. 3. 15 ff.: "Is this the scourge of France? / Is this the Talbot so much feared abroad," etc.; E. K.'s note to *Shep. Cal.*, "June"; and Hall's *Chronicle*, Hen. VI, an. 31 (ed. 1809), p. 230. Of

Montacute, i.e., Marquesse Montague, cf. *3H6*, esp. 5. 7. 10. Robert Gittings, *Shakespeare's Rival* (London, 1960), pp. 18-19, takes this passage to allude to Essex (with his Cadiz beard) and the young earls in his circle, Southampton (whose mother was a Montague), Rutland, and Bedford, and, by inference, to a connection between Shakespeare and the group.

ll. 81-82. *charge . . . wil duck*] This passage seems to carry a number of scatological equivoques. *charge,* privy; cf. *2H4* 2. 4. 51: "to venture upon the charged chambers bravely"; *LLL* 5. 1. 69-70 (a difficult phrase) "charge-house"; *Ham.* 5. 2. 43; and for the sense *duty,* cf. Fr. *devoirs, luck,* cf. Tilley L581: "Shitten luck is good luck"; and Grosse, *Classical Dict. of the Vulgar Tongue* (1823), "Luck, or Good Luck. To tread in a sir-reverence." *false fire* (discharge of blanks), flatulence.

   duck, i.e., bow, alludes to the fashionable elaborate salutations, as at l. 142. Cf. R. Niccolls, in *Londons Artillery* (1616): "the souldiers for their armes and furniture, both for seruice and shew, were well and rightly appointed, imitating the old Romans, in their garnish of feathers, which, as it is a sight braue and terrible to the enimie so it is goodly and delightful to friends" (in H. & S., 10:240).

l. 84. *the vnfrequented Theater*] The Theatre was closed on 28 July 1597; see Chambers, *Elizabethan Stage,* 2:397-98, who cites this passage as evidence that it was unoccupied in 1598.

l. 86. *Suited to those blacke fancies . . .*] See Babb, *Elizabethan Malady* (East Lansing, 1951), pp. 29 ff., who discusses at length the effect of blackness, from black bile, on the mind and sensibilities of the Malcontent; he quotes Du Laurens: The melancholy humor "tainteth and brandeth with blackenes [the animal spirit], which passing from the braine to the eye, and from the eye to the braine backe againe, is able to moue these blacke sights, and set them vncessantly before the minde," etc. *Suited,* a) appropriate, b) quibbling on the characteristic black suit.

ll. 86-87. *intrude, / Vpon possession*] This may, when joined with a common quibble on legal *suit*, allude to the current litigation over the lease of the Theatre, on which see Chambers, *Elizabethan Stage*, 2:398-99. Note *OED Intrude* 3, which quotes Coke: "He that entreth vpon any of the Kings Demesnes, and taketh the profits, is said to Intrude vpon the Kings possession."

l. 88. *ieast*] a) jester, who wore motley, b) romantic tale (on stage), rather than tragedy (?); cf. *OED Gest sb*^{1} 2.

ll. 89-94. The satirist's adversarius speaks the passages "what he? . . . you iest I see," and "A Papist?"

l. 95. *discarded intelligencer*] dismissed political agent or spy.

ll. 96-100. This attack is intended, it seems, against the rowdy's pugnacity as evidenced by his dress, and as such is typical with satirists. Cf. Lodge's description of the "incarnate devil" Lying, *Wits Miserie* (1596), *Wks.*, 4:41: "Who is this with the Spanish hat, the Italian ruffe, the French doublet, the Muffes cloak, the Toledo rapier, the Germane hose, the English stocking, & the Flemish shoe? Forsooth a sonne of MAMMONS that hath of long time ben a trauailer, his name is LYING, a Deuill at your Commandement." As Leishman shows (ed., *Parnassus*, p. 48), Rowlands includes Lodge's passage almost verbatim in *Letting* (1600), *Wks.*, ed. 1880, 1:32.

l. 96. *like to a king* Arthurs *fencer*] Probably a common expression; cf. Harington, *L. & E.*, p. 202: "Raynsford, a Knight, fit to haue seru'd King *Arthur*."

l. 97. *buffe*] the hard-wearing leather made of ox-hide, used by military men and sergeants. Cf. *Errors* 4. 2. 36: "A wolf, nay, worse; a fellow all in buff."

l. 98. *muffe*] "A depreciative term for a German or Swiss; sometimes loosely applied to foreigners" (*OED*). Florio, *Worlde* (1598): "*Stiticozzi*, swearing or swaggering muffs or dutchmen."

l. 99. *furrd sattin cloake*] perhaps the fashionable full-sleeved waist-length garment called the "Dutch cloak" (see Linthicum, p. 195).

l. 100. *Meddle not with him, hee's a shrewd fellow*] i.e., do not *mix* or fight with him; a variation of the "Meddle" proverbs, such as "Meddle with your match" (Tilley M747), drawing on the sense "equal, match" of *fellow. shrewd,* i.e., shrewish, malicious.

ll. 103-19. G. now turns to the Flatterer of Parasite type. As the parallels should indicate, he draws largely from Lodge's *Wits Miserie* (1596), *Wks.,* 4:27-29. Though the description is general and somewhat typical, G. has someone in mind, Shakespeare or Nashe, it would seem, probably the latter, though the evidence is insubstantial. Nashe suffered from the system of patronage, "prostituted his pen," and had some doings with the Earl of Southampton, to whom he dedicated *Choice of Valentines,* his bawdy poem. The reference to "Gue" would be relevant, if Harvey is indeed the Gue of Ep. 11 (see the note). Moreover, we would be expected to take *Don Pacolet* as a passing allusion to Nashe's poem, since Pacolet was the dwarf in the old French romance of *Valentyne and Orson.* See note to Ep. 24 for other generalizations and references which could support the assignment. Much of the evidence, it should be admitted, might hold as well for Shakespeare.

l. 103. *my lord and foole*] Cf. Overbury, *Char.,* ed. Paylor (1936), p. 8: "A Flatterer is *the shadow of a foole.* . . . Hee will play any part upon his countenance, and where hee cannot be admitted for a counseller, hee will serve as foole"; Dekker, *Gull's Hornbook,* ed. 1812, p. 22, whose Flatterer is a fool who "for the excellency of his fooling [is] admitted both to ride in coach with [his lord], and to lie at his very feet on a trucle-bed."

l. 104. *Gue*] On this blind performing baboon see Ep. 11, and note.

Commentary [209]

l. 106. *can make choyce of*] is able to choose. Alluding to *Choice of Valentines* (?).

l. 108. *wit of waxe*] a) i.e., without flaw, perfect; cf. *Rom.* 1. 3. 77; Tilley D553; b) i.e., servile in imitation, impressionable (*OED* 2b).

   fresh as a rose] By this time a stale comparison; proverbial (Tilley R176).

l. 109. *He playes well . . .*] Cf. Overbury, *Char.*, ed. Paylor (1936), p. 55: "If his Patron be given to musicke, hee opens his choppes, and *sings*, or with a wry necke falles to tuning his instrument."

l. 110. *soothes . . . vp*] encourages, approves of; *up* is emphatic. With this and below cf. Lodge, *Fig, Sat.* 1 (1595), *Wks.*, 3:9: "He is a gallant fit to serue my Lord / Which claws, and sooths him vp, at euerie word; / That cries, when his lame poesie he heares, / T'is rare (my Lord) t'will passe the nicest eares." And *Wits Miserie*, 4:26 (of Adulation): "If he meet with a wealthy yong heaire worth the clawing, O rare cries he, doo hee neuer so filthily." See also Ep. 68, with note. The *soothe* here, along with the *laugh* of l. 115, below, may suggest *South*ampton, Wriothesley (*ris*).

l. 112. Elderton *would not haue fathered*] Again, cf. *Wits Miserie, Wks.*, 4:16: "but turne him loose to write any Poeme, God amercie on the soul of his numbers: . . . yea ELDERTONS nose would grin at them if they should but.equall the worst of his Ballads." References to the famous ballad-maker (d. 1592?), noted for his inebriety, red nose, and licentious ballads, are frequent. On Elderton see H. E. Rollins, *SP* 17 (1920): 199-245, esp. p. 225. The play on the name occurs in Nashe, 1:280: "father Elderton." Alluding to *son*nets (?).

l. 114. *The story of* Don Pacolet *and his horse*] i.e., a nonsensical story, one poorly told and probably in bad taste. Ap-

parently a variation of the "tale of a roasted horse," on which see
Ep. 21, and Tilley T44. Pacolet, in *Valentyne and Orson* (trans.
from Fr. by H. Watson, 1565?), creates a wooden horse capable
of conveying him instantly to any desired place. Sidney uses
"*Pacolets* horse" in his description of dramatic actions that fail to
honor the unity of place (*Apology*, ed. Smith, 1:198). And
Overbury, in his criticism of the poor playwright (*Char.*, ed.
Paylor [1936], p. 77), states that "the itch of bestriding the
Presse, or getting up on this wodden Pacolet, hath defil'd more
innocent paper, then ever did Laxative Physicke." Some such association may be present here (quibble, *discourse*), and there
may be a play on the woman's *placket*. A lost anon. play *Valen-
tine and Orson* was ent. S.R. 1595, and Henslowe made
payment for another on 19 July 1598 to Hathaway and Munday.
Cf. *Wits Miserie, Wks.*, 4:26, 28: "he hath all the Sonnets and
wanton rimes the world of wit can offer him"; his "discourse is
. . . too often sauced with Hiperboles and lies."

l. 115. . . . *and iest*] The compositor may have missed "can"
(and perhaps an additional word), which would be appropriate
syntactically and metrically.

l. 116. Simile non plus *the best*] a) comparison extraordinary,
non plus ultra, b) one most perplexing, embarrassing, causing a
state of *non plus*. With the general sense, cf. Harvey, 2:212:
"Vncouth Similes, daintie monsters of Nature"; *EMO* Ind.,
ll. 26, 363: "absurd simile's," "adult'rate simile's"; 2. 1. 10:
"how he confounds with his *simile's*?"

l. 117. *like* Pace *his wit be ouer-awde*] Alluding, it seems, to Dr.
Pace, whom Stephen Gardiner replaced as Secretary in 1529,
and about whom Holinshed says (ed. 1587, 3:907): "being con-
tinuallie abroad in ambassages, and the same oftentimes not
much necessarie, by the cardinals appointment, at length he
tooke such greefe therewith, that he fell out of his wits." Note *H8*
2. 2. 130: "he ran mad and died." There was also one John Pace

(1523?-90), jester to Henry VIII and the Duke of Norfolk, called "madde J. Pace" by Cardinal Allen (see *DNB*), and whom Nashe refers to as a writer of "loueletters in rime" (3:10). For the bawdy, cf. Shakespeare, *Sonnet 51:* "Then can no horse with my desire keep pace."

l. 120. *Deep mouth'd*] loud and sonorous, esp. desirable to "fill the cry" of the pack.

l. 122. *Well fare his hart*] A common expression of good wishes, here, as often, ironic, (*OED*); cf. l. 58, above. *hart*, a) mistress, b) deer; cf. *FQ* 3. 2. 42: "But thine my Deare (welfare thy heart my deare)."

l. 123. *puisnes of the Innes of Court*] Cf. the type in Ep. 22 and Satire III passim; Amoretto in *III Parnassus*, likewise devoted to field-sports, his mistress, and to displays of wit; and Overbury's "*Fantasticke* Innes of Court Man," *Char.*, ed. Paylor (1936), pp. 45-46.

l. 124. *to make sport*] a) to engage in diversion, completing the chase figure; b) implying sexual dalliance; cf. *Oth.* 2. 1. 224: "the act of sport."

l. 127. *Merchants ruffe, that's set in print*] One smaller than a courtier's—little and diminutive," according to Middleton (ed. Bullen, 8:69)—which maintained its shape for a longer time.

l. 131. *light heeles*] As a phrase, usually applied (beyond dancing)·to promiscuous girls, their heels going up as they go down. With this line cf. Heywood's four epigrams (*Wks.*, ed. Milligan, p. 132) on "Light comyng and goyng," and similar plays on *light* at Eps. 47, 61, and Satire VI. 108.

l. 132. *th'embrace beneath the knee*] "But the nobles and those who have travelled abroad . . . greet each other with bared head and a bow, sometimes gently gripping each other on the outside the knee" (Thos. Platter, *Travels in England* [1599], trans. Clare Williams [London, 1937], p. 183). *Vd* 4. 2. 85-89: "There soone as he can kisse his hand in gree, / And with good grace bow it below the knee, / Or make a *Spanish* face with fauning cheere, / With th'Iland-Conge like a Caualier, / And shake his head, and cringe his necke and side," etc.

l. 136. *curried*] The general metaphor in the passage is from the treatment of horses or leather (*dawbe, oyly, prick-*). It may be based on some expression such as that in *Misogonus* 2. 3. 51 (ed. Brandl): "Tauke thou of rubbinge horses and of such riffe raffe."

l. 138. *Speake to him woe to vs*] Probably based on the popular proverb "Woman is the woe to man" (Tilley W656).

ha'te] have it. There may be a glance at the "hai" (It. "you have it") of the fencer, the home-thrust, suggested by "prick-song." *Hai* and *prick-song* occur together in a *Romeo* passage (2. 4. 19-26), the one that refers to Tybalt as the "captain of complements"; note, below, "Dictionary of complements" (l. 143).

l. 140. *What braue Saint* George . . .] Based on a popular, ironic comparison, implying stiffness and rigidity, it seems, as well as general chivalric bravado. Cf. Lyly, *Euphues, Wks.*, ed. Bond, 1:260: "Lyke Saint *George*, who is euer on horse backe yet neuer rideth"; and Tilley S42.

l. 142. *right ducke, pray God he be no Frier*] Proverbial; cf. 1530 quote in *OED Duck*; *Jew* 2. 1. 25 (ed. H. S. Bennett): "And duck as low as any bare-foot friar"; and Nashe, 3:78. "The Spaniard's courtesy was then held in universal estimation" (Singer, in Davenport, ed., *Poems of Hall*, p. 205).

l. 143. *Dictionary of complements*] Probably "compliments," alluding to alliteration; cf. *Cyn. Rev.* 4. 3. 19-20: "Yes, but you must know, ladie, hee cannot speake out of a dictionarie method"; Sidney, *Apology*, ed. Smith, 1:202; and *Astrophel*, 15.

l. 144. *Barbers mouth of new-scrapt eloquence*] Lyly refers to
the trade as the "babbling arte" and to "melancholy" as "a word
for a barbers mouth" (*Midas* 5. 2. 168, 101, ed. Bond). Cf. also
Gull's Hornbook, ed. 1812, p. 177: "if you itch to step into the
barber's; a whole dictionary cannot afford words to set down
notes what dialogues you are to maintain, whilst you are doctor
of the chair there." Pun (?), *Barbers* = *barbarous*.

l. 145. Synomicke Tully *for varietie*] Alluding to Cicero's guidelines for oratory. *Synomicke*, exhibiting synonyms, from Fr.
synonymique, though its complete function is unclear. It almost
certainly provides the clue to the likely play on *Tully*. In a passage in which he presents an extended comparison of Harvey to
a barber-surgeon, Nashe mentions an "old *Tooly*" (3:14), who
McKerrow thinks is probably not the actor of the name but
rather some well-known character of Cambridge. In the passage
Nashe also refers to a Williamson, barber, who had been called
upon to deliver a philosophy lecture. Harvey had complained
(1:69) that Cambridge men make no distinction "between the
learned and vnlearned, *Tully* and *Tom Tooly*."

l. 146. *Madame Conceits gorgeous gallerie*] Ridiculing the craze
for such titles, alluding to Thos. Proctor's *Gorgeous Gallery of
Gallant Inuentions* (1578), and perhaps Anthony Munday's *Banquet of Daintie Conceits* (1588). Cf. *SV In Lect.*, ll. 45-48: "You
Castilio, . . . / Let me alone, the Madams call for thee / Longing to laugh at thy wits pouertie."

l. 147. Castilio] i.e., Castiglione, whose *Il Cortegiano* (pub.
1528), trans. Hoby (1561), as *The Courtier of Count Balthazar
Castilio*, G. has in mind throughout much of this satire. G.'s
portrait of the courtier resembles Marston's; consider, e.g., *CS*
1. 19-50:

> Come *Briscus*, by the soule of Complement, . . .
> But oh! the absolute *Castilio*,
> He that can all the poynts of courtship show.

He that can trot a Courser, break a rush, . . .
Can quaintly sow wits *newe* inuention . . .
He that can purpose it in dainty rimes . . .
Tut, he is famous for his reueling,
For fine sette speeches, and for sonetting; . . .
And yet's but Broker of anothers wit. . . .
Come come *Castilion,* skim thy posset curd . . .
Take ceremonius complement from thee,
Alas, I see *Castilios* beggery.
Cf. also Harvey, 2:263.

l. 149 ff. Cf. *Venus,* ll. 260, 279-82; (for bawdy) Middleton, *Black Booke,* ed. Bullen, 8:21: "The third rank, quainter than the former, presents us with the race of lusty vaulting gallants, that, instead of a French horse, practise upon their mistresses all the nimble tricks of vaulting, and are worthy to be made dukes for doing the somerset so lively"; and Juvenal 1. 60-62.

ll. 153-54. *popish merrit* . . .] i.e., by works (horse tricks) rather than by faith.

l. 158. *wife's bated by some quick-chapt youth*] i.e., a) harassed, b) refreshed (?), and c) perhaps has her price lowered (*OED v*2 4) by a fast-talking youth(?). Among many references to shop-keeper's prostitution, see, e.g., *SV* 3. 185-86, 5. 78-79; *CS* 1. 63; *Greenes Newes* (1593), ed. McKerrow, p. 51; Harington, *L. & E.,* p. 175.

l. 159. *mistres minkes*] A term for a prostitute or promiscuous woman, apparently used esp. of the tradesman class; cf. Nashe, 1:173: "Mistris Minx, a Marchants wife." In *Faustus* the charac-ter Lechery is addressed as "Mistress Minkes."

l. 161. Cf. the speaker in *Choice of Valentines,* Nashe, 3:405, as he enters the brothel: "I hearing hir so ernest for the box / Gaue hir hir due, and shee the dore unlocks. / In am I entered: venus be my speede."

l. 165. Bloome *is Ordinary*] Presumably the same as "Bosomes Inne" of Nashe, 3:14, otherwise referred to as Blossom's Inn (McKerrow, ed., Nashe, 4:308), in Saint Lawrence Lane near Cheapside. See Sudgen, "Bosom's Inn." With the passage cf. *CS* 2. 114-16.

l. 166. *good fellowes all*] i.e., rowdies, boon companions, thieves—Warner's example of an "Ironized Terme" (*Albions England*, 9. 53 [1597], p. 241).

l. 167. *by the eares*] i.e., quarreling; proverbial (Tilley E23).
    vie stabs] Possibly based on "vie stakes."
    exchange disgraces] Based, it would seem, on the technical terms of combat, "to give th'Exchange disgrace."

l. 168. *bandie daggers at each others faces*] cf. "to look daggers." *faces* may glance at bluffs or face cards. Rowlands has a passage probably based on this, in *Letting*, Ep. 22, *Wks.* (1880), 1:28, which includes this line.

l. 169. *Enough of these then, and enough of all*] Based on the proverbial patterns "Bear this, bear all" (Tilley A172) and "Enough is enough" (E159). *all* caps the major aspect of the city, its *vanity* (ll. 8, 61, 65, 80, 102, 155), through allusion to "Vanity of vanities . . . all is vanity."

l. 170. *I may thanke you . . .*] Ironic, as at *AYLI* 3. 2. 238-39: "*Jaques.* I thank you for your company, but, good faith, / I had as lief have been myself alone."

l. 172. *my follies view*] my view of follies (?).

ll. 173-74. *tis supper time, / The horne hath blowne*] i.e., between 6:00 and 7:00 P.M. Horns were blown at the Inns of Court; see H. & S., 10:197. These last lines may contain the ironic invitation usually in the form "come up to supper," on which see H. & S., 9:462.

Satire VI

Here, in a stance more philosophic than is his usual practice, G. exposes the tyranny Opinion holds over thought as a result of a disregard for Reason in the minds of men, and the consequent loss of virtue. The attitude that Opinion is inferior to Reason as an index to Truth (and thus virtue) had long been a leading feature in the epistemologies of most philosophies, including that of Plato, Aristotle, the Stoics, and Neoplatonists. But G.'s concern derives primarily from the recently revived interest in Stoicism, which gave special attention to the inadequacy of Opinion. For most of his ideas he turned to the first chapters of Lipsius's *Two Bookes of Constancie*, trans. in 1594 by John Stradling, especially bk. 1, chap. 5, which sets forth the sources and effects of Reason and Opinion:

> First you are not ignorant that man consisteth of two parts, Soule and Body. That being the nobler part, resembleth the nature of a spirit and fire: This more base is compared to the earth. These two are ioyned together, but yet with a iarring concord, as I may say, neither doe they easily agree, especially when controuersie ariseth about souerainty & subiection. For either of them would bear sway, and chiefly that part which ought not. The earth aduanceth it selfe aboue the fire, and the dirty nature aboue that which is diuine. Herehence arise in man dissentions, stirs, & a continual conflict of these parts warring together. The captains are, REASON and OPINION. That fighteth for the soule, being in the soule: This for, and in the body. Reason hath her offspring from heauen, yea from God: and *Seneca* gaue it a singular commendation, saying, . . . *That there was hidden in man parte of the diuine spirit.* This reason is an excellent power of faculty of vnderstanding and iudgment. . . . For, you are deceiued if you think al the soul to be *Right reason*, but that only which is vniforme, simple, without mixture, seperate from al filth or corruption: and in one word, as much as is pure & heauenlie. For albeit the soul be infected and a litle corrupted with the filth of

> the bodie and contagion of the senses: yet it retayneth
> some reliks of his first ofspring, and is not without cer-
> taine cleare sparks of that pure fiery nature from
> whence it proceeded. [Ed. R. Kirk (New Brunswick,
> 1939), pp. 80-81]

It should be clear that G. follows this, as he does several other places in Lipsius, and thus, ultimately, Epictetus and Seneca. He is likewise, as usual, either under Marston's influence or else sharing the same influences with him. Marston is occupied with Opinion (cf. "To The Worlds Mightie Monarch, Good Opinion"), although nowhere so specifically as G. is here, and constantly assails the overthrow of Reason by brute sensuality, following Epictetus and Seneca. For general parallels see *SV 8*, with Davenport's notes, and for a number of specific parallels, which Davenport lists (p. 259), see *SV In Lectores*.

Right Reason for the Neostoics is *"A true sense and iudgement of thinges humane and diuine,"* and Opinion, its opposite, *"A false and friuolous coniecture of those thinges"* (Lipsius, pp. 79-80). This is usually the sense of G.'s major terms. But frequently, especially late in the satire, Opinion becomes more specifically "public estimation" and is associated thus with the multitude, the "breath of the vulgar." For a discussion of this common Eliz. sense see P. Ure's note on Opinion in *MLR 46* (1951): 331-38. For contemporary attitudes toward Opinion see Ure's references; the second stasimon of the chorus in Daniel's *Cleopatra*; Cornwallis, *Essayes*, ed. D. C. Allen (Baltimore, 1946), pp. 54-55; and the figure Opinion in Jonson's *Hymenaei*, discussed in depth by D. J. Gordon in *JWCI 5* (1945): 134-40. For Stoics on Opinion see, along with Lipsius, Epictetus, *Discourses*, trans. W. A. Oldfather (London, 1925), 2. 11. 13-18; Du Vair, *The Moral Philosophie of the Stoicks*, trans. Thomas James (1598), ed. Rudolf Kirk (New Brunswick, 1951), pp. 67, 75, 82; and Charron, *Of Wisdom*, trans. Samson Leanard (1630), p. 70. Thoroughly Neostoic in every respect, this satire should have place in any general discussion of that philosophy in its English Renaissance phase.

l. 2. *state*] Condition in general. Cf. the opening lines of *Vd* 4. 6: "I wote not how the world's degenerate, / That men or know, or like not their estate"; and Horace, *Sat.* 1. 1. 1 ff.

l. 3. *Natures manumission*] A central idea with the Stoics, for whom Nature is Right Reason, both innate and implicit in the universe. Cf. Lipsius, bk. 1, chap. 5, p. 81: "To obey [Reason] is to beare rule, and to bee subiect thereunto is to haue the soueraintie in al humane affaires. Whoso obeyeth her is lord of al lusts & rebellious affections"; and cf. "Variety," sometimes attr. to Donne (in *Elegies*, ed. Gardner), ll. 47 ff.: "The golden laws of nature are repeald, / Which our first Fathers in such reverence held; / Our liberty's revers'd, our Charter's gone, / And we made servants to opinion," etc. Marston makes the same point in similar language at *SV* 11. 204 ff., as does Chapman, "A Hymne to our Saviour on the Crosse" (in *Poems*, ed. Bartlett), ll. 213-14.

l. 7. *various*] variable.

breath] A type of things unsubstantial, and along with the proverbial *wind* a basic metaphor in the satire.

l. 8. *smooth brow*] a) pleasing and agreeable, but also b) pejorative, as in Rowlands, *Letting*, Sat. 6, *Wks.* (1880), 1:82: "smooth-fac'd neate Dissimulation."

On the Renaissance tendency to "hypostatize" the abstract Opinion, see Ure, pp. 332-33. The satirist has in mind the emblematic and thematic qualities of Fortune or Change, for which see the extended description in H. R. Patch, *Goddess Fortuna* (Cambridge, Mass., 1927), chap. 2. "The idea of Fortune's change," says Patch (p. 43), "is symbolized in her smile or frown." Here she is also the Goddess of Love, the fickle mistress of fashionable love poetry (see Patch, pp. 90 ff.), with the "galley" possibly reminiscent of Petrarch, suggesting literary imitation.

l. 11. *her cold northerne gales*] Cf. *Twelfth* 3. 2. 27-28: "You are now sailed into the north of my lady's opinion."

l. 12. Fanonian *praise*] It is tempting to correct to *Favonian*, the favorable west wind, a not uncommon term, from the Latin. But perhaps the satirist assumes this sense, joining it with that of the lady's *fan* or the weathercock *fane* (*vane*), the fan being frequent as a conceit for the lady's favor or disfavor (usually ridicule)— see, e.g., *Cyn. Rev.* 5. 3. 106; *EMO* 2. 3. 201—and the fane as an emblem of fickleness. On *wind* meaning "favor" see McKerrow, ed., *Nashe*, 4:203; on the propitious west wind see Tilley W445.

perry] a) a favorable gust at sea, often fig. for social or political currents, with the possible extra sense of b) jewelry or gifts (*OED sb*2)—as favors from the lady—as with Chaucer's Fame (*House*, ll. 1393-94): "But, Lord! the perry and richesse / I saugh sittying on this godesse!"

l. 13. *the soules bright* Genius] i.e., its guide and tutelary spirit, controlling through discursive Reason and Understanding the lower activities of the inferior, earthy Vegetable and Sensible Souls. See J. B. Bamborough, *The Little World of Man* (London, 1952), pp. 30 ff. Cf. *SV To Detraction*, ll. 7 ff., and *Proem. in lib. tert.*, ll. 15-16: "Be thou my conduct and my *Genius*, / My wits inciting sweet breath'd *Zephirus*," with Davenport's notes.

l. 14. *to safe conduct vs*] Standard Eliz.; implying "by royal priviledge or authority."

l. 15. *lifes intricate* Dædalian *maze*] For this usual symbolic view of the maze see Natale Conti, *Mythologia*, 7. 9. (1581), p. 732. Suggested by Lipsius, p. 82: "whoso hath this thred of *Theseus* [Reason] may passe without straying through all the laborinths of this life."

l. 16. *buffuld*] i.e., "baffuld," a) duped, hoodwinked, b) subjected to public disgrace, a term used of the degrading of recreant knights (cf. *FQ* 6. 7. 27), who, among other indignities, were hung up by their heels. A spelling not met elsewhere, perhaps suggested by Lat. *bufalus = bubalus*, buffalo, wild-ox, here meaning our "buffaloed," and alluding to the Minotaur, possibly obliquely to cuckoldry. Cf. Daniel, *Rosamund* (*Wks.*, ed. Grosart, 1:98), l. 485: "The Minotaure of shame kept for disgrace."

ll. 18 ff. *Thy slaue, thy shadow* . . .] With these lines cf. Lipsius, p. 82: "there groweth a communion and societie betwixt the soule and the bodie, but a societie . . . not good for the soule. For she is therby by litle and little depriued of her dignity, addicted and coupled vnto the senses, and of this impure commixtion OPINION is ingendred in vs, *Which is nought els but a vaine image and shadow of reason:* whose seat is the Sences: whose birth is the earth. Therefore being vile and base it tendeth downwards, and sauoreth nothing of high and heauenly matters," etc.

   out-bearded] defied; also implying venereal disease.

l. 23. *soules, bodies Queenes allie*] i.e., the soul's (the Queen of the body) nearest ally. Cf., generally, *SV* 11. 233-34.

l. 27. *kept vnder*] i.e., in subjection or servitude. Cf. 1 Cor. 9:27: "But I keep under my body, and bring it into subjection." Cf. *SV* 8. 116-17.

l. 29. *the worlds vpside downe*] Nashe refers to such an alehouse sign (3:315): "it is no maruaile if euery Alehouse vaunt the table of the world turned vpside downe, since the child beateth his father," etc. Described as "still common" by J. Larwood and J. C. Hotten, *History of Signboards* (1866), p. 462. For a discussion of this as a popular medieval topos ("le monde renversé") see E. R. Curtius, *European Literature and the Latin Middle Ages*, trans. W. R. Trask (New York, 1953), pp. 94-98.

ll. 31-40. This passage appears in *England's Parnassus*, under "Reason."

ll. 34-35. extenuate / His fore-ceited mallice] Alluding to the legal "malice aforethought," and involving a pun on *fore-sated*, such that *extenuate* takes on the added sense "to make (the body, flesh, a person) thin or lean" (*OED* 1), or specifically in medicine, "to render thinner (the humours or concretions of the body, etc.)" (*OED* 1b).

l. 39. politist] i.e., politician, in the sinister Eliz. sense of crafty intrigue. Not listed in this form in *OED* before 19c.

l. 44. distempered] deranged, mentally imbalanced; *distemper*, "to upset the right proportions of."

ll. 45-50. Quoted in *England's Parnassus*, under "Opinion."

l. 45. various as light change] i.e., variable as easy deception, fickle. Perhaps a metaphor from the clipping of coins, although the earliest entry in *OED* for this *change* is 1622; or from music, meaning "modulation."

l. 46. For the use of the rhetorical formula "now-now" ("*nunc-nunc*") in description of Fame see Patch's long note in *Goddess Fortuna* (1927), p. 55. For Fame as harlot, fully suggested here, see Patch, pp. 56-57.

Court-like friendly] i.e., hypocritically.

l. 48. Displeas'd with her] i.e., "along with her," or "with her displeasure." *her* refers to "humour" (l. 47).

l. 50. Soothing her no with nay, her I with yea] Common in accounts of flatterers. Cf. Hall's parasite, *Vd* 6. 1. 50, who "soothes, and yeas, and nayes on eyther part"; Guazzo, *Civile Conv.*, ed. 1925, 1:80, 84; and Tilley Y4: "Peradventure Yea peradventure Nay," with related N101, M34, W66. On the proverb of the woman's "nay" meaning "yea," which may be here, see H. E. Rollins, *Paradise of Dainty Devices* (Cambridge, Mass., 1937), p. 238n. "Aye" was frequently written "I" as they were pronounced alike.

l. 51. *weigh this feather*] i.e., esteem or value, with a play on (O-)*pinion*.

l. 52. *censure*] judgment, opinion, not necessarily adverse.

l. 54. *Cobler*] Along with the "Ale-konner" of the next line (an inspector or "connoisseur" of ale), proverbial "know-it-alls" and busybodies. Cf. "Ne sutor ultra crepidam," and Tilley C479, 480.

l. 56. *arbitrate*] i.e., "arbitration": judgment, absolute decision.

ll. 57-67. Quoted in *England's Parnassus*, under "Occasion." With this passage cf. Charron, *On Wisdom*, trans. Samson Leanard (1630), p. 70: "[Opinion is] a vaine, light, crude, and imperfect iudgement of things drawne from the outward senses, and common report, setling and holding it selfe to be good in the imagination, and never arriving to the understanding, there to be examined, sifted and laboured; and to be made reason which is true, perfect and solide iudgement of things: and therefore it is vncertaine, inconstant, fleeting, deceitfull, a very ill and dangerous guide, which makes head against reason, whereof it is a shadow and image, though vaine and vntrue. It is the mother of all mischiefes, confusions, disorders: from it spring all passions, all troubles. It is the guide of fooles, sots, the vulgar sort, as reason of the wise and dexterious."

l. 60. Smithfield of iaded fancies] The place of Bartholomew Fair and the cattle market. The horses sold there, usually called "jades," were proverbially poor (Tilley W276). Cf. *Twelfth* 2. 5.144-45: "I do not fool myself, to let imagination jade me."

ll. 60-61. th'Exchange / Of fleeting censures] Cf. Florio, *Second Frutes* (1591), p. 141: "A man must giue no more credite to Exchange and Poules newes, than to fugitiues promises, and pliers fables."

ll. 68-70. For critical attitudes toward Chaucer in the end of the sixteenth century see those in Caroline F. E. Spurgeon, *Five Hundred Years of Chaucer Criticism* (Cambridge, 1925), esp. p. x: "Chaucer still holds his place as prince of English poets. . . . Now, however, begins to creep in that general belief which clung so persistently to the minds of all writers of the seventeenth and eighteenth centuries; that Chaucer was obsolete, that his language was very difficult to understand, his style rough and unpolished, and his versification imperfect."

l. 68. *carpe*] Influenced by Lat. *carpere*, to pluck, tear at, etc., and thus metaphoric with *gulls*.

l. 69. *other-some*] i.e., certain others.

l. 71. *the mark is out of* Gowers *mouth*] i.e., he is past his prime; Bacon, *Sylva*, 754 (in *OED Mark* 10c): "At eight yeares old, the Tooth is smooth, and the Hole is gone, and then they say, That the Marke is out of the Horses mouth." *Gowers* would rime with *horse*.

l. 72. *trick of youth*] See Satire I. 38 and note. Gower is preferable to current irresponsible, perhaps lascivious poetry. *trick*, as in "jade's trick," continues the horse metaphor.

l. 73. *grandam*] i.e., archaic. Cf. Sidney, e.g., *Apology*, ed. Smith, 1:196: (of *Shep. Cal.*) "That same framing of his stile to an old rustic language I dare not alowe," etc.; and Jonson, *Disc.*, ll. 1805-6 (H. & S., 8:618): "*Spencer*, in affecting the Ancients, writ no Language." *Deep* here, along with *profound-* below, alludes to Spenser's complexity and seriousness, his "deep conceit" (Nashe, 3:323).

ll. 75-76. *giuing praise, / And grauity*] Cf. E. K.: "For if my memory fayle not, Tullie, in that booke wherein he endevoureth to set forth the paterne of perfect oratour, sayth that ofttimes an auncient worde maketh the style seeme grave, and as it were reverend: no otherwise then we honour and reverence gray heares. . . . for in my opinion it is one special prayse, of many whych are dew to this poete," etc. The same praise occurs in Beaumont's Letter in Speght's *Workes of Chaucer* (1598).

l. 76. *profound-prickt layes*] Alluding to *FQ* 1. 1. 1. Cf. *II Par-*

nassus 4. 1. 1180: "A gentle pen rides prickinge on the plaine."
-prickt, a) written, as the "pricked" notes of music, and b) sewn
(*OED* 4b), as in the adornment of cloth, a metaphor throughout
the passage (including *maister-peece, cunning,* and probably
layes, through a pun on *lace*). Cf. Gascoigne, *Jocasta* 2. 1 (ed.
Cunliffe, p. 269): "tried truthe / Doth beste beseeme a simple
naked tale, / Ne needes to be with painted proces prickt, . . . /
Where deepe deceit and lies must seeke the shade / And wrap
their wordes in guilefull eloquence," etc. The comparison to tex-
tiles is frequent in descriptions of *FQ;* note, e.g., George Wither,
preface to *Halelujah* (1641): "For which cause, such *composi-
tions* [as by implication *FQ* is], may be resembled to *Garments*
of whole Silke, adorned with gold lace."

It may be, finally, given the play on *Gowers-horse* above,
that G. plays on *Spenser-Fencer* and thereby alludes to some
form of the proverb "A (cunning) fencer reserves his master-
piece," for which Tilley F187 gives 1616 as the early date; with
the sense of *prick* "to pierce, wound."

l. 78. *he's a Lucanist*] Alluding to Quintillian's dictum that
Lucan was "magis oratoribus quam poetis imitandus" (*Inst.
Orat.* 5. 1. 90). A natural comparison to Daniel, as both had
written of civil wars, one frequently made by contemporaries
and not always implying criticism—see, e.g., Meres, *Wits
Treasury,* ed. Smith, 2:316. G. seems to recall Spenser's praise,
in *Colin Clout,* ll. 420-24: "Yet doth his trembling Muse but
lowly flie, / As daring not too rashly mount on hight, / And
doth her tender plumes as yet but trie / In loves soft laies and
looser thoughts delight. / Then rouze thy feathers quickly
Daniell," etc. For the negative sentiment, which seems to have
been common, cf. Jonson, *Conv.,* ll. 23-24 (H. &. S., 1:132):
"Samuel Daniel was a good honest Man, had no children, bot no
poet"; ll. 66-67 (p. 134): "that Lucan taken in parts was Good
divided, read alltogidder meritted not the name of a Poet"; and
Drayton, Epistle to Henry Reynolds, in *Agincourt, &c.* (1627),

Wks., ed. Hebel, p. 207: "Some wise men him rehearse, / To be too much *Historian* in verse; / His rimes were smooth, his meeters well did close, / But yet his maner better fitted prose."

ll. 79-84. This passage admits of several possibilities. It has been taken to refer to the play *The Dumb Knight* (1596?, pub. 1608), the plot of which, as has been remarked, is fraught with inconsistencies. In the address to the play, Lewis Machin refers to the "strange constructions" and to "sharp critical censures" which the play has received, and attempts by reference to his collaborator, Markham, to excuse himself: "hauing a partner in the wrong, whose worth hath been often approued, I count the wrong but half wrong, because he knows best how to answer for himself: but I now in his absence make this apology both for him and me." It is now assumed that Machin is responsible for the subplot, added after 1607 (a portion, it is thought, taken verbatim from *Every Man In*), and Markham for the main plot, presumed to be the play for which Henslowe paid "Marcum" thirty shillings in 1596. For a discussion of the foregoing, see F. N. L. Poynter, *Bibliography of Gervase Markham* (Oxford, 1962), p. 38n. and pp. 56-61.

The context would seem, however, to refer to poetry rather than drama. If we understand *form-content* for the "plot"-"Subiect" of the passage (for Elizs. *plot* was less specific than ours, meaning plan or design, outline), then the passage may allude to Hall's ridicule of *The Poem of Poems, or Sion's Muse* (1596) at *Vd* 1. 8. 7-16, for its attempt to express the erotic imagery of Solomon in terms of the fashionable love sonnet. This reading would account for the references to the pseudo-Virgilian *Culex* and the *Batrachomyomachia*, attr. to Homer, both of which treat light subjects seriously. (But then *The Dumb Knight*, in its absurdity, may be parodic.) On Markham's style in general, its mixing of ribald and serious—which may be the point here—see J. H. H. Lyon, *A Study of "The New Metamorphosis"* (New York, 1919), p. 139.

Finally, as Robert Gittings has pointed out (*Shakespeare's Rival* [London, 1960], p. 12), *rich* (l. 83) is a punning allusion to Lady Rich, Penelope Devereux, Essex's sister, the Stella of Sidney's sonnets, to whom Markham dedicated his long poem *Devoreux* in 1597. This poem, which may well be the allusion in this passage, purports to treat of the death of Walter, brother to Essex, at Rouen in 1591, but it gives instead extended and fulsome praise in epic style to Essex, Lady Rich, and her sister, the Countess of Northumberland. To this volume G. contributed two complimentary sonnets (signed "E. Guilpin"). G. here, perhaps sensitive to some criticism of the poem (it seems not to have been well received), attempts to vindicate it either by referring to its praise of Lady Rich, or else, having had recently a change of heart toward Essex (see the severe attack on Fœlix at Satire I. 63-76), seeks ingeniously to disclaim his clear support of Essex in the complimentary verse, or both—while at the same time covering Markham by hinting that the poem should be taken as mock-heroic. That G. should include Markham at all in his roll call of poets is suspect, it would seem.

Gittings constructs his thesis that Markham is the "rival poet" on the basis of this passage. Taking *soare* to mean "harm, spoil, wound or make sore" and *Falcon* as an allusion to Shakespeare, he paraphrases the last couplet: "Markham, though accused of triviality [for Gittings *plot*=*subject*], is enriched by addressing his verse to Lady Rich, and in so doing may spoil and fly as high as the more showy work of another writer, the 'Falcon.' "

l. 82. *vnkind*] glancing at the natural law of "kind" (i.e., of tragedy).

ll. 85-86. Drayton's *condemn'd of some* . . .] Mrs. K. Tillotson (ed., *Wks.*, 5:138) takes this to refer either to the general criticism, of which there was apparently more than has survived, for his borrowings from Daniel in *Idea's Mirror* (1594), or else to the attack on Drayton for plagiarism by Hall, whom G. (along with

Marston) was against. See the "Plagiarie sonnet-wright" who has
taken "whole Pages at a clap for need / From honest *Petrarch*"
in *Vd* 4. 2. 84, 6. 1. 251-52; and see 1. 7. 11. Note also Davenport's conclusion (pp. xlix-lviii) that while Hall may not have
him only or esp. in mind (Daniel fits as well or better), Drayton
might nonetheless have felt uneasy about the criticism. Perhaps
out of extreme sensitivity to such criticism, as Mrs. Tillotson implies, he removed several of the most obvious borrowings in the
1599 edition, and thereafter defended himself.

In the first two lines G. neatly summarizes the well-known
theoretical and practical concern at the end of the 1590s about
the two attitudes toward imitation: slavish copying or the
essential process of variation in art. See H. O. White, *Plagiarism
and Imitation during the English Renaissance* (Cambridge,
Mass., 1935), esp. his discussion of Drayton's *IM*, pp. 148-50.

l. 87. *sicke*] envious, corrupt (?). Cf. *H8* 1. 2. 81-83: "What we
oft do best, / By sick interpreters (once weak ones) is / Not our
or not allow'd."

ll. 89-90. Drayton has achieved the three names (*nomen, prae-
nomen, cognomen*) customarily granted the Roman slave when
freed since he is freed from "slavish" imitation.

l. 92. *sirnam'd* Golden-mouth] By Charles Fitzgeoffrey, in *Sir
Francis Drake* (1596), ed. Grosart (1881), p. 21, st. 26; repeated
by Meres, *Wits Treasury*, ed. Smith, 2:316.

ll. 93-96. *The double volum'd* Satyre . . .] Alluding to Hall's
Virgidemiae, which appeared in two volumes (ent. 31 Mar. 1597
and 30 Mar. 1598), the title, from "virgidemia" or "virgin-
demia," meaning "a harvest of rods" (see Davenport, ed.,
p. 159). The "other-some" (l. 95) is Marston, whose "*Reactio,*"
inserted between satires 3 and 4 in the second (?) edition of
Certaine Satyres (ent. 27 May 1598), is a sustained attack on
Hall's criticism of contemporary poetry. For a full discussion of
the quarrel between the two, with a tentative timetable and rele-

vant references, see Davenport's introduction to his edition of Hall, pp. xxviii-xxxiv.

l. 94. *Rods in pisse*] Proverbial for "punishment in store" (Tilley, R157).

l. 96. *clap'd* Reactioes *Action on his back*] i.e., figuratively, brought a suit against him (legal "action"), from the method of the bailiff or officer ("shoulder-clapper") in arrest. Perhaps to imply beating—"action of battery"—with *re*=*stripe* (*OED Ray* sb4 1); cf. *Rom.* 4. 5. 115: "I'll re you"; and Nashe, 1:93: "clapt many Brandes vppon theyr backes."

There may be a play on "Acteon." Marston figuratively cuckolds Hall (his muse) by writing satire himself, horns being usually *clapped* on. Shakespeare seems to make the same play on the name at *Wives* 3. 2. 45. Note also *Trimming of T. Nashe* (1597), in Harvey, 3:34: "Thy wit, thy wit, *Tom*, hath no roddes in pisse for thee . . . twill quite destroye thee: *Acteon* (as wise a man as you) no wayes could escape it, for all his loue to his hounds, . . . but was deuoured of his owne dogs." Hall had specifically referred to Marston as "a mad dogge," playing on his pseudonym "W. Kinsayder" (see *SV* 10. 51).

ll. 97-102. *Nay euen wits* Caesar, Sidney . . .] Perhaps in allusion to the *Astrophel* volume (1595), which is esp. moist in its praise. The imagery suggests Nashe's preface to Sidney's *Astrophel* (1591), 3:331: "Fayne would a seconde spring of passion heere spende it selfe on his sweet remembrance: but Religion, that rebuketh prophane lamentation, drinkes in the riuers of those dispaireful teares which languourous ruth hath outwelled. . . . Thou only [Countess of Pembroke] . . . keepest the springs of *Castalia* from being dryed vp," etc.

The criticism of Sidney probably alludes to his mannerism of using compound adjectives, esp. in *Arcadia*, and which he justifies in *Apology* (ed. Smith, 1:204). Hall noticed this trick of Sidney's style and criticized those writers who abused it (*Vd*

6. 1. 258-62): "others marre it with much liberty, / In Epithets to ioyne two wordes in one, / Forsooth for Adiectiues cannot stand alone; / As a great Poet could of *Bacchus* say, / That he was *Semele-femori-gena.*" But it seems unlikely that G. would take this passage to be critical of Sidney. Perhaps "affectation" is, generally, the failure to observe decorum in character-speech, which is the sense in *Apology* (ed. Smith, 1:202). Note, thus, Jonson, *Conv.*, ll. 511-13 (H. & S., 1:149): "Lucan, Sidney, Guarini make euery man speak as well as themselues, forgetting decorum, for Dametas sometymes speaks Grave sentences"; and cf. the similar ll. 17-19 (1:132).

l. 101. *for*] in spite of, for fear of (?).

l. 103. *play the two edg'd sword*] i.e., "kill o' both sides" (1625, *OED Two-edged* b), meaning "they are as applicable to the service of Falsehood, as of Truth" (1661, *OED*). A variation on "play at two-hand-sword," which occurs in *Courtier*, trans. Hoby, Tudor ed., p. 140, where the figurative sense, if any, is unclear.

l. 104. *both-hand playes*] The quasi-proverbial "play with two hands," i.e., falsely, corruptly. Cf. Heywood, *Wks.*, ed. Milligan, p. 36: "she can plaie on bothe hands, / Dissimulacion well she vnderstandes." Referring to "Ambidexter," frequent for double-dealing, esp. for bribe-taking lawyers, which is the metaphor here—*iudgments, playes,* pun *pleas:* cf. Preface to 1609 quarto of *Troil:* "of *Playes* for *Pleas.*"

l. 106. *phantastique winds*] a) i.e., absurd opinions; cf. "winds of praise" (*OED* 14b); b) imaginary *wines*, c) turns (?)—as in Middleton, *Micro.*, *Wks.*, ed. Bullen, 8:116: "Now windy parasites, or the slaves of wine, / That wind from all things save the truth divine, / Wind, turn, and toss, into the depth of spite." The *wine-cask* = *head* comparison is a favorite with the satirists.

l. 108. *Light minded* . . .] i.e., a) frivolous, b) wanton, as usual.

The three details are appropriate, respectively, to the three groups, and contain quibbles, as, e.g.: *parts,* a) roles, b) capacities, c) "privy" (?) parts.

l. 110. *quaint iest, . . .*] Appropriate, still, to the three groups, and of multiple signification. *quaint iest,* with a play on Chaucer's "quaint"; *crosse-poynt,* a) dance step in the galliard, b) crossed (and therefore fanciful) lace fastening hose to doublet; cf. "cross-gartered" and the context of Nashe, 3:224; *well-touch'd,* i.e., played.

l. 112. *breake againe*] i.e., deliver again; cf. *To break one's mind, OED Break* 22. All the above *break:* jests, points, music; and, always in the satirist's mind, "to break wind."

l. 113. *wone the bell*] i.e., the prize, at that time a bell. Cf. the Caius of Ep. 68.

ll. 115-56. Cf. Tilley L464: "To fear the loss of the bell more than the loss of the steeple."

l. 117. Cf. the similar Pollio of Eps. 26, 27.

l. 121. Cf. the fastidious Pansa of Ep. 52.

l. 123. *Thy haire's all short enough*] Presumably the usual glance at venereal disease.

l. 124. smug'd] made smart, neat.

l. 125. A blessing of Rose-water] Barbers after trimming applied perfume to face and beard. A "blessing" is a small quantity over and above the measure.

ll. 129-30. *shall a free mind / Sicke of Cockneys Ague, feare the wind?*] i.e., disgusted with a wanton's or perhaps Londoner's fever (affectation), presumably; including a play: the already sick needing no longer to fear the danger. For the relevant senses of cockney see K. Muir's note to *Lear* 2. 4. 122 (New Arden). Perhaps the satirist, like the spoiled child, no longer trembles

before the wind (from his master's rod, the "wooden censure" of
below): he faces his critics. The phrase "Cockneys Ague" doubtless owes something to "cook's egg" or "cock's egg"; cf. Florio,
Worlde (1598): "*Caccherelli*, . . . egs, as we say cockanegs."

l. 133. *mittigate*] Perhaps implying the sense "to free from
acridity," for which the *OED* gives 1633 as earliest entry.

l. 134. *veriuice of his snap-haunce hate*] G. varies the common
phrase "crabbed and snappish" used of satirists and other ill-
humored persons. For *veriuice*, see Satire I. 149 and note. *snap-
haunce*, the lock released by a trigger, or a firearm equipped
with such a lock. Leishman has a long speculative description of
the "Crabbgunne" of *III Parnassus* 4. 2. 1725, which, if there
was such, may apply here. For the sense cf. *CS* 2. 2, and *SV* 4.
131-32: "And old crabb'd *Scotus* on th'organon / Pay'th me
with snaphaunce, quick distinction." *snap-haunce* plays on
"back-biter."

l. 136. *deepe mouthed*] loud.

ll. 136-37. *as soone disioynt / His grind-iest chaps . . .*] i.e.,
break his jaws, which sharpen or crush jests, teeth being
grinders, and *disioynt* being an Eliz. critical term descriptive of
poor style. Related to the Latin proverb "genuinum frangere in
aliquo," "to break one's jaw on a person," to criticize severely.
Cf. Persius 1:114-15 and Ovid, *Meta.* 7: "Vipereas rumpo
verbis & carmine fauces." Cf. parallels in Nashe, 2:185-86;
Florio, *Montaigne*, ed. J. I. M. Stewart (New York [1933]),
p. xxii; Jonson, Ep. 58, H. & S., 8:45.

ll. 139-54. Epictetus, called "the central inspiration of European
neostoicism" (M. Higgins, *MLR* 39 [1944]: 342), and esp. in-
fluential with Lipsius and Du Vair, was known to Englishmen
largely through these disciples and commentators and through
the *Encheiridion*, available for some time in the Latin translation
and commentary by Simplicius and in Sanford's translation

(from the French) called *The Manuell of Epictetus* (1567). For his attitude toward Epictetus in this passage, and for his general Stoic position, G. seems clearly indebted to this little book, as well as to Lipsius and Du Vair, but I do not find specific borrowings. Marston appends the name "Epictetus" to the conclusion of *CS* 5 and mentions him again at *SV Proem. in lib. sec.*

On Epictetus's slavery, which determined the tone and temper of his whole life, see W. A. Oldfather's introduction to the Loeb edition. Of his obsession for freedom, Oldfather says, "I know no man upon whose lips the idea more frequently occurs" (p. xvii). This passage (like the entire satire) probably owes a general debt to Horace's 2. 7, which likewise treats of the Stoic paradox that only the philosopher is free; cf. 83-88: "Quisnam igitur liber? sapiens, sibi qui imperiosus," etc. Persius's fifth also treats the thesis that all men, philosophers excepted, are slaves.

l. 139. *perfect libertine*] Cf. *OED Libertine* 1: "Rom. Ant. a freedman, one manumitted from slavery." To contrast with the usual sense of *libertine*.

ll. 141-42. *a powre / To calme content*] If *calme* is a verb, then "a force (body of men) to pacify contention." But perhaps "a capacity for peaceful happiness."

l. 143. *busie Polypragmons*] i.e., meddling busybody (*OED*), from the Greek.

ll. 147-48. *Thy vertue-purged soule, thy* Genius . . .] i.e., by virtue purged. Alluding to the efficacy of the purgative (*OED* 11); cf. Donne, "To the Countesse of Bedford," ll. 89-90 (ed. Milgate): "Take then no vitious purge, but be content / With cordiall vertue, your knowne nourishment." *vertue-Genius-inclinations* suggests sidereal influence.

l. 152. *Mechanick mates*] i.e., base fellow's, *mechanick* used contemptuously for one engaged in manual labor, or in practical rather than speculative application; the phrase occurs in Nashe, 3:311. *Mate* functions in the sense "one of a pair," giving thus (*contra* "philosophick") an aspect of the soul, perhaps with a pun on *meat*, referring to "Vegetable" or "Sensible" souls.

l. 155. *perfect temperature*] i.e., sound, sane mental disposition, based on an unalloyed or proper combination of "humours" in the body. Cf. Lat. *temperare*, "to mix in due proportion."

l. 156. *Socratique*] With a quibble; cf. 1538 quotation at *OED Temperature* 2: "*Crasis*, a greke worde, sygnyfieth complexion, temperature, or mixture of natural humours."

l. 158. *Audacity*] i.e., "good audacitie," *Cyn. Rev.* 5. 9. 40-41; cf. *LLL* 5. 1. 4-5. Note Heywood, *Apology*, ed. 1841, p. 28: "This it held necessary for the emboldening of their junior schollars in any publicke exercise. . . . It teacheth audacity to the bashfull grammarian."

l. 162. *Black-men*] See note to Ep. 68, l. 2.,

l. 163. *many headed*] Often applied derisively to the populace, after Horace, *Ep.* 1. 1. 76: "belua multorum es capitum."

l. 165. *vulgar breath*] Cf. Lat. "popularis aura."

l. 167. *their sent of Garlike . . .*] The association of garlic-breath with the poor was common. Garlic, like onions, was thought to be a remedy against the plague.

l. 168. *for hainous*] i.e., be grievously offended. Cf. the same sentiment in *SV Proem. in lib. sec.*, ll. 13-14.

ll. 171-72. *some Chaundler slopt a mustard pot . . .*] Allusions to the uses of waste paper or waste books by Chandlers are frequent, esp. in Nashe; see, e.g., 1:192, 265; 2:180; 3:35, 330, etc. Cf. also Ep. 70 above.

ll. 173-78. *Or perfum'd Courtiour . . .*] A second use of such paper, referred to by Nashe, 1:305; *SV* 10. 35-38; *Gull's Horn-*

book, ed. 1812, p. 122; and, which may have informed G.'s treatment, Harington, *Ajax*, ed. Donno, pp. 65-66.

l. 177. *stile*] With quibbles on a) a sharp pointed instrument (Lat. *stilus*), and/or b) the steps over a fence; cf. Dekker, *Satiromastix* 1. 2. 270-71 (ed. Bowers), Asinus of a book he is reading: "The whoorson made me meete with a hard stile in two or three places as I went over him."

l. 178. *arse-smart*] the plant water-pepper; "Arsmart . . . because if it touch the taile or other bare skinne, it maketh it smart" (*OED*, 1617). Pun (?), *arse* = *ars*.

    tickled breech] a) i.e., squeamish or overly precise, b) loose or easily moved (scatological, cf. *OED* 3b).

ll. 179-82. As ballads were sung in the taverns ("to the payle"), "ale-knights" came to typify insensitive critics. Cf., e.g., Nashe, 1:23-24, who refers to "our new found Songs and Sonets," which "euery ignorant Ale knight will breath forth ouer the potte, as soone as his braine waxeth hote." Hall, *Vd* 6. 1. 193-94, pretends concern for "How it shall please ech Ale-knights censuring eye, / And hang'd my head for feare they deeme awry."

l. 180. *weeuil, mault-worme*] i.e., topers, figurative from the insects which destroy or "consume" grain; cf. Nashe, 3:383.

    barly-cap] likewise a tipler, a term of uncertain origin. *OED* lists this as its first entry. Probably related to "barleyhood," as Dyce suggested (ed., Skelton, *Dame Elean.*, 1:107), which may be a corruption of "barly-wood," i.e., "barly-mad."

l. 182. *a proper man*] "a handsome man." Harvey had referred to Nashe as Greene's "fellow-writer, a proper yong man" (1:170), which Nashe ridiculed (1:288, 3:130). G. seems to have taken a number of ideas in these concluding lines from the Nashe-Harvey quarrel.

l. 184. *Epethite of Pretty*] Marston's critic, "That newe discarded

Academian," gives a similar judgment: *"that's prety, prety good / That Epethite hath not that sprightly blood,"* etc. (*SV* 6. 90-94). "Epethite" is "pedantical" diction; cf. *LLL* 1. 2. 14 ff.; 4. 2. 7; 5. 1. 13.

ll. 186 ff. The repetition of "Ile" in this passage, along with the presence of "ouer-weene" and "Gallant," suggests that G. alludes to Harvey's criticism of Lyly and deliberately exploits it. Harvey has (2:7): "I am none of those, that greedily surfet of selfe-conceit. . . . He that thought to make himselfe famous with his ouerweening and brauing *Il'e, Il'e, Il'e,* might perhaps nourrish an aspiring imagination to imitate his *Ego, Ego, Ego,* so gloriously reiterated in his gallant Orations" (alluding to Cicero). Nashe criticizes the "I'le, I'le, I'le" at 3:103.

l. 186. *Gallant . . . Caueleire*] Probably with plays on *gall* and *cavil-er.* Pasquil, after *Pasquil's Returne* (1589), was often called "Cavaliero."

l. 187. *ouer-weene*] Harvey used *ouer-weene* (1:178) and Nashe ridiculed it (1:294).

ll. 189-90. With these lines cf. *SV* To Detraction, ll. 23-24: "Spight of despight, and rancors villanie, / I am my selfe, so is my poesie." The Marston lines are, according to M. Higgins (*MLR* 39 [1944]: 342), "a sort of stoic self-sufficiency intensely idiosyncratic in form."

INDEX

Index

A Note about the Book

Designed and composed by The University of North Carolina Press, Chapel Hill, North Carolina, the text was set on a CompuWriter II in ten-point Paladium, leaded three points. The paper is sixty-pound Hopper Natural Bulk Opaque, manufactured by Georgia-Pacific Corporation, Stamford, Connecticut, and the endsheets are eighty-pound Ivory Text Teton, manufactured by Simpson Lee Paper Company, San Francisco, California. The cloth is Roxite Linen Finish, manufactured by Holliston Mills, Inc., Norwood, Massachusetts. The volume was printed by Thomson-Shore, Inc., Dexter, Michigan, and it was bound by John H. Dekker & Sons, Inc., Grand Rapids, Michigan.

The title page and the ornamental woodcuts from the 1598 edition of *Skialetheia* are reproduced by permission of the Folger Shakespeare Library, Washington, D.C.